Prospects of England

PROSPECTS OF ENGLAND

Two thousand years seen through twelve English towns

Adam Nicolson & Peter Morter

Weidenfeld & Nicolson
London

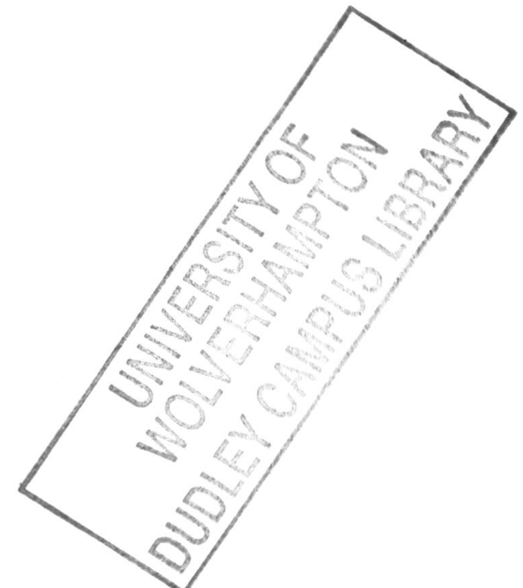

First published in Great Britain in 1989 by
George Weidenfeld & Nicolson Limited
91 Clapham High Street, London, SW4 7TA

ISBN 0 297 79578 3

Typeset by Florencetype Ltd, Kewstoke, Avon
Printed in West Germany

For Sonia and Olivia

Acknowledgments

I have many people to thank in these twelve towns for their hospitality, patience, guidance, and understanding. I cannot name them all but I am especially grateful to the following: in Chichester, Alan Redman and Michael Moore; in Glastonbury, Mr and Mrs Norman House and David Bromwich at the Somerset Local History Library in Taunton; in Alnwick, Bill Hugonin, Colin Shrimpton, Lord and Lady Richard Percy, Janet Purvis, Rev. Joseph Marren, Adrian Ions, Katrina Porteous and all the girls in Carrick's; in Chipping Campden, Brigadier Atkinson, Jeremy Green and Geoffrey Powell; in Woodbridge, the staff of the County Library, as well, of course, as Sonia and Peter, the admirable Morters, Marcus the dog and their beautiful daughters; in Blandford Forum, Ben Cox, Charlie Lavington, Archie Gibbs, Fred Wood, Mr and Mrs J.O.R. Tupper, the staffs of the Dorset County Record Office in Dorchester and of the County Library in Blandford; in Monmouth, Kirstie Buckland, Stephen Clarke, Sue Chivers, Mr Astley in the Planning Department and the Colonel of the Royal Monmouthshire Royal Engineers (Militia); in Weymouth, Doris Eastwood, the splendid Town Crier, and Colin Ellis in the Planning Department; in Buxton, June Barclay; in Whitby, Doreen Postgate, David Green, the staffs of the County Library and of the Literary and Philosophical Society; in Hebden Bridge, Freda Kelsal, Dr Betteridge, the staffs of Calderdale Archives, the County Library in Hebden Bridge and of Pennine Heritage, Sam G. Helliwell, Betsy Collinge, Mr and Mrs Atach of Heptonstall and Bert Tucker; and in Letchworth, Doreen Cadwallader and the staff of the First Garden City Museum.

The discretion and expertise of the editors and designers at Toucan Books Limited cannot be overestimated. My heartfelt thanks to them all, especially Robert Sackville West and John Meek.

The maps of Weymouth on page 97 and of Blandford Forum on page 73 are reproduced by permission of the Syndics of Cambridge University Library. The map of Chichester on page 14 is reproduced from a document in the West Sussex County Record Office, by permission of the County Archivist. I am also grateful to Michael Willis of Aerofilms.

ALNWICK
WHITBY
HEBDEN BRIDGE
BUXTON
WOODBRIDGE
CHIPPING CAMPDEN
MONMOUTH
LETCHWORTH
BLANDFORD FORUM
GLASTONBURY
CHICHESTER
WEYMOUTH
PM
THE PROSPECTS
MCMLXXXIX

Contents

Introduction

'THEY ARE ALL the same,' the highly educated and rather beautiful woman said to me as I was beginning to write this book. 'All English towns start with some kind of Saxon cemetery, don't they? A workman discovers it one day halfway under the gasometer. Then there's the Norman replanning and "burgage plots" '—she laughed —'the granting of fairs, something called borough status, the dissolution of the priory, the rising gentry, an outbreak of cholera or something else disgusting, a boom in trade—it's usually buttons or stockings—a new Town Hall in 1810 (described as "blandly neo-classical"), a sudden splurge of back-to-back housing after the railway turns up, an Arts and Crafts almshouse, a local memoirist, eventually a bypass, a conservation area, a one-way system and a board on the outskirts saying *Bumpton Regis—England's Gem.*' (In fact, for boards on outskirts, nothing can beat Blandford Forum's: it says 'Blandford—an Interesting Town'.) 'And then,' this lady went on, smiling deftly, 'comes the last stage of all: the author, notebook in hand, sensibilities on offer, concerned for the social realities and what he likes to call the "urban fabric".'

It was not quite a death-blow. I did not bother to tell her that there are few moments I enjoy more in life than arriving in a small town for the first time. A town is there, waiting to be known, waiting to be consumed, a rich and complicated thing, with its own ways of being, its own revelations.

The woman was wrong in another way too. Of course it is possible to give a generalized history of small-town England. But to do that is to blot out what is interesting about these places. It is the specifics of each town, its dominance of its own world, its own internal dynamics, which make it so intriguing. The towns are small, each small enough to be seen as an entity: particular events—the building of a bridge, the arrival of a duke—can be seen sending ripples into every corner.

Nevertheless I hope that something larger emerges too. Each of the twelve chosen towns has enjoyed a moment or a period when it has come into its own, when the forces at work within it have brought something to fruition, giving the town its enduring personality. It might be the influence of the Percys at Alnwick or of the Bastards at Blandford Forum, the holiday ideals in Georgian Weymouth or the ideology of the mill-owners in nineteenth-century Hebden Bridge. The twelve towns in this book are arranged according to the chronological order of their 'shaping moments', so that together they form a continuous story of town life, from the planning of Roman Chichester to the radically nostalgic ideals of the Garden City in early twentieth-century Letchworth.

It is extraordinary how dominant the inheritance from these shaping moments can be. The way the young people of Glastonbury hang around on the street today, for example, is simply unintelligible unless you are aware of what happened to the town in the early sixteenth century. In the same way a café in present-day Alnwick is laid out according to a pattern defined for it before the Norman Conquest. A string of events in the late 1780s dictates the employment pattern throughout the town of Weymouth today. This is what this book is about too—the presence of a town's past, not only in its physical structures but in the lives of people who live there.

I like all of these towns. I would most readily live in Alnwick; but I would take a foreigner to Weymouth if I wanted to show him England at its most relaxed; and I would choose Letchworth as the best example of English democratic ideals. But what is it that unites these towns, that makes all of them likable? The overriding quality is an almost physical aesthetic pleasure in the actual shape of the place: the miracle of Chipping Campden High Street, for instance, which William Hogarth identified as 'the line of beauty'; or, perhaps even better, the apparent curve of Weymouth's Esplanade—actually an optical illusion, for it runs dead straight on the map for a mile.

There have been some catastrophes in the towns in this book. The council building in Weymouth is a disgrace. The new supermarket in Alnwick and the shopping centre in Buxton are both worse. Nevertheless, in most places these lessons have been learnt, and development in the middle of these towns is now usually *too* cautious, anything beyond a little Georgian pastiche being considered too daring.

Are there any general rules? There is, I think, only one useful distinction to be made: between the plan and the elevation. The street plan should be sacrosanct. By far the greatest damage has been done when very large buildings have been erected where their predecessors were small and when holes have been cut in streets, particularly for traffic. Supermarkets and modern shopping arcades should be banned from town centres because not only do they destroy the town plan, but their service-ends are hideous, they need large car-parks, and they bring lorries into streets which are not suited to them. Towns dating from before 1900 need to be tight-knit to feel right. Gaps look like bad dentistry. This is not to ban modernity. As long as the scale is right and the plan is unchanged, any building that seems good at the time should be allowed (providing, that is, its elevation is well-designed and it is built in good materials). Planning departments should not be allowed to insist on pastiche as they now are, almost without exception. Endless pastiching of what is already there will turn a town into an indecipherable mixture of real and fake, with the result that the real is devalued and the meaning of the town is drowned in later bastardizations of itself.

This is important because towns act as extraordinarily articulate records of the life that has been lived in them. Disputes have naturally arisen between the inhabitants of towns, because there is always pressure on resources and space; these problems were often taken to court to be settled. Because the townsfolk have been literate for a long time, it is in these court records, therefore, that a great deal of the history of town life survives. Individuals emerge early. Petty ambitions and sinking failures, every means that people have devised for mutual sustenance and exploitation—all have left their traces. But those records only come to life when they are examined in the context of the town itself, its streets and buildings. A town plan is a metaphor of what the town has wanted to be and what it has become. The deliberately cleared stage-set of the marketplace at Blandford Forum, the rectilinear cross-streets of Chichester, the contrived privacies and open spaces of Letchworth: all of these represent different ideals of town life, the social and physical arrangements people have desired, sometimes struggled over, had imposed upon them.

Peter Morter and I planned this book together and his illustrations are an integral part of it. They are consciously in the tradition of town-drawing that dates back to the seventeenth century. Both in the ground-level street-scene and in the 'Prospect'—a slightly distant view from an often imaginary height—the *Scenographer*, as he was called, showed the town off to its best. Town prospects were almost always engraved and printed, not painted in oils, as a country house and its landscape might have been; they were civic things, to be shared and distributed, unlike the single vision which would be hung on the private drawing-room wall. In a way the prospect-drawer was always a propagandist for the town he drew. He was a visual editor who aimed, as Peter does, to show the town at its happiest, ignoring whatever detracted from the spirit of the place and bringing out the essentials, as a photographer can almost never do in a town.

In *Sculptura*, a book published in 1662 on the art of engraving, John Evelyn expressed the hope that scenographers would 'entertain us with more landskips and views of the environs, approaches and prospects' of English towns, 'which other countries abound with, to the immense refreshment of the curious'. The immense refreshment of the curious has been our purpose here too. But we hope for more than that. There was a salutary experiment performed a few years ago by two brain scientists, Doctors Bennett and Rosenzweig. A population of rats was divided into three groups. One was set scurrying around a rich and complicated environment, full of delights and surprises—the rat equivalent, in fact, of a small English town. The second group was confined to a boring and uniform place, where there was no joy in exploration and where life was as dreary as in a modern flat decorated with extreme minimalism. The rats were allowed to lead these lifestyles for a time, were then killed and afterwards their brains were weighed. The brains of the rats who had been scurrying around the small-town environments *actually weighed more* than those of the rats who had remained in their modern apartments. That is, perhaps, no more than one might expect. The shock comes with the third group, however. These rats were allowed to *see* the interesting streets but were not allowed to walk around them. When their brains were weighed, the results showed that they were no heavier than those of the modern apartment rats. That is the salutary lesson: you have to get out there.

CHICHESTER
Sussex

Part of CHICHESTER with the Cathedral a

EXPLANATION
A St Peter's Church
B Bell Tower
C North Street
D The Market Cross
E East Street
F South Street
G The Deanery

athedral Church of the Holy Trinity

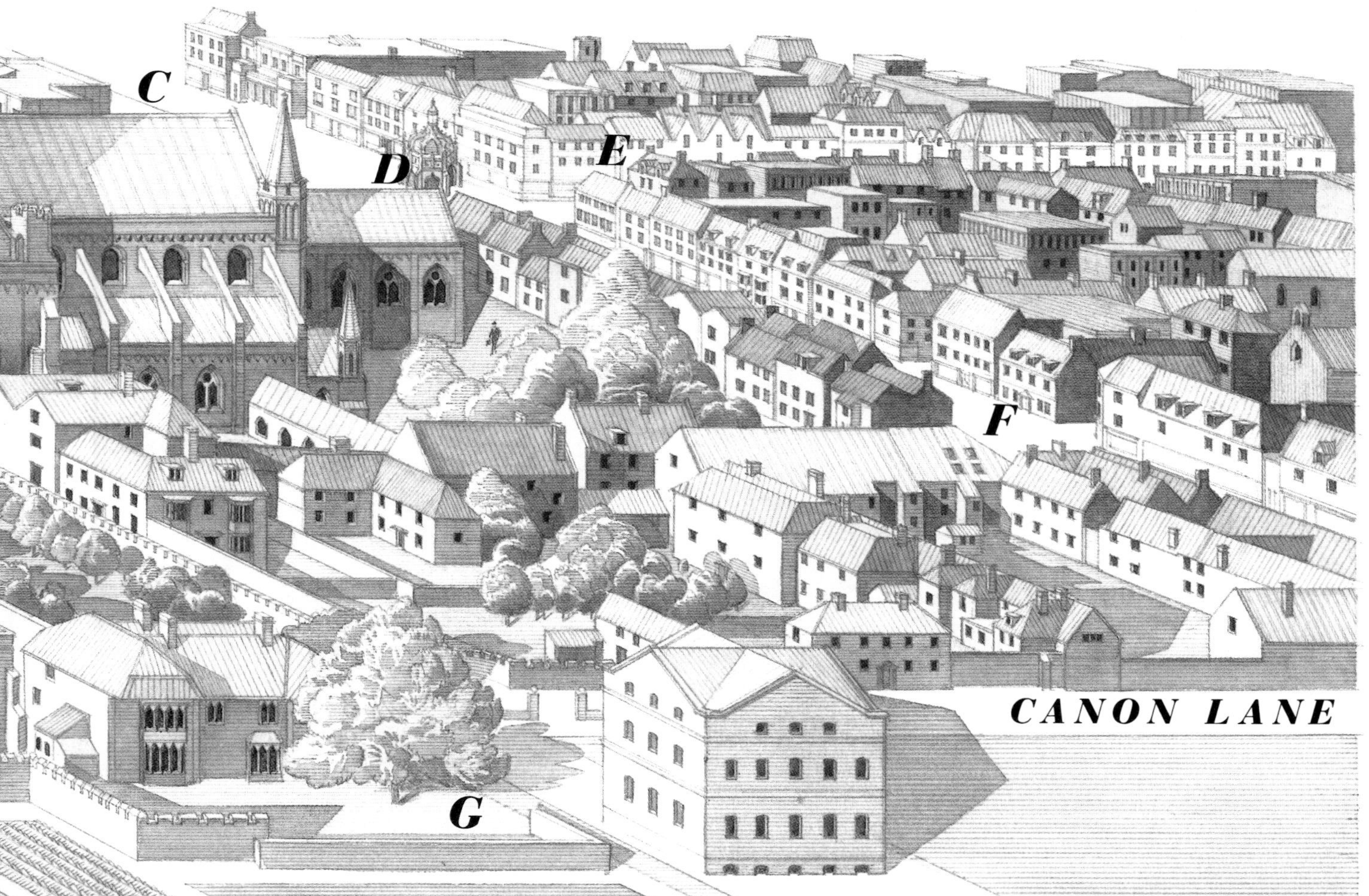

precincts in the south-west quadrant of the city

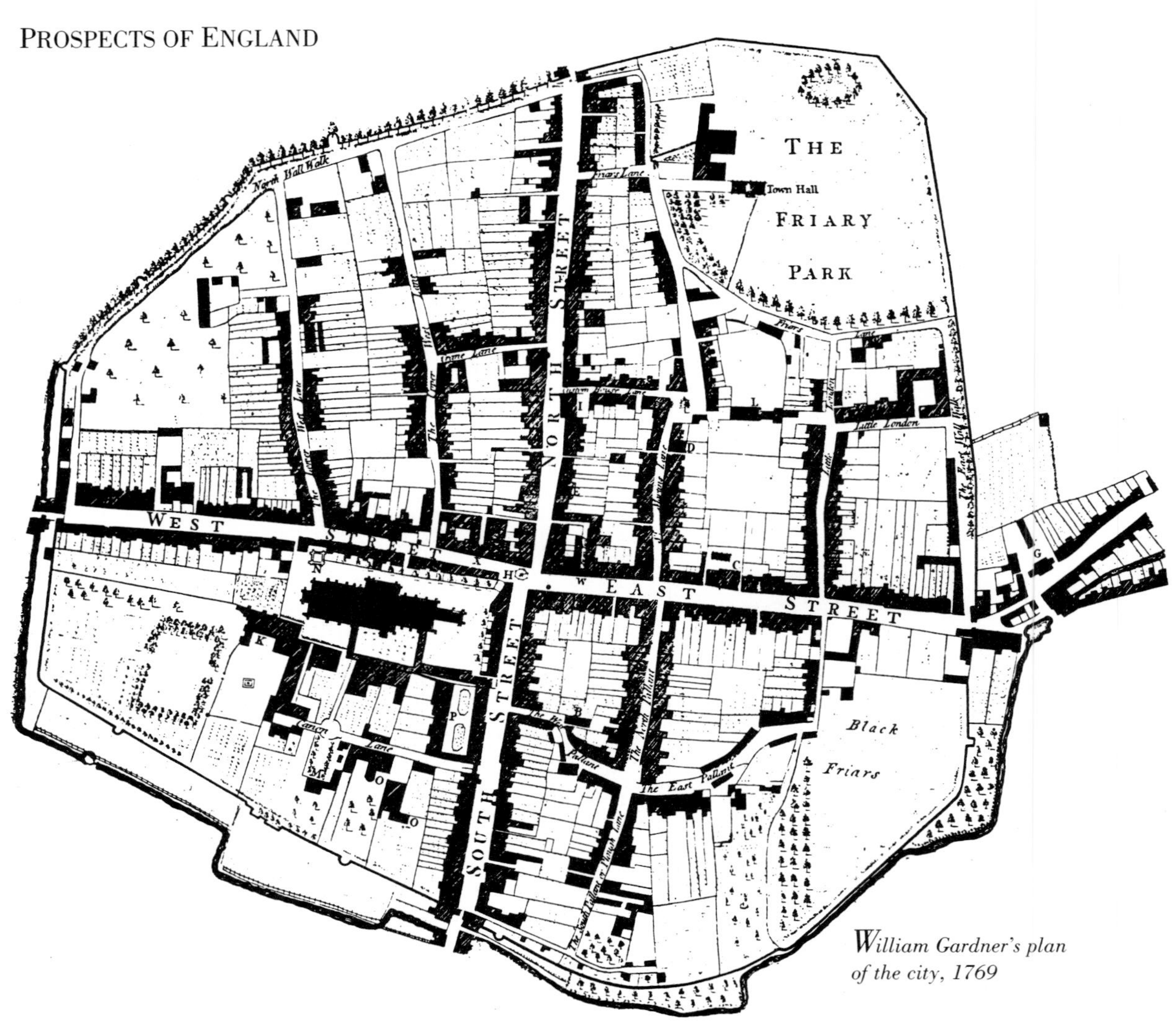

William Gardner's plan of the city, 1769

HOUSE PRICES in CHICHESTER today are determined by the line of a wall put up by its citizens in the third century AD. A house inside this Roman wall, the circuit of which is still virtually complete, is worth double its equivalent outside. Asked why, the estate agents say that outside the wall: 'You feel that you are there, but you are not quite there. You're in Chichester, but you're not *in* Chichester.' It is the difference between the urbs and the suburbs, the thing itself and its accretions.

If you go out through the wall at Northgate (the gate itself demolished like the others in the eighteenth century) and turn left, you will quickly come to the archway into the yard of Frederick Hill Ltd. Here, if anywhere, you can understand the exclusivity of the walled city. The corrugated iron sheds of the builders' yard are leant up against the outer face of the wall. There is a stark and revealing difference between the two elements in the scene—the plain height of the flint wall itself, grand and simple in its conception, and the busy clutter of a working yard at its foot. The one is austere and uncompromised, the other nothing but its details.

The wall has been repaired and refaced many times—by Alfred, often in the Middle Ages, in the eighteenth century when a promenade was made along the ramparts, and again recently. But the core is Roman and above all the *idea* is Roman. It may be that the wall was not originally built for defence—there is no sign about its construction of hurry—but to mark the Emperor Caracalla's decree in AD 212, by which Roman citizenship was awarded to all free subjects of the Empire. The aim of the wall was simply to circumscribe the town. A stone wall made the town distinct from its surroundings, establishing it as a place of order and arrangement, even of grandeur, quite different from the detailed mess of everything next to it. The wall, in short, defined the urbane.

That is a Latin word. The idea of the town, along with the cabbage, the turnip, the parsnip, the poppy, the pansy, the rose and the goose, was introduced to Britain by the Romans. And there is one incident which illuminates the sudden arrival of this urban idea in Britain. Preserved from AD 51, the moment almost exactly when Chichester was coming into being, it concerns a question asked by Caractacus, the hero of the Celtic resistance against the Romans. He was a chieftain of the Catuvellauni and had left his own people to fight the Romans in South Wales and then in the mountains of Snowdonia, staving them off for eight years until betrayed by his allies, the Brigantes, in the northern Pennines. When he was finally captured and taken to Rome to be exhibited there as a transoceanic savage in the marble streets, he turned to his Roman hosts, blasé with triumphs, with the exotic displayed in their cosmopolis as casually as fruit in a supermarket stall, and asked 'why do you, with all these great possessions, still covet our huts?'

The question lies at the meeting of two worlds. Not only the question, but the whole scene: the mustachioed chieftain, his hair greased, his skin naked except for the chains, its muscled surface oiled by the producers of the Claudian triumph, his bearing famous through history for its nobility; the perfumed spectators, the washed curiosity of the imperial intelligentsia, regarding with interest this other-world figure from beyond the limits of Empire, for whom the city was almost inconceivably foreign. This scene, a bringing together of the before and after of the urban experience, marks some sort of beginning. Here in the streets of Rome, where the city is a stage for political drama, is the start of our own urban history. The way Chichester is now is not strictly understandable until you have heard that story because Chichester is a Roman thing set down in Britain. It is a political artefact and—in a scuffed, changed, rubbed-down way—it still embodies, as a sort of manifesto, Roman ideas of civility and urbanity.

What was here before? In Chichester the answer is almost certainly *nothing*, or virtually nothing. An early Iron Age round house has been found in Sadler's Walk and some huts in the Cattlemarket, but apart from these the excavations in the city have found only a few Iron Age coins and pots. Roman Chichester grew on this green-field site. The first buildings here were a military camp and depot connected with the invasion in AD 43. For the following thirty years or so, the new town had a slightly stuttering beginning—little more than a small village outside the military depot, with some light industrial works and a frankly obsequious dedicatory inscription to Nero. In the early AD 70s, however, the situation changed radically.

Since well before the invasion, the Celtic people in this southern part of Sussex—the misnamed Regni,

The yard of Frederick Hill Ltd outside the north wall. Nowhere in England is the difference clearer between the urbs and the suburbs, the town itself and its messy accretions.

meaning 'the proud, the stiff ones'—had been allies and clients of the Romans against the other Celts in Britain. The king of the Regni, Tiberius Claudius Cogidubnus, was probably a friend of Vespasian. Possibly educated in Rome, his two imperial Roman names precede the royal Celtic one, and he was installed here very much as an Harrovian Maharajah would have been in India. His spectacular palace, Fishbourne, a mile or so from Chichester, built by Italian craftsmen, was the largest and most sumptuous Roman building north of the Alps. He had been loyal to the Empire throughout the early troubles of Roman Britain, providing troops in AD 60 to fight Boudicca during her rebellion. Nine years later, after a period of savage civil war in the Empire, Vespasian became Emperor and, partly as a reward for the loyalty of Cogidubnus, partly as a conscious wooing of the Britons, Chichester, or *Noviomagus Regnensium*, the Newmarket of the Regni, was in effect refounded. It now began to take on the form which has governed it until today.

The strict planning of Roman towns, and of the military camps which imitated them, was not simply an exercise in imperial rationality. The Romans saw it in some way as a ritual and symbolic act. There were three elements of crucial importance: the boundary, the centre and the two main streets which crossed there. All three remain important in the shape of Chichester today.

Throughout the Empire there was a fixed pattern to the founding of a town. A white ox and a cow would be yoked to a bronze plough, the ox on the outside of the boundary, the cow on the inside. Leading a procession, the founder, perhaps Cogidubnus in this case, would have begun to plough 'the first furrow' at the southwest corner (the only place today where the green fields come up to the wall) and would have continued in a wide circuit, establishing the limits of the future town. The ploughman covered his head with a flap of his toga and ensured that all the earth fell *in* towards the town. Any clod that fell outwards would be picked up by his followers and thrown inside the furrow. When the plough came to the site of a gate, it was taken out of the ground and carried over to the other side. *Portare*, to carry, is the root of *porta*, meaning gate. Throughout the Empire, the walls, which always had this sacred origin, were administered by the priests; they were objects sacred to Terminus, the god of boundaries. The gates on the other hand, where the sacred plough had been lifted, were always subject to civil jurisdiction.

Once the limits had been established, a hole, called the *mundus*, the world, was then dug in the centre of the town. First fruits and other unspecified good things, or even soil from Rome were all thrown into the hole which was then covered. The augur, whose title is preserved in the midst of the English ceremony of in*augur*ation, would stand on the central spot and draw out with a staff, both on the ground and in the air, the cardinal points around which the town was to be fixed. All sorts of oracles would be consulted. The behaviour of a goat, a cow, a falcon, a crow, a snake or a swarm of bees could all be relevant. An animal would be sacrificed and its liver inspected. A town was never planned without the inspection of a liver, because different parts of a liver were believed to correspond to different parts of the sky and the plan of a town was conceived of, in some senses, as a map of the sky. As Hyginus Gromaticus, the late Roman philosopher, wrote: 'The origin of the setting up of boundaries is heavenly and its practice invariable . . . Boundaries are never drawn without reference to the order of the universe, for the decumani [the east-west streets] are set in line with the course of the sun, while the cardines [the north-south streets] follow the axis of the sky.' Chichester is aligned in exactly this way, as is apparent from the site of Eastgate. It is now a rather complicated traffic intersection but the Roman origins are clear. East Street, laid along the course of the sun, meets, in a precise but obtuse angle, the line of Stane Street, running northeastwards from here to London Bridge. That angle is the meeting of the ritual and the practical.

No one, perhaps, has ever been more impressed by the ordained regularity of Chichester than the young Eric Gill. Until 1897, when he and his family arrived from Brighton to settle in Chichester, Gill had been obsessed by railway engines. 'I saw Chichester,' he wrote in his autobiography. 'It had simply never occurred to me before that day that towns could have a shape and be, like my beloved locomotives, things with character and meaning. If you had been drawing "engines" for years and were then suddenly taken to such a city, you would instantly see what I mean. I had not been training myself to become an engineer, I had been training myself to see Chichester, the human city, the city of God, the place where life and work and things were all in one and all in harmony. . . . It was a town, a city, a thing planned and ordered—no mere congeries of more or less ordered streets, growing like a fungus. . . . Here was no dead product of mathematical calculation, no mere sanitary and convenient arrangement. Here was something as human as home and as lovely as heaven. . . . Chichester is more than usually serene and orderly. The plan is clear and clean and rational—a thing of beauty having unity, proportion and clarity.'

Can an English town ever have had such a paean sung to it? But Gill is right. The plan of Chichester is a *mappa mundi*, a cross inscribed within a circle. The four main streets aligned on the cardinal points meet—in a slightly crooked way—at a central umbilicus: Chichester's navel, the market cross, which was put up in 1501 by Bishop Storey. If you get here at nine o'clock on a weekday morning you will see a Roman principle at work. All the clerks of the businesses in the town meet under the pale limestone of the gothic canopy to exchange letters. It is a place for a few minutes every morning of rubber bands and brown envelopes, of gossip and flirtation. It is the perfect example of a town plan working equally efficiently on the symbolic and the practical levels. The social, economic and physical centres of Chichester are for a moment united in that daily event.

I have, of course, exaggerated the surviving Romanness of Chichester. There has been a great gap in the past. The picture of Chichester in the fifth century recovered by the archaeologists is one in which the Romanness of the place has disappeared, leaving a haphazard and rather squalid occupation in timber buildings. The street plan now, if one is to be honest about it, is far more that of the tenth-century Saxon town, refortified by Alfred as one of his *burhs* against the Danes. It was at this stage that these cardinal streets acquired their slight wobble, where their Roman predecessors would have followed a perfectly straight line. And for anyone less intent on Chichester's origins, the impact of the Middle Ages would dominate the city: the Norman cathedral with its splendid fat needle of a spire (a perfect nineteenth-century replacement for the medieval one which collapsed in 1861) is its greatest building; one of the largest and best-preserved medieval almshouses in the country, St Mary's Hospital, is here; the large park cut in the northeast corner of the town surrounds the site of the Norman castle erected there soon after the Conquest; and the southeast quadrant, known as the Pallants, as it was the 'pale' or reserve belonging to the Archbishops of Canterbury, has an entirely medieval street plan.

Nevertheless, despite the great amnesiac period of the Dark Ages and the huge medieval contributions to the fabric of Chichester, I will persist in seeing it as a Roman city. It is possible—and I would advocate it—to walk around these streets in a sort of antiquarian trance, to see the ghost outlines of its distant origins floating hazily under the modern streets, the urban and imagined equivalent of the crop-marks left by rural villas.

There is one place, in the south aisle of the Cathedral, where you can see more than this and still look directly into the distant past. A hole several feet deep has been cut in the cathedral aisle; it is roofed in glass and floored with a fragment of a second-century mosaic. (It is a clever and slightly bogus bit of drama. The fragment was actually found several feet away and moved into the cathedral for effect. And there was no need to put it so far underground. Nevertheless it provides exactly what one needs: the surgeon's view into the layers beneath.) With this as your inspiration, and the detailed reports of excavations in the city as your guide, you can begin to walk the streets in the double-vision trance. As you move along North Street past W.H. Smith's, Sainsbury's, Acres the Bakers and the Rediffusion television-hire shop, you are tracing the frontage of a string of Roman shops.

Further up North Street, under the clumpy brick arcade of the eighteenth-century Assembly Rooms, you will find a large Purbeck marble tablet that was discovered by builders in 1723 on a site nearby. It is the dedicatory inscription from a temple to Neptune and Minerva put up in the early AD 70s, with the blessing of Cogidubnus, who is named on the slab as the Imperial legate in Britain. This immense honour was shared by only one other non-Roman in the Empire: Herod.

In East Street there are Roman walls in the basement of the National Westminster Bank, the base for a column in front of Tesco's, a large building under Hogg Robinson's travel agents, a Roman sewer under Marks and Spencer, and another large building under St Martin's Lane which lies just to the west.

Outside the walls beyond the East Gate, in the Cattlemarket, are a couple of slightly more articulate memories. Two coins were found here dating from the Roman Republic—decades before the Claudian invasion—probably dropped by merchants from the Empire when Britain was still a struggling confusion of Celtic statelets. But more interesting are the remains from the Roman period. Several beetles were discovered in a Roman well here: of the various species found, some ate dung, some grain and flour, and others plaster and wood. A farrier's knife and an animal emasculator were found in a box nearby. From this evidence, it seems likely that both the cattlemarket and the granary in which the *annona*, the Roman grain tax, was stored were on this site. A little further to the east, surrounded and now partly impinged on by nineteenth-century housing estates, which grew up after the railway's arrival in 1846, is the low turf bank of the Roman amphitheatre. If you ask the way to it in the jumble of streets nearby, there will be a tinge of incredulity as the instructions are given; Chichester's amphitheatre is not the Colosseum.

Wherever a spade has turned over the Chichester earth, it has struck something Roman. Cemeteries have been found outside all four gates; at the south end of South Street, under Rumbelow's electrical goods store, the foundations of the town wall have been found continuing serenely where, above ground, they have been erased; several tessellated rooms of a town house were found under the Bishop's Palace; and another under East Pallant House . . . and so on for many hundreds of examples. If you are ready to succumb to the antiquarian enthusiasm, it can seem at times as though you are floating like a Buddhist monk a few feet above the level at which Chichester really exists. And if you stop for a minute to have a cup of coffee and a bun in Morelli's café in East Street, the effect is weirdly redoubled. Morelli's is done out in a good, if plastic, imitation of precisely the most vulgar kind of interior decor which would have graced many of the more pretentious houses in Roman Chichester—mirrors and brown sausage-coloured formica marble, floor to ceiling. It is not to be missed.

Of all the archaeologists' discoveries, those in the northwest quadrant are the most intriguing. This part of the city, heavily bombed in 1943, has been more completely redeveloped than any other during this century, and is now filled with council offices, a circular library and new housing. With each phase of destruction and rebuilding, the Chichester archaeologists have been able to investigate the Roman plan. For once the evidence is not fragmentary, but comes together as a convincing urban scene. In dig after dig (and anywhere that a trench has been made for pipes or foundations, over an area that stretches almost 200 yards north of West Street, under the Post Office

West Pallant House

4 West Pallant

9 West Pallant

Pallant House

and the telephone exchange, at the back end of Sainsbury's and Woolworth's and crossing the line of the modern Chapel Street) the same thing has been found: a three-foot thickness of gravel, the huge bulk of which was brought here in the AD 70s or AD 80s. This was almost certainly the Forum of Roman Chichester.

At its southeastern corner, now covered by the Dolphin and Anchor Hotel, the six-feet-thick foundations of a large and heavy Roman building were discovered during the war. This, on the prime site in the town, was probably the Basilica, the administrative centre for the district, controlled by the *Ordo*, a local council of a hundred property owners. It was surrounded by a pavement of eight-inch-thick sandstone slabs. In the Forum itself there were statues on high columns and to the west of it, behind the present Post Office and under the Continental café (which now occupies the deconsecrated church of St Peter), were the splendid town baths. These covered 6,400 square yards and were probably built by the same craftsmen who had erected the palace at Fishbourne to include underfloor heating, stoking rooms for the hot baths, a cold water cistern with its pump, and culverts and sewers, both bringing fresh water and carrying the waste away.

One or two Roman pieces—a stretch of stone guttering, a column base—can now be seen set in concrete near the entrance barrier to the Little London car park. They are mossy and neglected things, but from them, and from what the archaeologists have found and surmised, one can start to envisage the effect produced by the material scale of the Roman city. It must be remembered that the Celts had almost nothing in the way of a town; their semi-pastoral, semi-agricultural society did not invest its values in a fixed place. Celtic temples were often no more than holes in the ground or natural places—a grove, a single tree. Rivers were goddesses in themselves, needing no statues, nothing constructed. The Celtic world was itself in this sense fluid and unfixed. They had music and poetry but no writing. Throughout the three and a half centuries of the Roman presence in Britain, in which literacy penetrated far enough into society for obscene graffiti to be written (in Latin) on lavatory walls—nothing whatsoever was written in Celtic. It is as if the idea of writing, the fixed thing, and the Celtic mind were mutually exclusive.

For protection the Celtic tribes had built forts defended by ramparts and ditches, often but not always on hills. The largest of these the Romans called *oppida*—towns—but in essence they were little more than Zulu *kraals*, with large acreages of pasture inside them and a haphazard collection of round huts scattered within the ditches. There was little planning or arrangement.

The Celts concentrated on other things and the luxuries available to their aristocrats can still astonish: the torcs of twisted gold worn around the neck, in

23 and 25 North Street

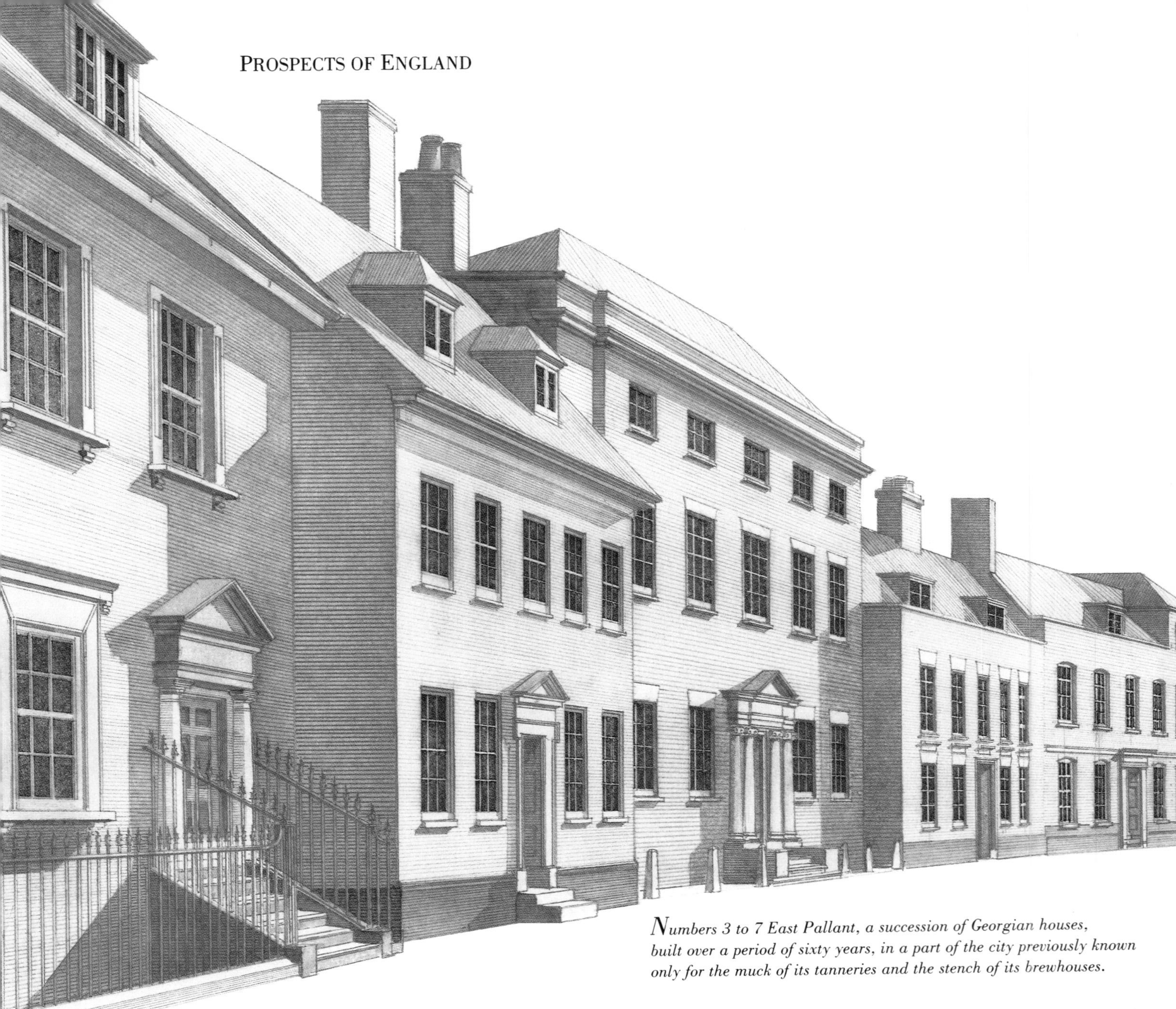

Numbers 3 to 7 East Pallant, a succession of Georgian houses, built over a period of sixty years, in a part of the city previously known only for the muck of its tanneries and the stench of its brewhouses.

which the braided metal is as thick as a python; the heavy bronze armlets which clasped the muscles of their upper arms; the mirrors, the long oval shields and the daggers, all decorated with the easy, near-animal curves of the Celtic imagination. The work and the substance in these objects could match anything in the Roman Empire, but what is significant about them is that they are all related exclusively to the body of the individual. They are the crowning artefacts of a society in which the great *individual* is the focus of its ideals and aspirations. The Celtic chieftain glitters in the mud of his kingdom. The Roman administrator—physically—is modest within the public luxury and substance of his surroundings. That is the central change brought about by the Romans in Britain. The focus moves from the physical body of the great man to the place in which he rules. No torcs but temples; not the dagger as a work of art but the forum, the basilica; not the song but the inscription; not the heroic stance but the reliable organization; not mud but gravel; not the kraal but the town.

The Roman historian Tacitus, writing of his father-in-law, Agricola, who was governor of Britain in the AD 70s, describes the cynical uses to which this Roman style was put: 'To induce a people hitherto scattered, uncivilized and therefore prone to fight, to grow pleasurably inured to peace and ease, Agricola gave private encouragement and official assistance to the building of temples [North and East Streets in Chichester], forums [off North and West Streets] and private villas [several miles outside the town]. . . . And so the Britons were gradually led on to the amenities that make vice agreeable—arcades [around the forum], baths [West Street] and sumptuous banquets. They spoke of such novelties as civilization when really they were only features of their enslavement.'

This is written as though the Romanization of the Celts was a complete success. There is evidence, however, from many Roman towns in Britain, that the Celtic aristocracy remained disdainful of urban life. At the abandoned town of Silchester, Chichester's twin forty miles to the north and now completely excavated, there are only twenty-five houses suitable for a member of the Ordo, which *always* consisted of a hundred local notables. Only a quarter of the ruling class took up urban residence; the rest remained in their country houses. Just as Chichester's great buildings reflected those at the palace at Fishbourne built a little earlier, it was always the country houses which led the towns in technical and artistic development. It may well be that town life for the Celtic grandees became, as it did for aristocrats later in English history, nothing but a part-time activity. Most of the year was devoted to their estates; the commercial and political business of town detained them for only a short season, when they would have taken lodgings. The severe distinction between town and country dwellers which emerged on the mainland of Europe never appeared here. The aristocracy remained attached to their land and when the entire Continental Empire was riven by peasant revolts in the fourth century, almost nothing of the kind occurred in Britain.

As a result, the life of Roman Chichester was, above all, commercial. The inscription on the temple in North Street reveals that it was paid for by '*collegium fabrorum*', a guild of craftsmen. Shops would have lined the Forum and the main streets, usually with living quarters at the back. On market days traders set up stalls in the porticos. A town of about 2,000 people, little smaller, for example, than Roman Paris, was provided with all the services one might expect. Chichester was the market for a port and all the primary goods which, for the first two centuries of Roman occupation, were drained out of Britain to satisfy the Continental appetite, would have streamed through here. Wool, corn, pearls, jet, dogs (especially bulldogs), baskets, bears (for the Colosseum) and oysters, as well as furs, hides and slaves from the north and Ireland, all contributed to Britain's adverse balance of trade with the rest of the Empire. It was an exploited colony in which the grandeur and order of the city streets were the tools of imperial flatterers.

The development of the town slowed after the death of Cogidubnus. Throughout the second century houses were improved with private bath suites, underfloor heating and coloured mosaic floors. At the end of the century Chichester was surrounded, in part, by an earth bank, to which the flint and mortar wall (faced with greensand blocks) was added a decade or so later. At this point Chichester probably became the capital of its own semi-autonomous city state. Prosperity continued and throughout the third and the beginning of the fourth centuries stone houses replaced the timber and clay buildings of the earlier town. The baths were rebuilt at least four times, each time increasing in luxury, elaboration and comfort.

In AD 367 a conspiracy of barbarians shattered the complacency of the province, as Picts and Scots overran the northern border. Chaos dominated Britain for two years until the towering figure of Count Theodosius restored national government. He refortified all the towns of Britain and solid, projecting bastions were added to the walls in all of them. You can still visit the one at the southwest corner of Chichester, accessible through the Bishop's garden. Another, at the southeastern corner has a pretty Victorian gazebo built on top of it. Originally they were designed as platforms for large stone-throwing machines. It had become a time of anxiety: troops were billeted on the townspeople to form a militia; German mercenaries were hired by the disintegrating Roman administration; in the last decades of the century, the stone buildings were robbed to repair the walls.

In AD 410 the leaders of the British towns wrote to the Emperor Honorius asking for help against an internal rebellion. He told them to look after themselves. This was no formal withdrawal of empire on the twentieth-century model. The province had been stripped of troops over many decades to fight, usually disastrously, in the endemic civil wars on the Continent. The administration of Britain had become almost impossibly complicated, as it degenerated from a single province to little more than a series of balkanized statelets. In some ways it was already a medieval world, in which membership of councils was hereditary and where half-Arthurian titles—the Duke of Britain, the Count of the Saxon Shore—had already replaced the classical Roman ranks. Chichester

became part of the defences of the Saxon Shore, contributing to the fleet that guarded its coasts against raiders from the north. You must try to imagine the late Roman scouting craft docking in Chichester's harbour a mile or two away, perhaps at Dell Quay, strangely camouflaged, as a contemporary described them, with 'the sails and ropes dyed blue like the waves . . . and the sailors wearing blue uniforms so that they may scout more secretly by day as well as night'. The fringes of empire had already begun to fray like a tattered cloth and the dialects spoken in the crumbled streets filled with barbarian words which the Romans could not understand.

In fifth-century Chichester the picture is of houses in decay and streets breaking up, of wattle partitions within rooms, of crude hearths built on top of the mosaic floors, of layers of rubbish and silt in the streets, of drains collapsed, of the great bath complex on West Street become a rotting hulk and destined to moulder there until the twelfth century, when the builders of the Norman cathedral would use it as a quarry. Mass-produced pottery and money ceased to be commonly used after AD 430, although the last gold imperial coin known in Britain, a solidus of Valentinian III, dating from about AD 450, was found enigmatically and in isolation outside the east wall of the town. After that, nothing but silence.

In the blank light of day you might now never guess that this was once a Roman city. Chichester is not Herculaneum. Instead, another period will grab your attention: the eighteenth century. At its beginning the town was poor and squalid. It was invaded almost daily by different markets with their attendant and varying stenches. The names of streets in which they were held have since been sanitized: Hog Lane has become the stinkless St Martin's; Crooked 'S' Lane off North Street was once Slaughter Alley. Part of the car park off Little London was the Oxmarket and cattle were also sold, at least in the summer months, when the trade and smell were at their height, along the full length of East, North and West Streets. Tanners and fellmongers, treating the mounds of animal skins produced by the slaughterhouses, and stinking more than any other tradesmen, pursued their business in the southeast quadrant of the city, the Pallants. (Of this atmosphere, there is one rather intriguing remnant in Chichester. Shippam's meat paste factory abuts on to the end of East Street. A giant chicken wishbone hangs outside the office door and the entire building emits a smell close to a combination of rot, cooking and dog. It is the most immediate historical experience in the town.)

As James Spershott, an eighteenth-century memoirist, rather comfortably remembered the old days before the great change, 'the city had a very mean appearance in comparison of what it has since arrived to. The buildings were in general very low, very cold and their fronts fram'd with timber which lay bare to the weather. . . . There were very few houses even in the main street that had solid brick fronts.' Houses were often slightly below the level of the streets and anything unpleasant could run down into them. The situation was different only in the cathedral precincts, where, as ever, old money made an effortless display of its bland dignity.

All this was to change in the years to come. The focus of Chichester life, which in the Roman city had been in the northwest quadrant and which had shifted in the Middle Ages to the cathedral and Bishop's Palace in the southwest quadrant, now moved again, across South Street to the Pallants. Here, above all, in a state of extraordinary preservation, you can see the way in which the eighteenth-century town remade itself. In a short period of a few decades the rotten squalor of medieval and submedieval Chichester was transformed. The new houses were not built half-below the streets, but were raised above them, a small staircase reaching up to the front doors. And here, quite consciously, in Chichester's own provincial

St Martin's Square, softened in the snow. A piece of informal—or at least half-formal—eighteenth-century town-planning, which in its slight juggling with order and symmetry represents the best of Chichester.

Renaissance, the classical ideal was brought back to the Roman city. The driving force was new money, derived from a boom in the corn trade and growing profits in more sophisticated goods from abroad. And the style in which the new well-being was expressed was the dominant aesthetic of the time—the Renaissance ideals of regularity and symmetry, transmitted through enough filters to make the result classical in reference but English in substance.

There is no dominant eighteenth-century town plan. The property boundaries may well be Saxon, and each statement of the new classical modernity is made on its own. Nothing is blocked together. That is the real delight of the Pallants—the way in which individuals come to a common purpose by slightly different and individually chosen routes. In East Pallant, one of the prettiest rows of houses in England, you can see this to perfection: No. 6 is quite plain and demure, from early in the century, while No. 5 is much swankier and built in about 1760, with a flamboyant three-part Ionic doorcase, and No. 4 is again from early in the century, but brought to a point by its small and utterly elegant doorcase, added about fifty years after the house itself was built. This beautiful street is exactly expressive of the English small-town character, its near self-importance, its drawing back from pretension and shunning of the exaggerated.

Just around the corner is a house that oversteps the mark. Pallant House—the name itself a faintly offensive assumption, claiming as it does a quarter of the city—was built in about 1712 by Henry Peckham, a young man on the make. He was a dramatic snob, banning the market in front of his house, removing its ancient market cross, and having two fake Elizabethan portraits of his ancestors painted for the drawing room. The house itself, in beautiful brick, also demonstrates it. Everything is frilled and flounced, finicky and flickering. As the crowning element of the façade, Peckham had a local sculptor top the gateposts on either side of the stair leading to the front door with a pair of ostriches, the bird in the Peckham coat of arms. They were so incompetently executed that the town immediately christened Peckham's residence the Dodo House. Small towns see through their man.

Do not end here. Go up North Pallant, across East Street and up St Martin's Lane along the side of Marks and Spencer (a shop, incidentally, which covers the area of what had previously been thirteen individual holdings, including all their gardens, outbuildings, stables and so on, and in which the kink in the southeast corner of the food department follows a medieval property boundary). A couple of hundred yards up St Martin's Lane, you will come to St Martin's Square. This little eighteenth-century space is oddly grand in a small way, like a Venetian campo, in which the arrangement is more than any one part. The place is both whole and without focus, and embodies some of the best of Chichester and perhaps of England.

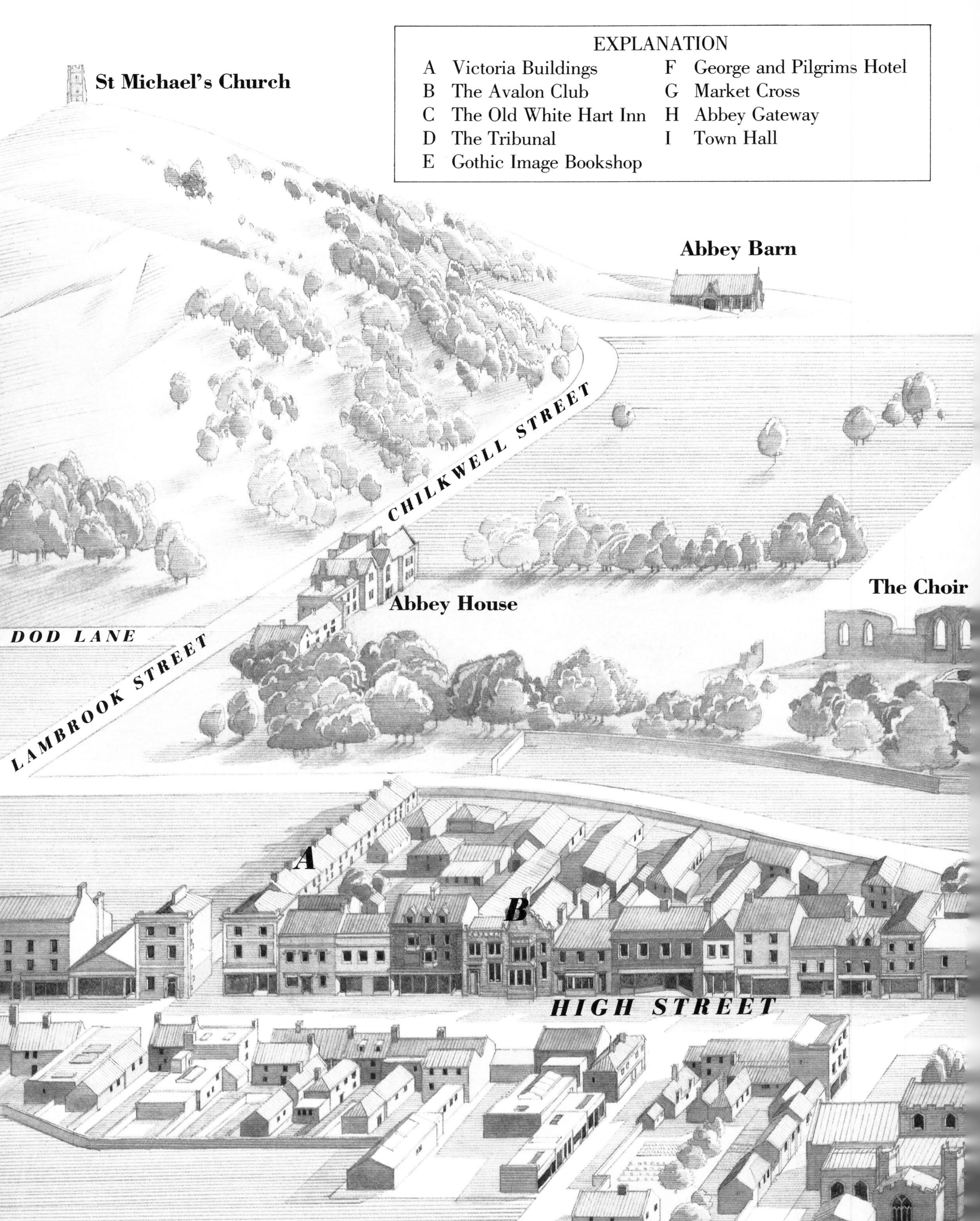
EXPLANATION
A Victoria Buildings
B The Avalon Club
C The Old White Hart Inn
D The Tribunal
E Gothic Image Bookshop
F George and Pilgrims Hotel
G Market Cross
H Abbey Gateway
I Town Hall
St Michael's Church
Abbey Barn
CHILKWELL STREET
Abbey House
The Choir
DOD LANE
LAMBROOK STREET
A
B
HIGH STREET

GLASTONBURY
Somerset

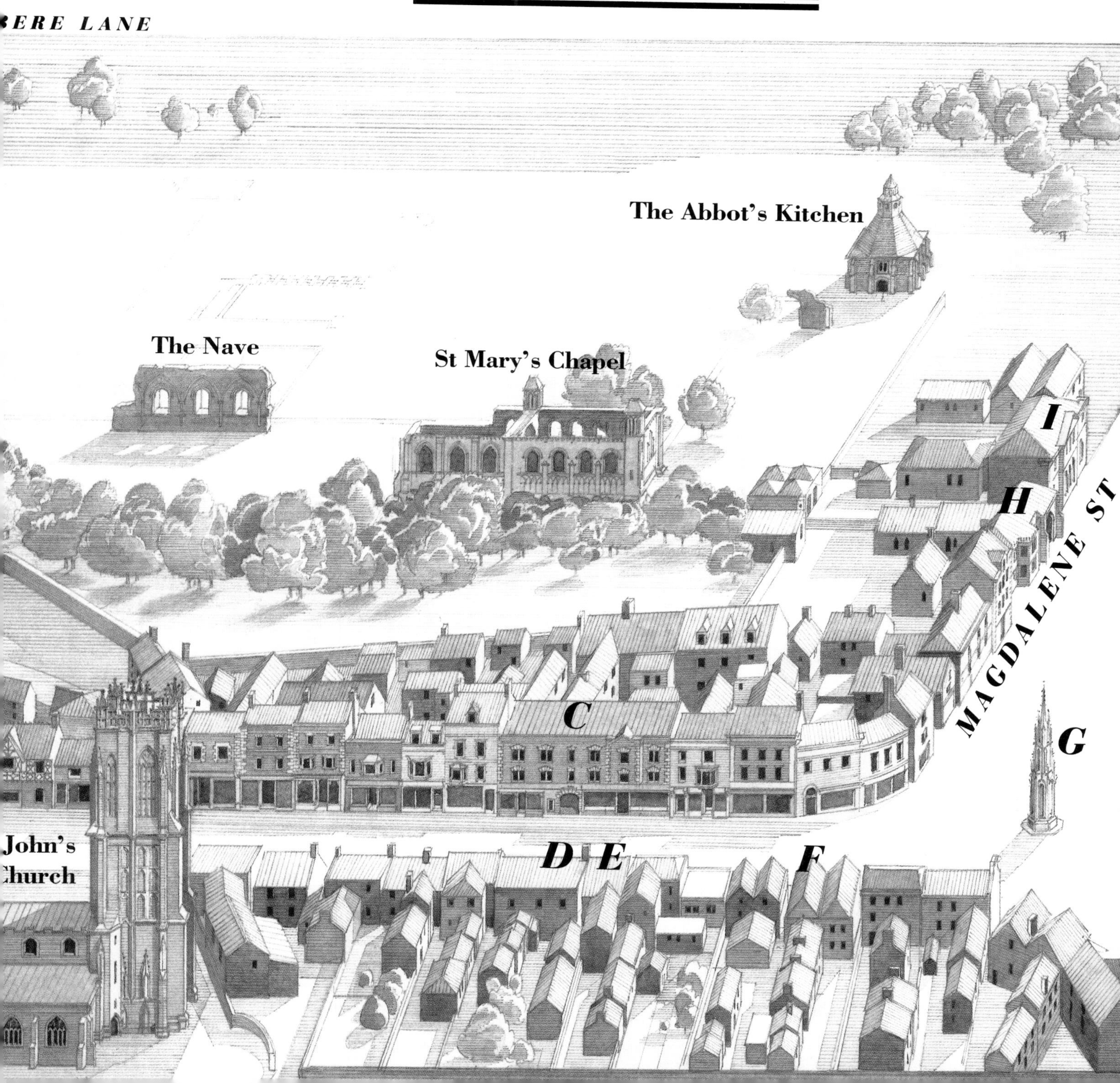

IF THERE is something about GLASTONBURY in Somerset which strikes you as bitty, even part-defunct, not entirely right in itself, this is because it still bears the mark of a town that was deliberately ruined. For the first thousand years of its existence Glastonbury was a company town. The immensely powerful corporation which had its headquarters here was, in the most frighteningly Stalinist of episodes, taken over by the government. Its assets were stripped, its power base broken, its chief executive and two of his assistants (falsely accused of crimes against the state) publicly humiliated and then hanged, the rest of the staff bought off or otherwise dispersed and—eventually—most of its buildings sold either as hard core for the new road to Wells or to any farmer or peasant who happened to be building a cattle shed or piggery nearby.

The corporation was Glastonbury Abbey, the sudden takeover its dissolution by the Crown in November 1539. To describe it in these terms is no exaggeration. You only have to look at the broad outline of the plan of the town today to see that its streets are draped around the four sides of a vacuity. The forty-odd acres of the abbey precinct are a lovely, rolling bit of countryside, filled with trees from romantic nineteenth-century plantings that frame the broken molars of the abbey ruins themselves. It is utterly unurban. At its eastern end, there is even a country house, 'the much admired and distinguished residence called "The Abbey House"', as the particulars of an auction held here in 1850 described it, 'in the "*Tudor*" style of architecture, the elevation of which is elegant and imposing in the extreme'. This 1825 house is now a retreat for Anglican clergymen.

The rural space which the abbey precinct has become eats the very heart out of Glastonbury. In the four and a half centuries since the Dissolution, Glastonbury has never made for itself a new, non-monastic and secular centre. As a result it has a shiftless and oddly uneasy atmosphere. The so-called market-place, at the bottom end of the High Street, is scarcely more than a slight widening of Magdalene Street which comes up to meet it from the south. Rather unenthusiastically, the local teenagers gather here in the evenings on the small terrace in front of the Town Hall (1818); the wilder members of the alternative Glastonbury society, attracted here by what one rather severe nineteenth-century historian called

The east side of the Market Place

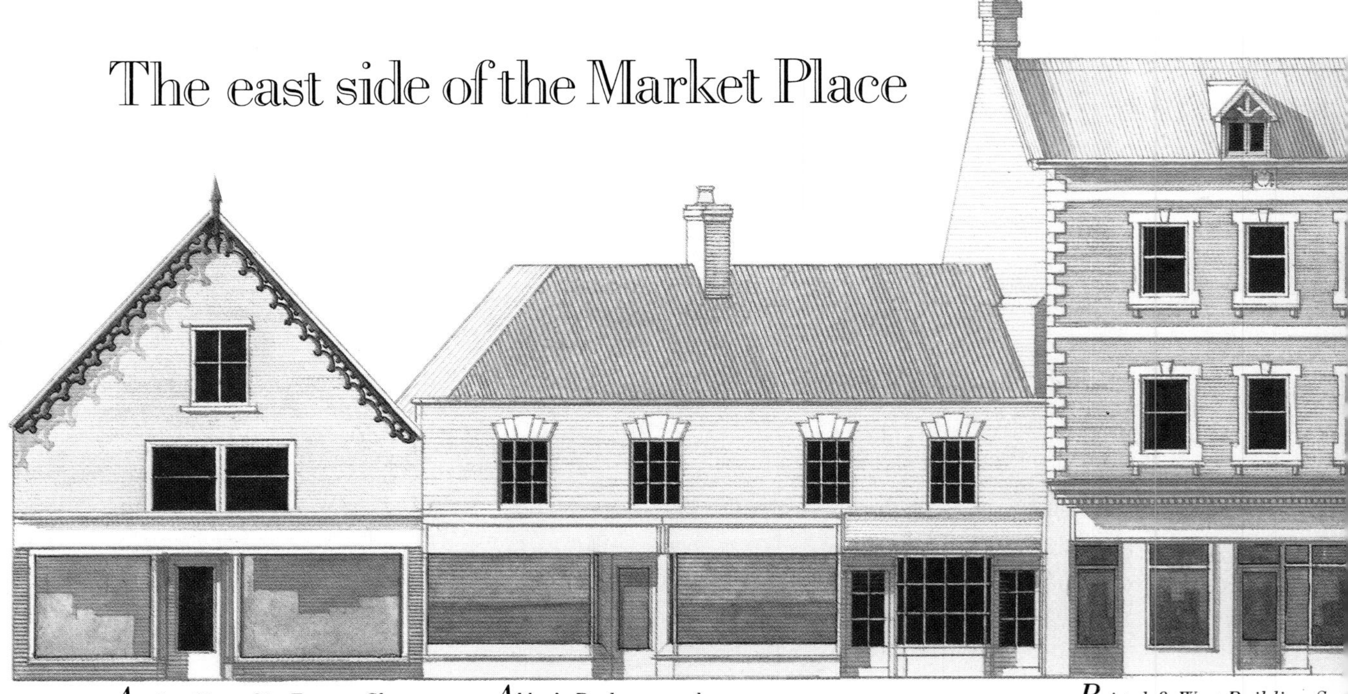

Avalon Sheepskin Factory Shop.
A medieval building with early nineteenth-century bargeboards.

Abbot's Parlour tea-shop.
An eighteenth-century front on a much older building, perhaps part of the Abbey school.

Bristol & West Building Soc
A mid-eighteenth-century shopkeeper's house.

'the mist of hobgoblin notions even now to be found floating over the district', sit by the war memorial in St John's churchyard halfway up the High Street, playing their guitars, meditating, or simply reminding the passing members of the bourgeoisie of their spiritual indigence.

Apart from these two rather marginal places, Glastonbury nowhere comes to rest. The town itself is a place of haste and discontinuity and the reason for this, quite simply, is that without a working, living abbey it lacks focus. I know of no other town which is so badly in need of its ghosts. Henry VIII and his commissioners disembowelled it and the story of Glastonbury is in essence a simple one: the all-important presence of the abbey, followed by its all-important absence.

The beginnings of this monastic town are sunk deep in a muddled and muddied pool of legend, propaganda, fraud, selective evidence, wishful thinking, credulity, sanctity, extraordinary coincidence, enigmatic remains, corrupted records and outright eccentricity. It is the realm of suggestibility, a rich compost in which the most flamboyant side of Glastonbury's life flowers as never before. It is surely the only town in the world where you can take a Mystical Tour (£10, about three hours, highly recommended, from a shop called Gothic Image in the High Street) on which a modern mystic will calmly and sympathetically conduct you around the sacred sites. This is Avalon, the Isle of Apples, one of the Isles of the Blest, where Arthur was buried, dead of his wounds at the last Battle of Camlann; down there, over the River Brue, is the Pons Perilis, where Sir Bedevere, at the third time of asking, cast the sword Excalibur into the waters; here too in AD 63, Joseph of Arimathaea came to evangelize Britain, bringing with him the Holy Grail, the cup in which he had caught the blood of the Saviour as He died on the cross. Joseph arrived first at Wearyall Hill on the western edge of Glastonbury. Here he planted his staff in the ground and it sprouted as the Glastonbury Thorn, a miraculous tree which flowers on Christmas Day. It was cut down by a maddened seventeenth-century Puritan who was blinded by a flying woodchip as he did so. Where the abbey now is, Joseph built the first Christian church in the country and buried the Grail at the foot of Chalice Hill.

What can you say? The literature surrounding these stories is vast and acrimonious. Sceptics and believers both pour out rivers of mutual scorn on the blindness of the enemy. Unless you have undergone the 'Glastonbury Experience' it is difficult to know what to think. There are stories of heavily pregnant women being drawn up the Tor on the eve of parturition by indefinable and irresistible forces; of apocalyptic thunderstorms accompanying the midsummer and midnight processions conducted on to the Tor by The Brotherhood of the Essenes and their leader, a woman known as *The Centre*. If one tends towards scepticism,

The Abbey Gateway and Porter's Lodge. A restored, part-medieval, part-eighteenth-century façade.

Town Hall, 1818, the ground-floor arcade originally open as a market.

however, there is at least one *fact* which has been dominant in the history of the place: since records began, Glastonbury —and the rest of England—has believed in its peculiar sanctity. This is not a place in which the sceptic, with his cool analysis of what might or might not be true, has ever thrived. The opposite has always been the case. Glastonbury was always the great *attractor*, the bringer-together of elements that began in other places, distinct and apart. In a more immediately intelligible way than the esoteric complexities of the Glastonbury mythomanes, this *attractability* of the town, its magnetism, has been of governing importance. In its heyday up until 1539, Glastonbury was never remote or cut off from its surroundings. It was the focus and organizing centre for them. It was the centre of its own spiritual and material world; it was always important to itself. And without the generally acknowledged sanctity of the place, that would never have happened. The Gothic Image mystics are only doing what comes most naturally to the town—making a perfectly good living out of an 'aura' which people like them have always understood to be there.

What, then, can be sifted as likely fact? There is no evidence of any Roman occupation of the abbey or the town, although remains of what might have been a Roman quay have been found at the foot of Wearyall Hill, Joseph's arrival point. The nearest relative to the winter-flowering thorn on that hill is to be found in Syria, spitting distance from Arimathaea. Something like a military outpost of the 6th century AD—the time of Arthur—has been found on top of the Tor, contemporary with and within signalling distance of the new fortifications at Cadbury Castle, the current favourite among Arthurologists for the site of Camelot.

When, a century later, the Saxons arrived here, Glastonbury was already a holy place. There were almost certainly huts here belonging to Celtic hermits and a crude church, both made from the willow that grows so easily on the Somerset wetlands nearby. This church, known as the Old Church in the records, was preserved until a fire destroyed it in 1184.

The holiness of the place was understood and confirmed by the Saxon kings who gave large tracts of land to the abbey. Three of them—Edmund, Edgar and Edmund Ironside—were eventually buried here. The magnetic attraction of Glastonbury ensured that not only land was accumulated by the abbey church but also an increasing number of significantly holy *bodies*. Those of Arthur and Guinevere, found in 1190, only a few years after the disastrous fire and certain to increase any revenue coming the abbey's way during a critical time, joined what was to become a faintly monstrous collection of relics. The list of them made in the fourteenth century, kept in the muniment room, reads to me (as a twentieth-century, non-Catholic) like a rummage through a vast and macabre attic. Whole bodies are somehow more acceptable than parts. There was a complete St Patrick and an uninterfered-with St Dunstan (the possession of whose body both Glastonbury, where he had been Abbot, and Canterbury, where he was Archbishop, repeatedly claimed). There were hundreds of parts of 'apostles, martyrs, confessors and virgins', as it says in the relic list, of bishops and abbesses, one Pope (Urban), King Oswald, Bede 'the doctor' and 'Gildas, the historian', unspecified 'innocents and other unknowns', the head of St John the Evangelist, many parts of the holy cross and the stone on which Christ's blood had flowed, a bit of Daniel and the beard of St Paul, 'one big arm bone of St Wynwaloe', 'the flesh and blood of St Thomas of Canterbury; also his bones' and unspecified 'teeth and hair'—it is an astonishing catalogue of sacred dismemberment.

It was one of the best collections in the country, each piece in its particular place in the great abbey church and each the object of veneration and pilgrimage. In the vision of medieval Christianity, of which this place was a cardinal point in England, the idea of the Incarnation, of God becoming flesh, of holiness entering the physical body, was taken seriously enough for it to be recognized that the physical remains of a holy man or woman were also themselves holy. There is no conflict here between the spiritual and the physical; the one interpenetrates the other. And because of that intimacy, and the holiness of remains which follows from it, the remains were, in themselves, *healing*. It was the prospect of gaining health—both spiritual and material—from contact with or even proximity to the body of a holy man, that brought so many people on pilgrimages to the sites of relics. The number of pilgrims to Glastonbury before the Dissolution is not known, but it was large enough for the abbey to build a hotel for them in the High Street. It is still there, still a hotel and now renamed The George and Pilgrims, to catch both the secular and the religious trade. It is a sumptuously fronted building, panelled in good stone, and was probably built in about 1475. Five hundred years later the façade still has about it the air of a well-funded official building, on which no expense has been spared. It is pushed into the more humdrum surroundings of its purely commercial neighbours. Almost certainly, those visitors who stayed here would have had to pay for their board and lodging, and the construction of this smart building is more likely a sign of the abbey administration maximizing revenues than simply a reaction to the volume of pilgrim traffic. Pilgrimage was one of the few recognized forms of medieval holiday; it is obvious enough that an attractive inn would encourage the traveller to come.

This is to jump almost to the end of the story, but the string of connections between the inn, the relics, the idea of holiness and the management of the abbey's financial affairs is a good example of how Glastonbury —as an abbey and a monastic borough—allowed the spiritual to work alongside the practical side of life. After the abbacy of St Dunstan in the tenth century, it was never again a place of great sanctity. Monastic Glastonbury never had its mystics. But Glastonbury was always a place of order and integrity. It looked after its possessions; its abbots and monks (about eighty of them up until the middle of the fourteenth century; about fifty after that) seemed to have behaved well. The investigations into the state of the house that occurred at irregular intervals throughout the Middle Ages—often stimulated by the jealousy and rivalry of the Bishops of Bath and Wells for the rich, powerful and independent abbey in the middle of their diocese—almost never discovered anything seriously wrong. Abbot Walter Monyngton (1342–75) was reprimanded by the Bishop of Bath and Wells for providing disgusting food for the monks and for being rude to them when they wanted to see him. Abbot John Chinnock, his successor, was thought to be a little 'lukewarm and remiss in discovering and correcting offences'. These, though, were exceptions. Even when Henry VIII's lizard-minded Dissolution Commissioners came looking for laxity and corruption in 1535, they were forced to report to Thomas Cromwell that: 'at Glastonbury there is nothing notable; the brethren be so straight kept that they cannot offend.' Rather desperately in need of evidence three years later, and happily bribing to obtain it, all they could come up with was some dissatisfaction among the very young monks with the way they were being taught, and one objection to a little sodomy.

From the beginning the outlines of the Glastonbury régime are clear: in the background a richly numinous haze; in the medieval foreground a businesslike practicality. Glastonbury was a well-ordered place. Her town and her estates, alongside the life of the soul within the abbey precincts, were all perfectly maintained. It can be seen as a place of accessible holiness. You would not find the peaks of Christianity here but instead a high plateau. By the early twelfth century, after a slight hiccup at the time of the Norman Conquest, when some of its lands were stripped from it, only later to be returned, Glastonbury had arrived at this plateau of fulfilment. For the next four centuries, in a classically medieval coming-together of the *rich* and the *holy*, it was both one of the most sacred and the largest financial institutions in England. It was able to ride out almost any storm in either the economic or the political climate. Here, with the easy continuity of a liner in a swell, the Benedictine abbey, with the town around its feet, pursued its prosperous, litigious, conservative course. Its buildings were enhanced, its library and relic collection added to, its properties improved, its prestige enriched. It was a layered place: pagan myth, Celtic Christianity, Saxon and then Norman royal patronage. It had the essentially measured ideals of Benedictine monasticism—simplicity, community, enclosure, stability and obedience—and a vast estate spread across southern England of which this was the organizing node, the focus of a redistributive bureaucracy.

Next to this complex cultural institution—with its learning and seriousness, its money and sanctity—was the town, as parasitic and as necessary as any cluster of followers around a military camp or railway junction. As you walk the few streets of Glastonbury today, you are exploring a skeleton, the bones of a place from which the soft mobile elements that made it happen, have fallen away. But there is one aspect of monastic life which saves the story of Glastonbury, makes it restorable, fills the gaps with the memory of life. That is the obsessive care with which the administration of the monastery recorded what happened, what mattered and what was valuable. This written record, preserved in a well-ordered muniment room in the abbey, with a monk whose sole occupation was to look after it, was seen as the guarantee of the abbey's standing and possessions. When Edward III came to the abbey with his Queen Eleanor just before Christmas 1331, the climax of the visit came when the King was shown the assembled documents of the abbey, testimony to what it was and what it was worth. After he had seen them he confirmed all the liberties Glastonbury had ever enjoyed.

These were extensive. This town was in some senses the capital of a private monastic state. At its core was the land known since well before the Norman Conquest as the Twelve Hides. These 'hides' were parcels of land, nominally of 120 acres, which formed the basis for medieval taxation. The Twelve Hides had been granted to the abbey by Saxon kings. Over the years the abbey gradually enlarged their extent to take in wide stretches of both hill and lowland in Somerset. Within the Hides the Abbot was all-powerful. An inquest at Shaftesbury in 1275 found 'that no King, justice, sheriff, constable or other bailiff or official of the King, might come within the Twelve Hides in order to sue, examine, arrest or do anything which might disturb the Abbot or the monks.' The Abbot was said 'to hold the regality of the Isle of Glastonbury' and this was applied with all the pedantry of medieval legalism.

This judicial independence has left its own monument in the town. Just up the High Street from the George and Pilgrims Hotel is the Tribunal. This building dates from the fifteenth century, with a sixteenth-century façade added by the last abbot but one, Richard Bere. Nevertheless, it is certain that the abbey maintained a courthouse, probably on this site, from at least the thirteenth century onwards. In this building, which is now a local museum, the Twelve Hides Court met every four weeks, presided over by the abbey's steward—a layman and member of the county gentry, often a knight, a professional, paid a fee for services rendered—who was, in effect chief agent or factor of the abbey's estates. The bailiff of the Twelve Hides, another layman of the next rank down in the administrative hierarchy, acted as clerk or prosecutor. The court would hear all cases from the level of a manorial court—petty squabbles between people in the town, trespass, damage, failure to observe customs of the manor, minor debts and assaults, transfers of tenancy—to more serious things such as murder and grand thefts, which in more normal situations would be heard by the sheriff or assize court.

The Tribunal has been altered and restored since the Dissolution, and is now full of a rather incongruous collection of Iron Age spindle-whorls and crusty pots. It is, nevertheless, possible to imagine the court at work here. The townspeople on trial are kept waiting downstairs in the room at the front. Through the long windows looking onto the High Street they can see the faces of their neighbours peering in. There is a fireplace here, lit, warming. Their turn comes and they are summoned upstairs into the courtroom itself. The scale is small. At a table in the well-lit room sits the steward, an impressive and worldly figure, imbued with the automatic authority of his wide experience outside the rents and tenancies, the customary grazings and annual ritual which are the structure of everyday life for the ordinary townsman. The room is intimate and domestic; there is no dais. Logs burn in the fireplace here too. Unlike a modern court, no one here is a stranger to any part of the proceedings. Those sitting in judgement will be entirely familiar with the world of the man accused. Nor is he unfamiliar either with his judges or the sort of penalty they are likely to impose—more often than not a fine payable in money or in work to be done for the abbey. He is never removed to prison; the authority is not abstract.

It is a world of utter intimacy. No one and nothing would have been unfamiliar. Despite the strict definition and maintenance of class difference—the report made to Henry VIII late in 1539 on the Glastonbury estates owned by him at that time included 271 Bondmen 'whose Bodies and Goodes are at the King's Highnes pleasure', as they had been at the Abbot's—there was an astonishing ease of access across the class boundaries. From almost the last moments of Glastonbury's existence as an abbey, there is a glimpse of this closeness at work. A local man, John Lyte, had been lent £40 by the Abbot and one day shortly before the Dissolution 'he paid £10 of the said £40 to the said abbot in the little parlour upon the right hand within the great hall . . . it was immediately after the said abbot had dined, so that the abbot's gentlemen and other servants were in the hall at dinner.' Later 'On St Peter's day, at mid-summer, being a Sunday, in the garden of the said abbot at Glastonbury, whilst high mass was singing', Lyte paid the rest, taken aside by the abbot into 'an arbour of bay. . . . And at that time the abbot asked of the said master Lyte whether he would set up the said abbot's arms in his new buildings that he had made. And the said master Lyte answered the said abbot that he would; and so at that time the said abbot gave unto the said Mr. Lyte eight angels nobles.'

This almost Edwardian scene with its decorum, wealth, a hint of obsequiousness and perhaps of mild corruption, a settled comfort, rounded well-being (you expect everybody to be smoking cigars), with servants

to hand, dinner just eaten and the notes of sung mass coming across the garden to the shady arbour—how perfect an eve-of-cataclysm it is!

From the beginning, the abbot had been established in St Benedict's rule as a man of authority, the guarantor of order. He was always an administrator. As the possessions of abbeys grew he became increasingly concerned with running the abbey business rather than with the spiritual direction of the monks. In almost every monastery, from the thirteenth century onwards, the abbacy itself was endowed with lands held separately from those of the monastery. The abbot became a feudal magnate. As the radical Langland described him, the average abbot rode about as

> A pricker on a palfrey from manor to manor,
> An heap of hounds at his arse as he a lord were.

The Abbot of Glastonbury had, as his personal preserve, four deer parks, and did indeed keep a pack of hounds with which to hunt in them. For several centuries, the abbots' favourite manor was always at Meare, a few miles away to the west, where a small island stands up out of the lush wetness of the Somerset Levels, where there was an acre of vines and where a lake several miles round was filled with shoals of fat and edible fish. It was here that the last abbot Richard Whiting was arrested.

Meare was only one of about eighty-five Glastonbury manors spread across Somerset, Dorset, Wiltshire, Devon and Gloucestershire. Most of this vast 90,000-acre estate, some of the best farmland in England, was in the abbey's hands by the time of the Norman Conquest. Throughout the five centuries that followed, the abbey was a leading developer, particularly in the draining of the Somerset marshes, where flood banks and drainage ditches turned the marsh into valuable meadow and ploughland. By the time the abbey's annual revenue was calculated for Thomas Cromwell in 1535, it amounted to £3,311, compared with the Archbishop of Canterbury's £3,223 and Westminster

The west front of the tower of St John's Church in the High Street, probably built by Abbot Selwood in 1475. The pierced battlements and the elaborate panelling and buttressing make it a perfect example of the Glastonbury style: richness in a small space.

The fourteenth-century Abbot's Kitchen, the best-preserved in Europe, built in the grey limestone from the abbey's quarry at Doulting. Smoke from fireplaces in each of the four corners rose through internal flues to the crowning lantern.

Abbey's £2,409. On top of this huge monetary income was the revenue in kind—particularly the tithes from the livings the abbey controlled. The Abbey Barn in Glastonbury is only one of many from the monastic period still surviving in Somerset.

The huge estate was run from the mother church, but in a highly sophisticated way. The smallness of the Abbey Barn is a measure of how little physical produce was brought into Glastonbury itself. In a miracle of organization, the different parts of the estate were made to be mutually self-supporting. Timber from the wooded manors on the Mendips was brought down to be used on abbey projects in the marshy Levels. Abbey cattle from several manors were taken down in late summer to graze on the incomparable wetland meadows after the hay had been cut in June. Peat was dug from the northern Levels and transported—part of the way by punt on wetland rhynes—to upland parishes; limestone was quarried on abbey property at Doulting near Shepton Mallet and used in many parts of the estate; and large quantities of fish and eels were taken and distributed from the three fisheries at Meare, where the abbey fish-house is still standing.

Administratively, but not actually, all these goods passed through the abbey bureaucracy. Everything left its traces in the records there: the number of goslings born to the flock of geese kept at Longbridge Deverill; the ravages of murrain in the Monkton Deverill sheep; the late farrowing of sows, the early lambing of ewes; the blight on spring wheat in the drained meadows at Westonzoyland, the milklessness of the Baltonsborough cows and the grapelessness of the Wedmore vines.

Almost every monk in the abbey would have held some kind of office in the administrative hierarchy. At the top, the abbot would represent it on a national and international level. He was usually summoned to the House of Lords (but rarely attended), was occasionally a member of the King's Council and would personally supervise the constant litigation, either in Westminster or Rome, through which the abbey's rights and prestige were maintained. By the early fourteenth century, the monks were being paid what was in effect a salary, disguised as a clothes allowance. It rose from 30s. in 1307 to 53s. 4d. by 1369, at least three times as much as monks received in any other abbey in England.

As a monk progressed up the administrative ladder, more rewards and responsibilities came his way. In a fascinating system, which matched the abbey staff both to the abbey's resources and its needs (described fully in an abbey document from December 1303), each senior monk was allotted an administrative post, a set of properties with which to fund it and a set of duties to fulfil. The abbey lands in Somerset were given over to various abbey functions. The Prior, the Abbot's deputy, held Beckery, the low land just west of Glastonbury, where the sewage works and sheepskin factory now are. The Chamberlain was required to provide clothes, shoes, laundry, tailoring, spice and knives for the monastery from the proceeds of the manors at Monkton Deverill and Longbridge Deverill in Wiltshire and West Monkton in Somerset.

Each of these monastic officials was in effect running

a small subsidiary business of the great corporation. It became his career. From the abbot, who probably held about a quarter of the abbey's entire possessions himself, the pattern would extend through these upper offices to the pittancer, gardener, refectorer and sub-refectorer, the Master of Novices and the Master of Children, the succentor, charged with writing and illuminating manuscripts, and the sub-succentor.

The community of about fifty monks was attended by about eighty servants. Despite the Benedictine rule of silence and community, it would be quite wrong to think of the abbey as an island separate from its town. The abbey owned the town, policed it, had probably laid much of it out in the twelfth century, built both the Churches of St John and St Benignus, sorted out its every squabble in the Tribunal, kept a record of every land transaction in the abbey Muniment Room, provided employment for most of its people, received their rents and at harvest time their labour, supported their sick and ailing, fed and clothed their destitute and embraced, in short, the entire structure of their lives. Town was unthinkable without abbey. It is why, at times, Glastonbury can appear so bereft today.

A chaotically inventive piece of country Georgian in the High Street, now Glastonbury's most elegant Tandoori restaurant.

The reverse was also true. The town invaded the abbey. The precincts are now a sort of historical-associations park. Not so then. There were many and repeated complaints of the noise made by the servants around the cloisters. Pilfering for relatives in the town by the servants needed to be regularly punished. The abbey ran a school on the corner of the High Street and Magdalene Street, where 'poor men's sons were bred up as well as any Gentlemen's and were fitted for the universities'. The entire social structure of the town was melded with the abbey's. Until the beginning of the fourteenth century all the services required by the abbey were the prerogative of townspeople. Porter, gatekeeper at the main gate, chief baker, abbot's cook, monks' cook and three assistant cooks, butler and scullion—all these jobs were pieces of property which were owned, could be sold, let out and inherited.

The Pasturel family had by 1300 achieved something of a monopoly. For over two hundred years they had passed the master bakership from father to son and, by a series of astute marriages, had also managed to concentrate the portership and the launderership in their hands. This was too much and in 1317 the abbey decided to buy out William Pasturel. He was satisfied with an annual pension of £10, eight yards of cloth of the clerks' livery with suitable furs and maintenance for his son Richard and daughter Alice until they had been provided for by the abbey in religion and education.

This one small example among many shows exactly how intimate and domestic the abbey-town relationship could be. It was something that existed more at the level of the people involved than as a function of the offices they held. Every arrangement is more like a solution to a problem within a household or a family than an agreement between public bodies.

Of all the servants, the realm of the abbot's cook is most accessible today. The abbot's kitchen (the monks had their own, now demolished) is the most complete of all the monastic remains. It was built in the early fourteenth century, a thing of massive substance, with a fireplace in each of the four corners and an air of limitless and beautiful solidity. The cook was well paid. He received the revenues from the manor of Uplyme in Devon and £188 15s. from other manors with which to pay for the food. His perks were defined in 1309 as *half* of the following: nine helpings from every bull and cow; the offal of oxen, sheep, roe deer, kids, rabbits, lambs and hares; head of congar, hake, plaice, the heads and tails of skate, the tails of salmon and one out of every hundred red herring (most of this fish was bought in London). These grisly remains (what, you might wonder, happened to the *heads* of the salmon?) were almost certainly resold in the town by the cook or his boy. It is some measure of the quality of the peasants' diet that they were considered in any way valuable. The cook was bought out of these rights in 1340 for bread and beer and a house in the town.

The astonishing precision of these records is perhaps a sign that the hereditary servants had drifted into taking too much. They may well conceal a conflict between town and abbey. In April 1305 the Member of Parliament, Thomas de Bruton, complained in Westminster that the Abbot and Convent had enclosed for its own purposes 1,200 acres of what had been the townsmen's commons. This caused a rumpus and seventeen leading Glastonians (including Henry of Norway, Thomas the Plumber, Richard Little, John Strong and John Brown) were brought before the Twelve Hides Court and accused, in effect, of insubordination. Loyally, weakly and rather pathetically they all denied it had been they who had instigated the complaint. Who else could it have been? What else could they have done? This incident alone reveals the essence of the power relationship between monastic landlord and lay tenants-cum-servants. However much the people of Glastonbury might have wanted to claim their rights, absolute authority remained with the abbey.

Almost unruffled and essentially unchanged, Glastonbury sailed towards her demise. The accounts for 1539 are as full as ever: the Chamberlain has the gutters and roof of the new inn repaired; the sacristan has 2 albs mended and surplices repaired for Christmas; six new bell-ropes are bought; John Goldesmythe is paid 13s. 2d. for mending and gilding the foot of the senser in the Lady Chapel; ivy is stripped from the church . . . new brooms are bought, eight waggonloads of stone are brought in from Doulting, new pewter plates are ordered, King Arthur's tomb is cleaned, the Wednesday and Friday alms are still being distributed at the great gate of the abbey, and the girls of the St John's Church guild are given beer for a feast.

But Glastonbury was now almost alone. Virtually every other monastery in the country had already been dissolved. Glastonbury had given Thomas Cromwell the manor of Monkton Deverill the year before to appease him. But, as John Beche, the last abbot of Colchester had written in reproach: 'The king and his council are drawn into such an inordinate covetousness that if all the water in the Thames were flowing gold and silver it were not able to slake their covetousness.' Orders in Council deprived the abbot of his chaplain, steward and cellarer. In the spring of 1539 the 'superfluous treasures' were removed from the abbey by the royal commissioners, including the great sapphire of Glastonbury and part of a unicorn's horn. On 19th September the chief commissioner, Richard Layton, and his colleagues arrived suddenly to search the abbot's apartments 'for letters and books, and found in his study, secretly laid, . . . a written book of arguments against the divorce of the king's majesty and the lady dowager.' This evidence had almost certainly been planted. Abbot Whiting was found to have 'a cankered and traitorous mind'. He was taken to the Tower, and the Glastonbury treasures—5 lbs of gold, 400 lbs of silver, 450 lbs of gilt plate—were removed.

Whiting was interrogated. Cromwell made a note to himself: 'Item the abbot of Glaston to [be] tryed at Glaston and also executyd there with his complycys.' In November Whiting was taken to Wells and, as Cromwell had personally arranged, paraded there in public in a rank of thieves and rapists who were later hanged in chains at Meare. On Saturday 15th November he and two monks, John Thorne and Roger James, were put on hurdles, dragged through the streets of Glastonbury behind horses and then up the Tor where they were hanged; there Whiting, as a brutal joke of the time put it, 'swimming in ayre, and not water, *waved* with the wind in the place'. His body was quartered and the parts displayed in different places.

Within days the abbey had been closed up. The local gentry gathered for the spoils and the town of Glastonbury began a long decline. An attempt to foster a weaving community here in the middle of the sixteenth century, based on a core of French and

The Chapel of St Thomas the Martyr and the choir of the Abbey Church in ruins, the result of 'barbarous havoc' made in the eighteenth century.

Walloon emigrés, foundered on the townspeople's xenophobia and greed. The kersey weavers were cheated and abused; they left for Frankfurt.

Almost nothing else happened in Glastonbury for centuries. The locals developed a reputation for effective *overlooking*—casting the evil eye. A flood in 1606, a fire in 1658, Monmouth's rebellion thirty years later, when Judge Jefferies, sitting in the Tribunal, condemned twelve rebels to hang, and smallpox in 1723 all carried off their share of Glastonians. A brief rage for the Chalice Well waters swept through the town in October 1750 when Matthew Chancellor, an asthmatic farmer from North Wootton near Wells worth £40 a year, dreamed that he would be cured if he drank the water on seven consecutive Sundays. He did, he was, and within a few months tens of thousands had flocked to the well. Lists of cures were published—scrofula, blindness, ulcers, deafness—but in truth it had no curative powers. It was a national scandal. Chancellor was accused of fomenting papist sympathy, but it turned out he had been a member of the Church of England for sixty years. A scathing female correspondent of the *Gentleman's Magazine* said she could 'remember the time when the humour of the people ran as high for cow piss, for the cure of the same distemper; and that thousands would flock to St James's Park in the morning to follow the cows.' A little pump room, still there, was built on Magdalene Street but the fad was over by 1752, and Glastonbury collapsed back into its familiar hopelessness.

St Mary's Chapel in the abbey was used as a stable, the animals eating off the altar. The antiquarian William Stukeley arrived to deplore this state of affairs in the 1720s. 'A presbyterian tenant' had 'made barbarous havoc in the abbey ruins' selling off the carved stones to the highest bidder. The townspeople had bought some 'to build a sorry market-house contributing to the ruin of the said fabric and to their own; what they durst not have done singly, they perpetrated as a body, hoping vengeance would slip between so many: nor did they discern the benefit to the town from the concourse of strangers purposely to see this abbey, which is now the greatest trade of it.'

There is the voice of modernity. The Tor is climbed by 300,000 people every year. Glastonbury was described to me by a local conservationist as 'the heritage wing of the Glastonbury-Street unit'—Street being the town across the Brue valley which is the international headquarters of Clark's Shoes. All hopes for Glastonbury are now pinned on a bypass which will, it is thought, allow the 'personality shops' to thrive. No longer a town but a heritage wing, girdled with car parks but without a cattle market, a police station or a railway station, a town in need of its ghosts.

ALNWICK
Northumberland

IT ALL DEPENDS on which way you arrive. If you are coming from the south, up the Great North Road from Newcastle, you will reach ALNWICK in the clutter of its southern outskirts, a fire station here, a garage next to it, Hardy's new fishing tackle factory opposite, the general air of arbitrary space and the dribbling arrival which accompanies the twentieth-century edge of almost every English town. It is on this southern side that the town has, since the early nineteenth century, been allowed to expand from its medieval core into a series of privately owned fields.

As an experiment, stop the car here before you reach the middle and turn around. Go back to the A1, which now bypasses Alnwick to the east, and follow it northwards for a couple of miles until you meet the old road again, coming south from Berwick. Now, for one of the most astonishing urban arrivals in England, turn back again to Alnwick, southwards, the way an invading Scot would have come. The road passes through a belt of trees. Take it slowly. There, on the left, surrounded by the beeches, is a rather delicate eighteenth-century cross marking the site where Malcolm, King of Scotland, was killed in the winter of 1093. He was at the end of a campaign in which he had burnt most of Northumberland in revenge for the disdain with which he thought he had been treated by William Rufus the previous summer. Malcolm and his army were resting here when they were tricked and captured by the Earl of Northumberland and his steward Morel, who was Malcolm's own godfather. Morel murdered his godson. Most of the Scots army was slaughtered. On hearing the news Margaret, Malcolm's queen, sickened for three days and died of a broken heart. Here is one strain of Alnwick's history already: violence, high blood and trickery.

In front of you is a calm and grassy valley, with Capability Brown clumps pimpling and punctuating it, the lazy, dun River Aln sliding along the bottom. There is no sign of a town to be seen (here, you are less than a mile north of where you turned round before) and on the crest of the far ridge stand the serious, masculine battlements and towers of Alnwick Castle. (Remember what Vanbrugh said on coming to Northumberland: 'There is nothing here of the tame, sneaking south.') The castle has occupied that ridge since the twelfth century, controlling the crossing of the River Aln. It has been greatly altered since then, so that what you see now is the combination of fourteenth-century military efficiency, eighteenth-century whimsy and the manly style of a certain sort of Victorian Borders romanticism. It is unforgettable.

You drop down to the river. Parading on the parapet of the bridge is the symbol of Alnwick, or at least this side of it: the lion *passant*, with his flagpole of a tail stuck ramrod-like out behind him (unless, as happens every few months, you find him after some of the boys from the top end of town have broken off his tail, when all he looks like is Eeyore). This splendid lion is inseparable from Alnwick because it is the badge of the Percy family who have owned this castle and been lords of the manor of Alnwick continuously since 1309. Since then three Barons Percy, eleven Percy Earls of Northumberland, a Baroness Percy, a Duke of Somerset who was also Baron Percy, and eleven Percy Dukes of Northumberland have been able to call Alnwick theirs. Many of them, especially after the union of the crowns of England and Scotland in 1603 and the end of the border wars, never came near the place. Nevertheless, Alnwick cannot be understood except in the light of their influence.

You climb the steep hill (The Peth) towards the castle wall, zigzag around the massive, battered sandstone blocks of the barbican, its battlements surmounted by joky eighteenth-century figures, and find yourself suddenly injected straight into the streets of the town itself.

In this way, Alnwick is effortlessly self-dramatizing: it is a double place. Its southern outskirts have spread into the private property of its citizens. Its northern edge is rigidly defined by the castle of the Dukes of Northumberland beyond which stretches their park and demesne. This seigneurial control of the whole northern flank of the town was to have a crucial effect on Alnwick's development in the nineteenth century and still governs its appearance today. These two elements—they can be called, perhaps anachronistically, the civic and the ducal—are in some senses almost equal. Even the look of Alnwick conveys this. The castle does not, as at Richmond in Yorkshire, loom over the town. Its walls are curiously hidden as you walk about the streets. There is no sense here of the loyal burgesses gathered at the foot of the ducal throne. Far from it. The development of Alnwick, and of the Alnwick frame of mind, has occurred within the

Alnwick Castle from the valley of the Aln: a mixture of fourteenth-century military efficiency, eighteenth-century whimsy and the manly style of Victorian Borders romanticism.

Part of ALNWICK seen from the south showing the Market Pla

double matrix of castle and town, each jostling against the other, each sometimes courting and wooing, sometimes fighting and defeating or occasionally, gracefully, giving way before the rival.

The town was here first. It is, like most English settlements, undatably old but, in the astonishingly conservative way of urban topography, the pattern of land use from before the time that Alnwick came into being still governs what happens in the body of the town today. Return (if you are not impatient with this yo-yo treatment of a place) to the southern, civic side. You will be coming up the Alnmouth Road. You pass another Percy lion, his tail a perch for twelve pigeons, on top of a column put up by grateful tenants of the estate in 1816. The road drops and arrives at the rusty, rubbed hulk of the fifteenth-century town gate, called Hotspur Tower. Manoeuvre carefully through its narrow opening (efficiency addicts have been anxious to knock it down since the eighteenth century) and you find yourself in Bondgate, the broad central street of

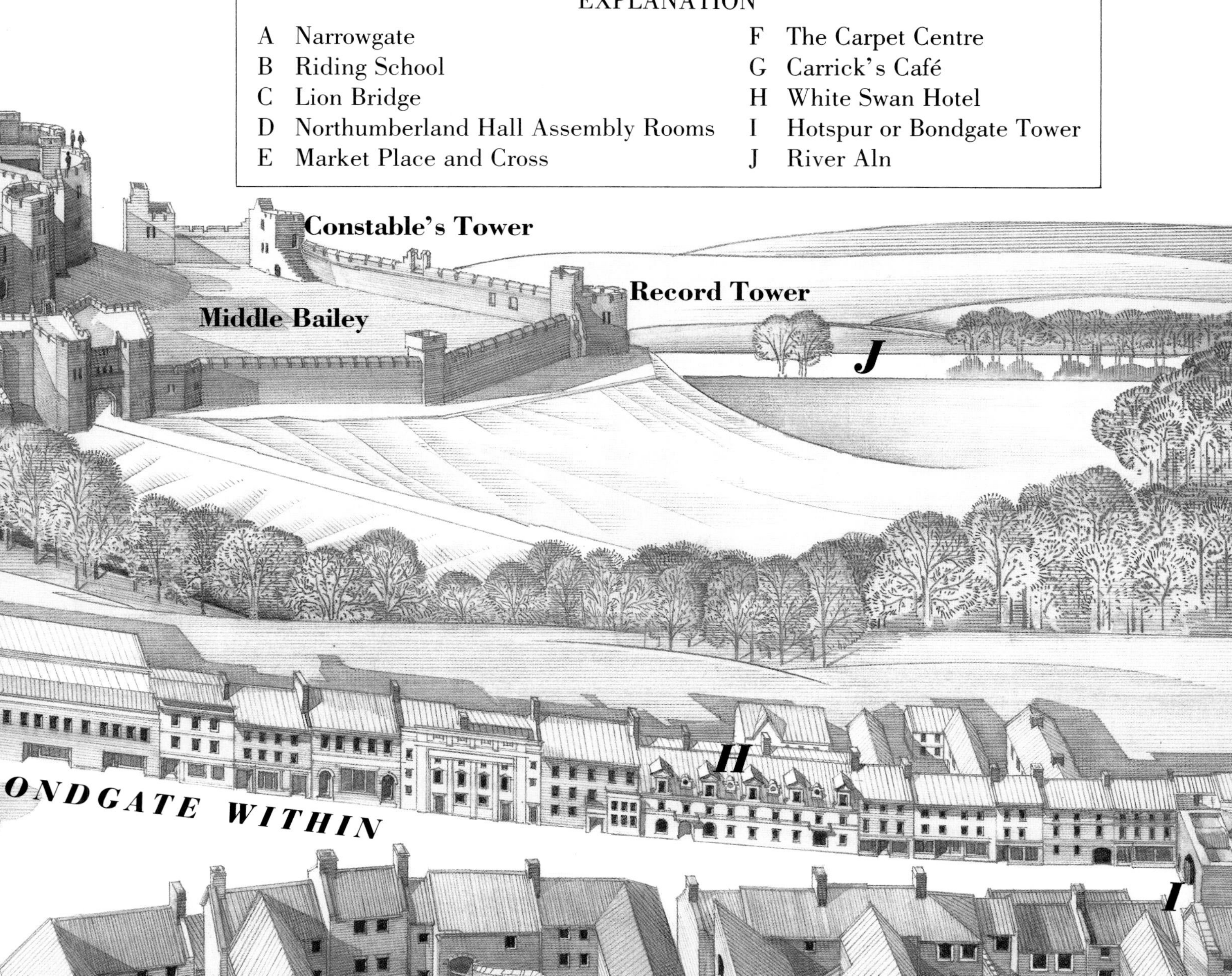

nd the Hotspur Tower with the Castle overlooking the River Aln

old Alnwick, called, slightly absurdly, 'the business district' by the local council. It means the banks are here.

You have disregarded everything so far. You have paid no attention to historical relics, to the sensitivities of historical geography. You have been holding back for the climax of early Alnwick: the Carpet Centre. Or more strictly the brown litter-bin and red post-box on the pavement immediately in front of it. The point is this: the street leading in from the east divides here, branching either side of the Carpet Centre, with its green 1920s dome and its bargain reductions. One branch continues north-westwards, still called Bondgate and then Narrowgate, on towards Eglingham and Wooler; the other, called Market Street, Clayport Street and Clayport Bank, moves smoothly south-westwards towards Whittingham and Edlingham. This wishbone fork at the heart of Alnwick is the oldest thing in the town. Where we now decide to walk past the northern windows of the Carpet Centre (berbers) to

Woolworths, or past the southern windows (axminsters) to the Queen's Head, Anglian travellers in the seventh century would also have made their (less luxurious) choices.

You must now demolish the entire town centre and take everything to ground level to see it in the clarity of its plan. Within the fork of Bondgate is an agglomeration of buildings (including the Carpet Centre) which without any doubt represent the rigidification into stone of what were originally market stalls. The plan makes it clear. The three streets of Bondgate, Market Street and Fenkle Street (*fenkle* means angle in the Northumbrian dialect) make a neat triangle, with a road out at each corner. This was the original market place or village green of early Alnwick, open across its whole width and bordered on each of the three sides with the houses of the villagers. That pattern is evident today in the visual and psychological distinction between the almost smooth (i.e. planned) line of the buildings framing the triangle and the compression and confusion of almost everything in the middle, with cramped passages and jutting corners between the originally haphazard plots.

It is always the pattern which survives rather than the fabric and if you want to get an idea of the town-planning of the early Middle Ages go into Carrick's café in Bondgate. Inside it is smooth with formica and bright with space-age lighting. The waitresses will tell you anything you need to know about Alnwick and its habits (knickers stolen off washing lines on the Cornhill Estate, the absolute difference between Upper Barresdale—rough—and Lower Barresdale—not so bad, but then she came from there). Before you get carried away on this line of conversation, remember to notice the *shape* of Carrick's. It is extraordinarily long and narrow, diving miles back like a plastic tunnel from its narrow shop frontage. The reason is that the building occupies almost to its full extent what later came to be called a burgage plot. This thirteenth-century term describes something that was probably in existence before the Norman Conquest. There is no great mystery about it. It is simply a long, narrow piece of land (here largely built over by the modern café) with a house at its head, facing on to the green-cum-market, and with the yard-cum-garden stretching out at the back. Along the outer sides of Bondgate, Market Street and Fenkle Street these burgage plots, of a standard width of thirty feet and a varying depth of four hundred feet or more, stretched (and to a great extent still do) back from the street frontages like the long tasselled fringes of a rug.

It is one of the most rational arrangements imaginable. Everyone had access to the green and its water, which now emerges in the fountains (called 'pants' in Alnwick) on Market Street and opposite the famous Carpet Centre. The lines of plot-head houses, with barriers across the three entrances, created an unbroken corral within which beasts and people could be gathered against the depredations of rustlers and wild animals. Each house had its own piece of land on which vegetables could be grown and hobbies pursued. It is also, if you imagine the middle of the triangle free of its present impedimenta, a wonderfully spacious arrangement for the hundred or so households arranged around the green. In fact, it has almost everything you could want of a town plan: sociability married neatly to individuality; clarity and a certain complexity; a mixture of turning in towards the green and turning out towards the world; an immovable sense of place. Don't try saying any of this to the waitresses in Carrick's; you will get a funny look and may well be called a 'scabby lad'.

This geographical and social system was in existence before a castle was built here. It is tempting, but perhaps sentimental and wrong, to see it as the epitome of the self-sufficient community. The arrival of the Normans represents a sort of cataclysm for Alnwick, the berthing of another vast, powerfully organized and alien culture on the north side of town. With the Normans came the Great North Road and the link with the body of the rest of the kingdom to the south. Norman Northumberland became the border march of England, an in-between zone permanently contested, fought over and burnt by both the English and the Scots and also by more independent gangs who lived in the hills and did freelance damage whenever they felt like it or got the chance.

This era of border violence lasted, virtually without diminishment, over half a millennium, from the Norman Conquest until the union of the Scots and English crowns in 1603. These hills and valleys were the Lebanon of medieval England, a zone of political chaos and warlordery, of Gallowaymen swarming over the Cheviots 'naked except for their knives', of Flemish mercenaries raping women, mutilating priests and then being slaughtered themselves; of a general, casual killing, and in all of this a hazy line (from which none benefited more than the Percys) between service to the

On the corner of Fenkle Street and Narrowgate is a former Savings Bank built in 1835. This beautifully branching street-scene represents one of the original openings into the green-cum-market-place of tenth-century Alnwick.

king and self-aggrandizement.

At the bottom end, there was nothing whatsoever romantic about this lawless world. One story from very late in the period, 1532, will be enough to show the nastiness of it. A member of the appalling Scottish Kerr family had boasted in front of his King that he would burn a town of the Earl of Northumberland's, 'within three miles', as the Earl's own account of it runs, 'of my poor house of Warkworth [the Percy castle a few miles south of Alnwick], where I lie, and give me light to put on my clothes at midnight. Upon Thursday at night last, came thirty light horsemen into a little village of mine called Whitell, having not past six houses in it . . .; and there they would have fired the said houses, but there was no fire to get there, and they forgat to bring any with them; and took a wife being great with child in the said town and said to her, "Where we cannot give the Lord [Northumberland] light, yet we shall do this in spite of him", and gave her three mortal wounds upon the head and another in the side with a dagger; whereupon the said wife is dead and the child in her belly is lost.' The weak bravado, the flaccid wit, the bread-and-butter evil, even the incompetence over the fire—how many times must these things have reappeared in minor, unrecorded incidents in the Borders.

But as George Tate, the splendidly liberal and forthright nineteenth-century historian of Alnwick, wrote: 'Bad men perpetrating unjust deeds, like the wolf when seizing on the lamb, have always some excuse for their iniquity. . . .' And what was the grand excuse offered for their iniquity by the great men of the Borders? It was, above all, the astonishing glamour of their own lives. Consider for a minute the figure, in 1377, of Henry Percy, the first Earl of Northumberland, thirty-five years old, Marshal of England, commanding at the beginning of the year all English forces in France, with his personal retinue made up of a hundred men-at-arms and a hundred archers, all wearing the Percy lion and crescent on their surcoats; returning from France to dine in London with John of Gaunt at the house of a Flemish merchant; championing John Wycliffe in front of the King; coming north to the Borders and raising an army of ten thousand which he then led on an incendiary campaign through the lands of the Earl of March.

The Earl's son was the most famous Percy of them all: Hotspur. Three glimpses of this figure reveal much of the brutality, beauty and, above all, physicality of this warrior culture. The first concerns Sir William Stuart of Teviotdale, who had fought on the side of the Scots at the battle of Homildon, and was tried (being an Englishman) for treachery and acquitted. Hotspur nevertheless considered him a traitor, kidnapped him and had him tried again before a jury of his own retainers who of course found him guilty. He was then executed, drawn and quartered.

The Douglas family of Cavers in Scotland still have a pair of lady's gauntlets, fringed with silver filigree, on which the Percy lion is picked out in pearls. These gloves were probably the love pledge which Hotspur carried hanging from his spear and which was won from him by Earl Douglas outside Newcastle in 1387.

When Hotspur was killed at the battle of Shrewsbury, not by Falstaff or Prince Hal, but by an arrow in the brain, shot from an unknown hand, there were many in the country who refused to believe he had died. To prove it, his body was exhumed from its grave in Whitchurch and 'bound upright between mill stones, that all might see he was dead'. It was then drawn and quartered and the various parts shown at Shrewsbury, London, Newcastle, York and Chester.

How did this glamorous, vicious, alien world impinge on the town of Alnwick? First of all, the castle and the outer bailey to the west of it (now an elegant, tree-lined Victorian street called Bailiffgate)

The 1824 Mechanics' Institute in Percy Street, with the door tailored to fit its fashionably Egyptian frame.

Part of the White Swan Hotel in Bondgate Within, rebuilt in the mid-nineteenth century, by the castle architect Salvin.

constituted a simple garrison presence, where the constable, in the early fourteenth century, maintained a regular troop of forty men-at-arms and forty 'hobblers' or light cavalry. In times of crisis—and this medieval borderland was addicted to crisis—the number could rise to three thousand or more. On the positive side, their presence stimulated the Alnwick market, but the deficit far outweighed that. Alnwick was burnt, by mercenaries nominally employed by King John, in 1216. In 1316 the Scots penetrated as far as Richmond in Yorkshire. The price of wheat was eight times that of normal and the people of the town were living on dog meat. As usual, banditti were roaming the district mutilating churchmen and robbing innocents. For centuries, the men of Alnwick had to contribute their quota to the watchers employed by the Warden of the Marches (more often than not a Percy). Every night six men watched out for the coming of the Scots over Alnwick Moor. As a rather futile attempt to impose some sort of border security, no one was allowed to speak to a Scotsman without permission from the Warden.

Despite all this, the town was burnt again in 1420. A royal licence was granted in 1433 to 'enclose, wall and embattle' it, and at some time after this the Hotspur Gate (wrongly named) was built. It was one of three—the others, now demolished, were on Clayport Street and at the very bottom of Narrowgate, about level with the Old Cross Inn. But money was short. The town was certainly still unwalled in 1473. By 1557, the Hotspur Tower was said to be in great decay and used only as a granary. It may well be that the wall, of which nothing is now to be seen except this one gate, was never completed. Certainly, until the middle of the nineteenth century when it was demolished to make way for an enlargement of the White Swan Inn on Bondgate, there was a heavily fortified pele tower *within* the line of the town walls, which does not say much for their effectiveness.

In these circumstances, it may seem surprising that any life could be maintained in medieval Alnwick beyond mere survival. Nevertheless, within the frightening and intimate embrace of feudal power, the town managed a vigorous and complex life. That extraordinary image of Hotspur's body crammed between the millstones speaks volumes about the nature of that power: the man is dead and so the power is dead. (In the world of modern government the opposite is true. Think of Lenin, Kennedy, Luther King: the man is dead *and so* the power lives on.)

This physicality of the medieval world controlled the way in which somewhere like Alnwick worked. Power was not only personal but intimately associated with place. The feudal system distinguished people from each other, both legally and socially, by their differing relationships to place. The arrangement of a town and its surrounding land was a blueprint for the arrangement of society.

Dodds Lane drops to its narrow opening on to Clayport Street. Much of nineteenth-century Alnwick consisted of lanes like this, threaded between some of the nastiest slums in the country which had gathered on the back-yards of the medieval burgage plots. Many have now been demolished; others, like this one, rehabilitated and improved.

To start at the bottom, there were twenty bondmen in Alnwick in the thirteenth century, each of whom held twenty-four acres off the lord on condition that they did work in his own demesne, ploughing, reaping, carting dung. They could not leave but they could not be evicted either. These semi-slaves, who had disappeared as a class by the end of the fourteenth century, may well have given their name to Bondgate.

Above them came the free tenants, who held land directly off the lord but not on the servile conditions of the bondmen. The whole of Bailiffgate, for example, was occupied by these free tenants, paying their rents not to the town authorities (of which this outer bailey of the castle did not originally form a part) but directly to the lord's steward. Free tenants had no rights in the town. If they wanted to pasture animals on Alnwick Moor, a privilege conferred on the town in its earliest charter, then they had to pay the town per animal. This class would also have rented space in the market place from the lord of the manor and kept their stalls there, and from that their alternative Alnwick name of *stallinger* arose—a stall-holder. It was in the lord's interest to foster the growth of the shops, bakeries and beerhouses in the centre of the market place (as well as the mills on the river below the castle) since he received their rents direct from the stallingers. The last remaining piece of evidence of the manorial control of the market place is in a plaque fixed to the western end of the Assembly Rooms there. This large, rather out-of-scale block was put up by the 3rd Duke in 1826 on the site of the butchers' shambles which his predecessors had controlled since the beginning of butchery in Alnwick. The plaque commemorates—a little sycophantically—the handing over of this virtually unused elephant of a building to the Urban District Council in 1919.

Above the stallingers, and representing the core of the town of Alnwick, came the burgesses, the freemen. Originally, any head of a household occupying one of the burgage plots surrounding the triangular green was by definition a burgess, *free* to enjoy the privileges specified in the charters granted by the lords of the manor in the twelfth and thirteenth centuries: to pasture beasts on Alnwick Moor; to attend the market without paying tolls; and, most important of all, to pay their annual rents not directly to the lord's steward but together in a lump sum, known as the 'borough farm'. This gave them some control of their own affairs and, more than anything else, recognizes something of the duality of authority in medieval Alnwick.

The burgesses organized themselves in a variety of different ways. First they became members of a guild. There were tanners and skinners (always important trades in a cow country), weavers, dyers and fullers, and tinners, braziers and smiths.

These guilds were famous for their raucous proceedings. The wonderful George Tate claims that nineteenth-century Alnwick mothers would still chide their children, 'Bairns, what a guild ye are making!' Each guild would elect an alderman and they, with others, would become members of the next layer in the town hierarchy, the 'Four-and-Twenty'. This was the supreme authority within the town, originally perhaps elected by all the freemen, but by at least the sixteenth century, a self-electing, self-confirming oligarchy. In 1731 they built themselves, on the site of the lord's beer houses, a Town House, or Hall, overlooking the market place. Here they appointed out of their own number their four executive officers, the Chamberlains. On the gutter head on the front of the Town House are the names of the four Chamberlains in 1790: Strother, Forster, Gibson and Hardy. The Chamberlains' principal task was to collect the borough farm and take it at Michaelmas to the lord's court in the castle, where the steward would receive them, swear in their successors as Chamberlains and then have a party.

This party—paid for, crucially, by the town and not by the castle—had, by the eighteenth century, become a terrific affair. The account for 1718: 'To the Castle 3 quarts Canary 7s. 6d., 3 quarts White wine 6s. 6d., 3 bottles Claret 7s. 6d., to Mr Coles Servant 2s. 6d., to his Groome 2s. 6d., to the Porter 1s., to the music at Arthur Gair 2s.' This was the generous and rather muzzy heart of the relationship between town and castle. There always had been some hazing of boundaries here. In the early days one of the Chamberlains was often a lord's man, called the Bailiff, who might even also act as steward. Out of this workable and trusting muddle came the end of Alnwick Borough as an independent political organization.

The actual story is too complex to go into here but the outlines are clear enough. The burgesses of Alnwick, having been in the beginning some sort of representative organization, had become, through a quirk of self-protective rule making, a narrowly based interest group. The right to be a freeman in Alnwick, which had originally been associated with property—the burgage plots ranged up along the streets—had become genetic: after the sixteenth century only the son of a freeman or his widow or the apprentice of either could become a freeman too. At the same time, the freemen, many of whom were now very poor, wanted increasingly to use the common property of the borough—principally Alnwick Moor—as though it were their own privately held ground.

Into this mess of small-minded confusion stepped the powerful and energetic figure of Sir Hugh Smithson, a charming Yorkshire baronet who had married the Percy heiress and who eventually became the first Duke of Northumberland. He set about making Alnwick, both castle and estate, a viable proposition and, in one of many schemes, managed, in the course of two long law suits, to deprive the town of its most important rights on the moor and to emasculate the borough by destroying its financial independence.

The whole story is told with indignant and endless relish by George Tate and nowhere in its history does the political geography of Alnwick as a castle town become more clear. He quotes an anti-ducal pamphlet called the *Craftsman*: 'You may recollect', it whispered adroitly in the ear of the freemen, 'that several of you were sent for in a private manner, at different times, and in small parties, by some agents of the great man to a certain public house in the town; and then and there your minds were poisoned with artful insinuations tending to excite you to seditious and tumultuary measures;—and in short nothing was left unsaid or undone to set your hearts against your old friends the Four-and-Twenty, with divers hints and insinuations about applying to the great man at the head of the Peth, and that he would undertake your cause and fight your battles for you against the Common Council [another name for the Four-and-Twenty]. Nay, so far did these gentry go, as to tell some of you, that the duke . . . would overthrow the Four-and-Twenty'.

The Duke did succeed, as was inevitable. These incidents were towards the end of the battle in 1778. Others, several years before, when the Duke's campaign was beginning, illuminate the corrupting forces at work. George Tate tells the story: 'Treachery had crept into the Common Council. . . . In September 1759, the Chamberlains met with Mr Green and *Mr Forster* to consider proposals . . . On May 8th 1760 "further proposals were approved of, and *Collingwood Forster* was sent to wait on Lord Northumberland, and authorised to settle and adjust with his Lordship the several points, which may happen to be in difference betwixt his Lordship and the Borough." Fierce contention there was in the Four-and-Twenty at this crisis, and so excited was Thomas Strother against *Col. Forster* that he seized him in his arms and attempted to toss him over the Town Hall stairs; but on the 6th of March 1762—one of the black days in the calendar of Alnwick—Articles of agreement were signed by both parties; and thus after a warfare of nine years [the first court case], the public rights were surrendered and a hollow peace was concluded. *Col. Forster* had his reward; he became steward of the Baronial Courts, chief electioneering agent of the lord, and clerk of the peace for the county.' Forster's house was in Fenkle Street, on the site of what was until recently part of the Nag's Head, and is presently a disused rump of a building backing on to the giant new (1988) Presto's which Alnwick District Council has for some reason allowed to intrude its vast and destructive presence into the historical core of the town.

The arrival in Alnwick of the energetic, reforming, tough-minded new Duke and his family in about 1753 coincided with the beginning of the town's economic resurgence. This section of the Great North Road had been turnpiked in 1741. The Hexham to Alnmouth road, via Alnwick and Rothbury, was itself turnpiked in 1753–4. The White Swan in Bondgate was enlarged and became the post stage. In 1785 there is the first mention of a workhouse, in 1807 a Correction House, in 1811 a Fire Engine House, 1815 a Dispensary, 1816 a Savings Bank, 1824 a Mechanics Institute and 1825 a gasworks. In 1833 Alnwick was to be included in Schedule B of the Corporation Reform Bill (how the deadweight of modernity arrives with that phrase!) which would have given it a mayor and corporation, but the Duke used his influence in the House of Lords to have it left out.

Meanwhile, north of the town, the Percy holdings were being consolidated. Bailiffgate, Walkergate and the originally separate little monastic town of Canongate were bought up by the estate, as well as the rear of the ancient burgages along the north side of Bondgate as far as Denwick Lane. This block of territory, in which many houses were demolished and their land incorporated in the park, in effect created a ducal boilerplate on top of the town. Just at the moment when Alnwick was expanding, its northern limit was more rigidly defined than ever before. As a result, Alnwick expanded southwards (for the better off) and (for the poor) teemed within the container of its now desperately constricted medieval centre.

The result is absolutely apparent today. If you walk through the ducal part of Walkergate and Canongate you can still make out the holes in the street pattern where houses were demolished, and appreciate the model village air of the pretty Victorian cottages built by the estate for its workers in the later part of the century, where retired estate people and their widows are still housed by the Duke today.

If you go a few hundred yards to the south, to the block of land between Market Street and the old archery ground of Green Batt, you are in a different world. Facing on to Market Street at the top is the grandest private house in Alnwick, with a Tuscan portico, a carriageway entrance to one side and an air of urban sophistication. It is now called the Old Post Office, but when it was built in 1797 it was a gentry house, like all of those (including Mr Forster's) along the smart north side of Fenkle Street which it faces. The social texture of Alnwick from the mid-nineteenth century until after the Second World War consisted of this relatively grand, gentry style bang up against the most squalid of disease-ridden slums. If you go up any of the little passageways which push between the houses on Market Street you will enter what was once one of the worst slums in England. Go up Correction House Lane. The dark, dank buildings are set close together. What had originally been intended as the garden of the burgage plot with a single house at its head became filled along this whole stretch in the nineteenth century with mean, cramped buildings. One typical burgage plot was covered in 1849 with the following buildings: a brewery, a candlemaker's, a cartwright's workshop, a washhouse (with a 'ragged school' over), eight single-room tenements let to paupers largely engaged in rag and bone collecting, a smithy, two coalhouses, two middens, a piggery, a privy, three two-room dwellings, a stable, a pub and a grocer's shop. Each of the tenements was let separately, with 8–20 people sleeping there at night on floor space of between 100 and 250 square feet. Many of them at this date may have been the Irish poor escaping the potato famine in Ireland.

Disease had never been entirely absent from Alnwick. The Black Death had done terrible damage in 1348. A 'hot and dangerous ague, whereof there be many dead' had gripped the town for two months in 1543. In the seventeenth century the market had occasionally to be held out of town because the country people would not come in for fear of plague. Worse than any of these was the 1849 outbreak of cholera which could find no conditions more congenial than the crowded poverty of the slum yards. In the single burgage described above (called Teasdale's Yard, fronting on to Fenkle Street and its site again now mostly occupied by the enormous Presto's) there were seventeen cases, five of them fatal. In all, 136 people died in the space of thirty days, three-fifths of them between twenty and sixty years old. Half lived in Clayport Street, where the drainage from the crowded yards at the back ran through the front houses. The lower part of the town (still the smarter), Canongate and Walkergate were virtually unaffected. The water in St Michael's Pant was found on investigation to be horribly polluted. The death rate per thousand, throughout the middle years of the century, never dropped below nineteen and occasionally rose to more than thirty. This is as bad as any third-world country today. (Ethiopia in 1984, twenty-four per thousand; Bangladesh, fifteen.)

The extraordinary social contrasts in Alnwick have diminished in this century. Before the war, as some of the older citizens remember, the Duchess Helen used to make her slow and elegant descent to the town, to Dodd's (now Curry's electrical goods), where Miss Barber, in the palest of lilacs and blues, would sell her a dress by Worth of Paris. A few yards away, in a dark and dirty house at the back of the Queen's Head, Spanker Anderson, the tinsmith, would be mending leaks in people's pots, surrounded by cabbage water and the smells of dense humanity. Now, scandalizing certain sections of Alnwick opinion, the present Duchess cycles to the famous Presto's to buy her own coffee and biscuits. The first thing I was told in the town was that there are no longer any live-in staff at the Castle. The butler and housekeeper sleep in their own house. At the other end of the scale, the slums have been cleared. New housing estates have been built out on the west side of the town. Many social problems persist. Depopulation of the surrounding area is putting pressure on the town's businesses. Unemployment, over 20 per cent among men, is double the national average and worse than anywhere else in Northumberland. There were 1,600 crimes committed in Alnwick in the first ten months of 1987, which is more than one for every five of the population. Despite these problems, Alnwick is a wonderful place. The District Council has made some appalling planning decisions in the last few years but Alnwick has managed, vociferously and vigorously, to survive them and if you come here you will find, in that curiously attractive Northumbrian speech, with its abrupt shifts of tone and its exact, sprung quality, one of the friendliest welcomes in the country.

The Percy lion passant on the bridge over the Aln. Nothing is more tempting than the tail: frequently repaired, as frequently broken off again.

As the flagship at the head of Campden, the Church of St James is the greatest communal gesture of the town. Most of what you now see, including the tower, the nave and the wide-open series of clerestory windows, was paid for by Campden's wool-merchants in the late fifteenth century.

CHIPPING CAMPDEN
Gloucestershire

The gateway to Sir Baptist Hicks's mansion, built in about 1620. The chimneys from the lodges on either side come up next to the archway and emerge under the twin, flame-shaped finials.

MAKE IT JUNE. Abandon your car somewhere and walk. Head north along the edge of the Cotswolds, England's inland riviera, with its laid-out ease and its folding-in of field, wall, manor house and barn. There are no more than slight curves in the landscape and the air is thick with privacy and property. Nothing is accidental here; everything is in agreement. There are no prisons; unemployment runs at under five per cent and Conservative majorities are vast. For every two people in work there is one who is retired. It is buffered, padded England; England in an armchair.

As the afternoon comes to an end and Wales, on the far side of the Severn, turns black against the sun, drop down to the east, away from the limestone ridge, into a small fold of a valley that holds in its slight crease the town of CHIPPING CAMPDEN. This is your arrival. The rough track dropping from Dover's Hill meets its first few houses—recent, town-edge things (Cotswold Rise, The Garden House); stiffens into tarmac; acquires a name (Hoo Lane—*Hoo* from the Saxon for the nose of a ridge); kinks a little and descends past the straight line of Westend Terrace. The lane drops between clematis and the first hints of urbanity—a pair of Regency doorcases, a frill-edged hood on a porch—and then injects you with the suddenness of which all good townscapes are made into the heart of Campden, the High Street itself.

It is the most beautiful street in England and—in the thickening light of a summer evening—the best arrival I know. For a long curving mile it extends in front of you, bulging at one point to accommodate some island houses in the middle. The street flows on past them, completely uninterrupted, until at the northern end it forks. One branch, called Leysbourne, continues north

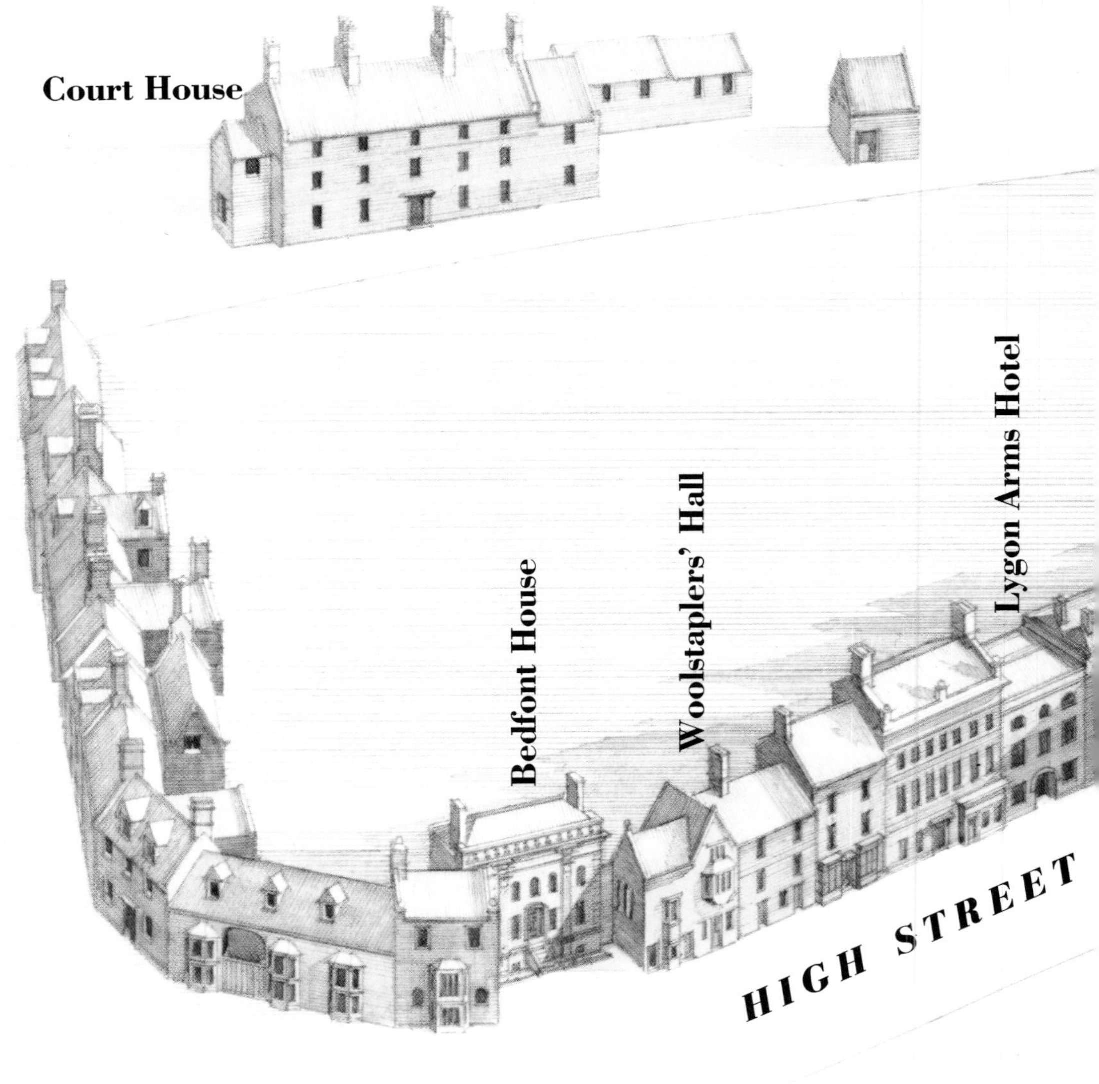

towards Stratford, the other moving off and slightly uphill to the great perpendicular church of St James. Here, the crocketted and pinnacled tower provides a tall and foursquare end-stop for any view along the street.

This continuousness, this image of urban agreement, is the great beauty of the town of Campden. It is a relatively recent thing. Only in the last decades of the nineteenth century were the last plots filled up. Before then the gaps were occupied by gardens and orchards with glimpses into the fields on either side. The town has slowly evolved to the point where every building now stands tight with its neighbour, shoulder to shoulder. Except in Leysbourne, where some seventeenth-century cottages were given a pretty and regular new front in the early nineteenth century, where Tuscan doorways with fanlights give on to the rural irregularities inside, there are no terraces in the street. Every building, from the fifteenth century to the twentieth, pursues its own end. Above the line of the street the roofline stutters; the height of the ridges step up and down. Chimneys cluster and then thin out. The sharp and angular Cotswold gables meet the suavity of eighteenth-century cornices with a complete nonchalance. Nothing is carried on from one house to the next. Each is a private property, cutting its own outline against the sky, but each is bound by the common line of the street. This part-conformity, part-individuality is one of the characteristics which make the High Street such a wonderful thing. It is a tangible metaphor of urban life, of the balance of cooperation, freedom and imposition on which the working of a town depends. It is a balance which at moments in the history of Campden—and we are living in one of them now—has proved very difficult to maintain.

But there is something else without which the look of Campden might be nothing: its stone. The valley in which the town lies is underlain by marlstone, which is

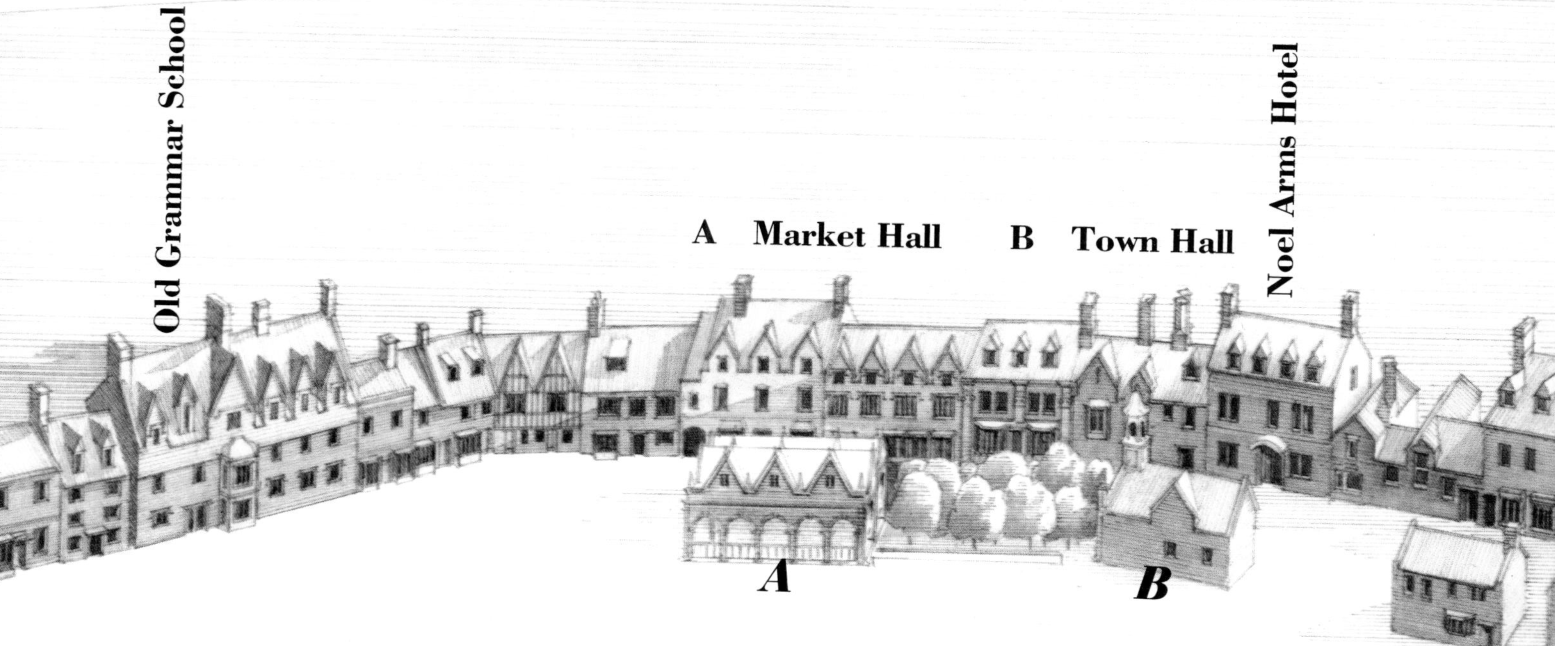

The High Street, CHIPPING CAMPDEN

no good for building. But the hills above it to the west are made of a beautiful cider-coloured limestone called the inferior oolite (inferior because it lies at the bottom of the oolitic sequence of rocks). It is composed of tiny spherical particles, honey-coloured caviare, each of which is made up of concentric layers of calcite. These little roe-like pearls were wrapped around specks of broken shell or quartz in a shallow sea about 170 million years ago when the Cotswolds were something rather like the Gulf of Aqaba.

Up on Westington Hill, a mile to the southwest of the town, you can still visit the quarry from which the stone for Campden came. Don't be shocked. Amey Roadstone Corporation owns it now and in their rather grim factory on the floor of the quarry they manufacture artificial paving slabs and walling stone. Enormous lorries from Guiting Quarry a few miles to the south bring in the aggregate which is then crushed here, mixed with cement and pressed into the artificial stone. Over forty men are employed at the quarry, a good proportion of them from Campden, and as you might expect in the Cotswolds, the whole operation is well screened by trees. No stone is actually quarried at Westington now. The seam of good building stone dribbled away in the 1940s, at least six centuries after the first pit was dug here. For a few years long galleries were driven into the quarry face to find some more but it was uneconomic. Now, apart from the ARC works, a large area of tummocky and broken ground is covered in rough woodland, the worked-over leavings of Campden's quarrymen.

Thank God for the oolite. It is thick with water and quite soft when first taken from the ground—you must imagine the carts lumbering down Westington Hill with the load—and when it is in this state the masons can work it. A fine, smooth, ashlar finish is easily achieved. Richly moulded copings for the gables and cornices for the chimneys can be cut quite crisply when the stone is young. Dated stones, finials and corbels, elegant dripstones around the heads of windows and doors were all within the compass of the Campden masons. It is these little dancing details that give any number of the buildings in the town a lift, a little shimmer on a façade, the rest of which can be kept strict and plain. Only when the stone dries out will it harden and develop a weather-proof crust. That crust is what you now see, speckled with lichen on the surface like the skin of a trout. You see a whole spectrum of

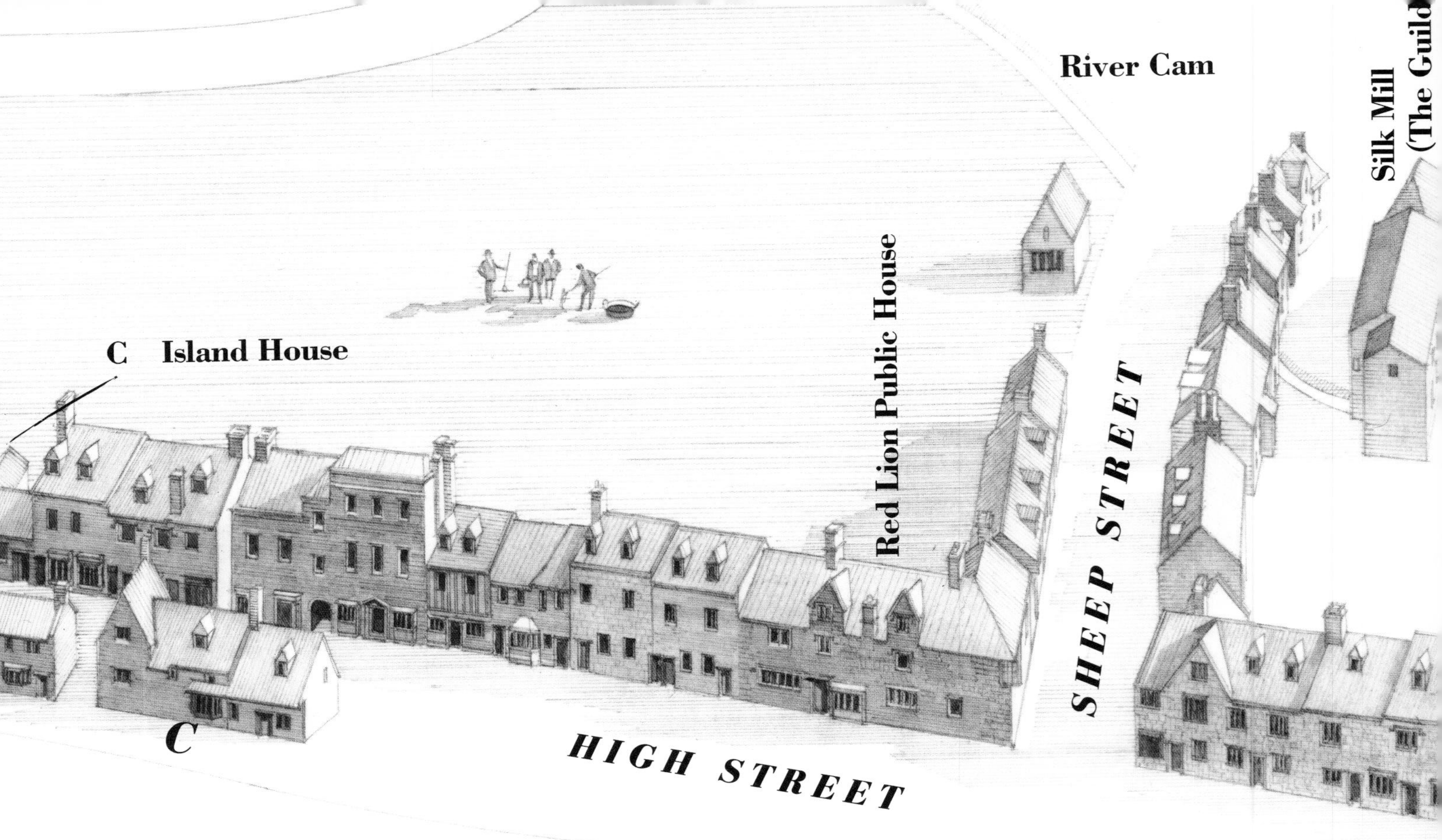

scarcely definable colours which vary in the different lights. The buildings, as J.B. Priestley wrote, are 'faintly warm and luminous, as if they knew the trick of keeping the lost sunlight of centuries glimmering about them.' The same quality extends to the roofs. They were made of oolite too, but of a slightly different formation, quarried a few miles south of Campden. The immensely heavy stone slates, weighing at least a ton for every ten feet square of roof covered, make the transition from wall to sky as perfect as it can be—a slight lightening in the colour of the stone. Little buttons of dark moss like fossilized hamsters crouch on the slates, and a line of solid stones along the ridge, cut into Vs by the masons, caps them off.

The stone is not a 'rustic' material. It looks dreadful when left rough. The practice of most landlords or breweries in Campden pubs of stripping the plaster from interior walls is bogus as the unfinished stones were never meant to be exposed. Only the public bar of the Red Lion has kept the nicotine-stained plaster as it should be.

Everywhere else in Campden, the stone is chic. In a way, it is the oolite which makes it a town and not a village. It is not a silk suit, but more of a well-pressed tweed. In fact, like a sort of adopted camouflage, there seems to be a great penchant for the Cotswold-stone-coloured tweed jacket among the retired gentlemen of the town. Go into the Noel Arms at lunchtime and you will find, pressed up against the bar, a row of faces surmounting what at first sight seems to be a rather beautiful oolitic wall. All the natural variations of colour in the stone are there—a slightly darker patch here, a curiously yellow, flaky one there, its neighbour heavy with lichen and moss, another coming out in bobbles and corbels. So it seems, anyway, until part of the wall turns to the gas flames of the concrete-log fire. Perhaps it is an unconscious decision; or perhaps it is part of the dominant ethic of those who have come to retire in the town that nothing should be allowed to disturb the place. A green tweed might be seen as slightly subversive, a hint that the wearer might approve of a fish and chip shop in the High Street.

These three elements—the stone, the long, fluid curve of the street itself and the wonderful insouciance with which different sorts of buildings are pushed up against each other without jarring—are the foundations for a certain myth about Campden. They give it a look of unplanned inevitability. The curve, the lack of strictness, the placidity of colour—they might tempt you into thinking that Campden has always been a place for rest, quiet, contentment, even the 'natural' life.

Nothing could be further from the truth. To begin with, Campden was a Norman New Town. It was set up as a Special Development Zone (a borough) at the end of the twelfth century, designed to attract new businesses to the area, with a guarantee of freedom from local taxation and a regular opportunity for trade (in the form of a three-day fair beginning on St James's Day). Beforehand, there had been a small village here, most of it probably clustered around a Norman church, but with outlying hamlets, as there still are today, in Westington to the southwest and Broad Campden to the east. In all there would have been about 300 inhabitants of various classes, including a few serfs. They probably farmed about 2,500 acres of open field, ran sheep on the wolds above and grazed cattle on the meadows by the river after the hay had been cut in midsummer.

The great High Street was almost certainly laid out with the founding of the borough. It was made to bulge in the middle to accommodate the stalls for the market. The main road down Westington Hill was diverted to run through the street. A plot was laid out for each of the burgesses, running then as they still do in narrow strips from the High Street to symmetrical service roads at the back, one still called Back Ends, the other Calf's Lane.

No building survives from the twelfth or thirteenth century, but literally hundreds of party walls between the individual plots, and the strictly marked line of the curving street are all a precise inheritance—strict to the inch—from the early medieval commercial venture. The outlines on a modern map record the intentions in a surveyor's mind of about 800 years ago. Such historical precision is a rare thing. Anything more tangible is rarer still. The only hints appear when things went wrong. A quarrel at the fair in the middle of the thirteenth century when 'the girls and lads were singing for pigeons', ending in a wounding with a barbed arrow and the theft of a book worth 20s.; the building of a small hut in the churchyard where a poor holy woman called Matilda was to live; a complaint that the shopkeepers were cheating on their measures of bread and beer; another that the people of Campden were arresting strangers from out of town (called 'foreigners' in 1274 as they are even today) if they were thought to be friends of a burgess's debtor; a fight at Westington in which two men were killed; a theft from the fish pond early one thirteenth-century morning when the thief claimed that he was hungry and only wanted some breakfast; an incident a few years later when Thomas ap Rice called Elizabeth Pratt 'a noughtye hore and an harraunte hore', apparently without justification; the attempted removal at the beginning of the fourteenth century of a curate who had turned out to be unruly and had taken to using 'raylinge wordes against the parishioners'.

These tiny, scarcely articulate fragments drape a few ribbons of flesh on the surveyor's bones. But, for the most part, they are court records and the picture they give of quarrel and petty violence is an unbalanced one. A more steady picture emerges from the evaluation made at the death of the lord of the manor in 1273 of the state of the town and parish. Compared with the village recorded in the Domesday survey of two centuries before, Campden had obviously thrived. By then there were about 700 people living in about 120 houses, many of them burgesses and free tenants. A list of all the principal citizens survives. Among them were the owners of four shops, the millers of four mills, the blacksmith, the reeve or Lord's bailiff, a nurse called Dionysia, a goldsmith called Robert, and several men whose surnames (de Fulford, de Cheltenham, de Saintbury, de Ilmington) show that Campden was already a regional centre, pulling in 'foreigners' because of its attractive commercial arrangements, a place that was no longer bound to plain subsistence agriculture, but had begun to bubble and strive with the tensions and excitements of a commercial life.

One element in the survey of 1273 catches the eye above all others: 'There is also a common pasture called the wold, where the lord can have 1,000 sheep of his own.' The tenants would have had at least as many themselves. Campden had become a wool town. For the next two centuries it boomed. Medieval England was a wool state almost as much as countries in the Persian Gulf are now oil states. Between 1260 and 1360 England was exporting about 32,000 sacks of wool a year, an annual total of about 5,200 tons, representing seven million fleeces. Campden was one of the most important entrepôts for the trade, gathering wool from the northern Cotswolds and the Welsh Marches. Behind the whole business stood the extraordinary Cotswold sheep 'with long faces and square bodies and the whitest wool', as Leland described them in the sixteenth century. More

There is a romantic emptiness to the site of Sir Baptist Hicks's mansion. The enormous Jacobean pile, which had cost £44,000, was burnt down in 1645 by a royalist garrison, perhaps by mistake, perhaps out of hooligan indifference to a thing of great and elaborate beauty. The pieces that remain hint at the Italianate extravagance of the work: a fragment of the south front; a pair of symmetrical banqueting houses; the great galleon bulk of Court House, still lived in by descendants of Baptist Hicks; and the charming, slightly eccentric display of the main gate and lodges. Outside them are the almshouses built by Hicks in 1612 for £1,000. In plan they are in the form of a capital I, a tribute, it is said, to the king, Iacobus Rex. Each of the twelve inmates received a pension of 3s. 4d. a week, and a ton of coal, a gown and a felt hat once a year.

Bedfont House: the only house stepped back from the line of the High Street, built in the 1740s for the Cottrell family.

persuasive propagandists, the poet Gower for example, could call this rather odd-looking animal 'The noble dame, the goddess of merchants, the beautiful, white, delightful.'

You can see what he meant: the sheep were walking money for those who were tough and clever enough to manage and develop the complexities of the growing international trade. Their markets were the great cloth factories of Flanders and northern Italy; the 'production line' was on these wolds and in the meadows at the back of the town just west of Sheep Street, where the animals were washed in the brook, shorn and their wool then pushed into the enormous sacks. Between here and Antwerp or Milan stretched a complicated commercial ladder which has been described as 'a pocket of capitalism in a pre-capitalist world.' The wool was a political commodity and the merchants had to deal with a constant manipulation of the trade by the Crown. Because the government needed the commercial network and skills which extended to letters of credit, bonded warehouses, restricted outlets and the idea of futures—the entire clip could be sold, to Italian merchants only, when still on the backs of the sheep—the merchants themselves were in a position to make huge loans to the king.

There was nothing folksy about the business. Its scale was vast. In the fifteenth century one of the Campden wool-tycoons, William Weoley—from a family, incidentally, which was originally Flemish—had to call in royal assistance to recover a debt of £1,180 from the Albertine Wool Company of Florence. At a time when the daily wage was 1½d., and a large and beautiful church could be built for £200, this represented in today's money something like £5 million.

With such high stakes to play for, business ethics were to say the least in a rather dubious state. Most of the *grands bourgeois* of Campden's great days as a wool town behaved disgracefully. In 1300 the Weoleys and the Grevels beat up and robbed a visiting merchant called Thomas Bishop. Throughout the century there was a steady stream of thefts and assaults. On one occasion even the vicar stole wool worth £300 from the Weoleys' own house. A few years later, records reveal the Weoleys stealing again, this time gold and silver from the Abbey of Evesham.

This is not the usually accepted picture of fat wool sacks and fatter burgers pursuing their respectable business ends in mutual toleration and comfort. It is more like Chicago than the Cotswolds. What effect did all this have on the life and shape of the town? It roughed out a commercial oligarchy which in some form or other has dominated Campden ever since and it gave Campden its first surviving stone buildings. In the High Street both Grevel's House, with its open-gobbed gargoyles, and the Woolstapler's Hall almost opposite are probably fifteenth-century wool-merchant's houses. Looking at them now, you are brought face to face with a reminder that Campden is not a natural outgrowth from its own soil. If it had been nothing but a local

Town Hall: an amalgam of fourteenth-century foundations and buttresses, an eighteenth-century façade and, slapped on top of it, a Victorian porch.

market it would now be only half the place it is. Foreign money has been pouring into the town from the fourteenth century to the twentieth. There has always been, in other words, a kind of symbiosis in Campden between the local and the 'foreign', between the indigenous and the alien rich, between—you could say—the stone and the money that paid for it.

The Grevel who built the house in the High Street is depicted in a brass on the chancel floor of the church of St James. He has grim, hooded eyes and a down-turned, fleshless mouth and is described in the brass not only as 'the flower of the wool merchants of all England', but more pointedly as 'a former citizen of London'. William Grevel, who came from an old Campden family, can be seen as one of the very first rich men who came to the Cotswolds to retire.

It was the semi-alien wealth of the Grevels, and of other great wool businessmen like them, that transformed the rather simple Norman church into the beautiful perpendicular building that is there today. In this wonderful church the oolite comes to a pitch of perfection. It is mottled on the outside, blushing darker here and there, and absolutely crisp inside the fluting of the nave piers. It is quite characteristic of Campden

Woolstaplers' Hall: one of the oldest houses in Campden, built in the fifteenth century by the wool-rich Calf family. It is now a museum with the largest collection of anti-poaching man-traps in the world.

Market Hall: given to the town by Baptist Hicks in 1627 as a market for butter, poultry and geese, it narrowly escaped demolition and removal to America in the 1930s.

that all this, cut in Westington stone, should be the work of an anonymous outsider.

The town's great international days were over after the middle of the fifteenth century. As more and more English wool was made into cloth in England rather than being exported raw, the need for an entrepôt like Campden disappeared. The stream was not big or fast enough to drive the new weaving mills, which gathered instead at the far end of the Cotswolds around Stroud.

Nevertheless, Campden did not immediately sink into an easy, golden somnolence. At the end of the sixteenth century and at the beginning of the seventeenth, two outside families in succession became involved with the town and with a curious symmetry they demonstrate the two sides of Campden's double-face: first resentment and rejection; then involvement and mutual profit.

Thomas Smith was a favourite page of Henry VIII. He had been with him at the Field of the Cloth of Gold in 1532 and had done well out of the redistribution of power and wealth in the sixteenth century. He married into part of Campden; he was granted the land that had belonged to Bordesley Abbey; the rest he bought up himself. By 1553 he owned the whole town and parish. There is no doubt that the arrival of this powerful man in Campden (you can see his armoured effigy resting in a small Renaissance pavilion next to the altar in the church) caused a great deal of resentment. The powerful local oligarchy, led by the rich Bonner family and others, made life as difficult as possible. Smith's cattle were prevented by force from grazing in certain fields. There was a fight when the Bonners and the ap Rices started to cut down Smith's woodland to the west of the town in Combe.

The bitterness of this power-struggle did not come to a head until after Thomas Smith's death in 1593. His son Antony inherited. He was probably a rather weak man, taking bribes as a Justice of the Peace and setting thieves free, including rather pathetically some Bonners, out of 'his own corrupt and pryvate affecon, for lucre, gayne and reward'. He also stole from the Church. The townsmen's reaction was intelligent enough. They borrowed £100 and acquired a new charter from the King by which Smith, the Lord of the Manor, was excluded from any significant decisions affecting the town. The new bailiffs, elected under the new charter by the burgesses of Campden, took their overlord to the Court of Star Chamber. At the hearing Smith repeated that he was 'lord of the Honour of the Towne' and that the complainants against him were 'his very tenants' dwelling within the compas of his Leet and Laweday'. It is the classic picture of old feudal rights, now weakened, struggling against the new force of a rising bourgeoisie. Smith claimed to no good end that his tenants had 'procured very indirectly of the King by synister informacon' their new town charter 'which tended greatly to his disturbance.'

Smith probably lost the case. No record survives. Eventually, having left no physical mark on Campden, he washed his hands of the town and died in Cirencester in 1609. Campden had won. The corporation he had forced them into setting up ran the town for almost another three centuries. In a very reduced form, as the Town Council, it is still there today. That conservative, urban, independent force—you could see it as the High Street in political form—is the only monument to the Smiths, a monument to their failure as lords of the manor.

A couple of years before he died Smith sold the manor of Campden to an altogether different man. Baptist Hicks was an astute businessman, riding the Stuart monarchy's need for credit. He climbed gradually from his silkmercer's shop in Cheapside in London, supplying costumes for James I's coronation in 1603, when he was knighted; lending the King £24,000 a few years later; becoming a baronet, Member of Parliament, Master of the Mercer's Company and leading member of the Virginia Company by 1622; making his biggest loan to the Crown of £150,000; and dying seven years later as Baptist, Lord Hicks, Viscount Campden. This tremendous man, vastly rich by any standards —he gave £100,000 to each of his daughters on their marriage—eased any difficulties he might have had with the townspeople by a largesse and style which Campden had never seen before and has never seen since. In 1612 he built and endowed a row of beautiful almshouses near the church. Water was piped to them from a little ogee-roofed conduit house on Westington Hill. A small market-house for butter, eggs and poultry was added in the middle of the High Street. The church was given a splendid new pulpit and a medieval lectern. He walled the churchyard in fine oolitic ashlar; he refounded the grammar school, which had fallen into the corrupt hands of some indolent burgers; he tried, with his influence at court, to have Campden made one of the Staple Towns through which the wool trade was channelled, but those days were gone and in that almost alone he failed. One cannot help thinking that it was the knowledge and memory of what had happened to the Smiths that encouraged most of his works. Baptist Hicks, quite consciously, *bought* the heart and mind of Campden.

Of the great palace which he built for himself next to the church, only the most poignant fragments survive. It was burnt down, perhaps by accident, in the Civil War. One short stretch of the south front still stands in a field, black in parts with seventeenth-century soot and the stones reddened by the fire. In front of it, the eight acres of terraced gardens are now grazed by sheep. A pair of ruinous pavilions, elaborate with strapwork and crowned by flame-shaped finials on the spiralling chimneys, hint at the Italian ornateness of the forgotten house and at the energy of the man who built them, a man—a glimpse of his life—who won a large part of Kensington, Campden Hill, one evening at cards. Only the double gateway next to the church is still complete, with a pair of stone houses on either side of it, their solid stone roofs following, perhaps not by accident, the same ogee curve as the High Street itself.

From the seventeenth century to the twentieth Campden followed the course already set out for it. Houses in the High Street were rebuilt or replaced at regular intervals. Some of the prettiest acquired a more modern front, with modillion cornices and pilasters that do not extend to the ground but stop short at the first floor—a strange Campden habit, seen in several places. The finest of all the yeoman houses, Bedfont House, was built in the 1740s by Thomas Woodward for the Cottrell family. It is absolutely typical of the town that the stone ornaments with which its slightly flaking, Venetian façade is decorated were stolen from the ruins, a mile or two away, of the mansion of Burnt Norton after the fire in 1741.

Campden continued to behave as it had done: there was more fighting in 1844 against the engineers who tried to bring the line of the Oxford, Worcester and Wolverhampton Railway through the town. A truncheon survives with the inscription '1844 Campden Glos. Defeat of Issambard (*sic*) Brunel—Oxford, Worcester and Wolverhampton.' When Edward Ashbee brought his Guild of Handicrafts here in 1902—about a hundred and fifty people from the East End of London—to set up a William Morris-type experiment in rural, craft-making socialism, the Campden shopkeepers quickly set up a double pricing system, one (higher) for the 'foreigners', another for the Campden people. The Guild only lasted a few years.

And what of Campden now? It is in a difficult situation. Its entrancing prettiness—greatly helped by Ashbee and the Guild, who rebuilt many of the houses and managed to get both the electricity and telephone companies to bury their lines down the High Street—has meant that large numbers of rich, retired people now live there. Almost all of the old houses are lived in by 'foreigners'. Most of the local people live in the council estates. The Town Council itself is dominated by foreigners, nine to two. The Campden Society, with many powerful connections, has over three hundred members, virtually all of them foreigners: with a brief to keep the town looking nice, it has squashed schemes for three housing estates. A new plan for fifteen relatively cheap 'starter homes', which will cost about £30,000 each, has been allowed to go through, with the idea that the children of local people will have the priority in buying them. Nevertheless, it will not make much of a dent in the social dominance of rich, old, retired people. There are few children in Campden itself, and virtually all the pupils at the comprehensive school at the northern end of the town are bussed in from up to fifteen miles away. Local employment is difficult because the Society and the District Council—there is some overlap between the two—do not want any big developments near the town. A family of local farmers wanted to build a large vegetable packing plant on Station Road, but that too has been disallowed. Perhaps the most pointed of all signals about the state of Campden today is that those same farmers have to bring Sikh labour in from Birmingham every day to pick their sprouts and spring onions. The recent sale of council houses has made the situation even worse. The draw of the town is so great that even those council houses are now beginning to be bought up by outsiders.

It is not a good state for a community to be in. There is, without any doubt, a good deal of resentment in the town. It has several layers. The local people do not like the influence exerted by the incomers. Various more or less exclusive clubs formalize the difference between those who are 'in' and those who are not. Nevertheless, those very club members like to think of Campden as a 'working community' and dislike too open a catering for tourists. Others, who themselves run a certain kind of smart tourist shop selling antiques and sheepskins, do not like fish and chips, ice-creams, and—bringing it full circle—the growing and packing of Brussels sprouts: they smell and the lorries are big.

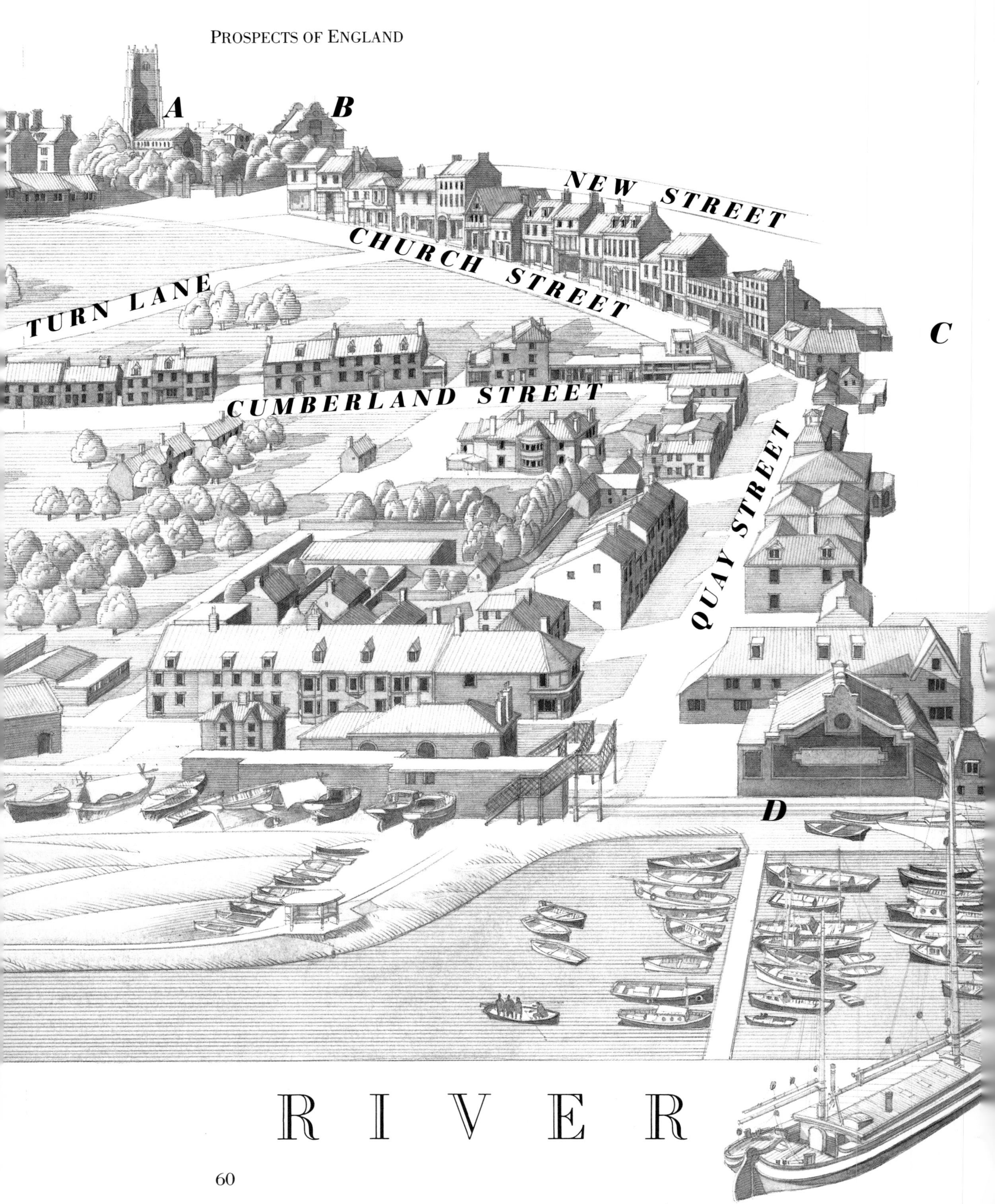
A
B
NEW STREET
CHURCH STREET
TURN LANE
C
CUMBERLAND STREET
QUAY STREET
D
RIVER

WOODBRIDGE
Suffolk

EXPLANATION

A	St Mary's Church	E	Quayside
B	The Shire Hall	F	The Tide Mill
C	Thoroughfare	G	The Granary
D	Jetty		

WOODBRIDGE—and this is meant to be a compliment —is an octopus. It is a mature, rather portly cephalopod which behaves in the way it might do only in the world of Dr Doolittle, comfortably basking on the sunny south-facing shore of a Suffolk estuary. Its clean, sleek head—its smart part, with well-dressed houses, the Shire Hall on Market Hill and the church—rests on the upper part of the slope. From there its long, gradually untidier arms trail down towards the waters of the River Deben, in the end slithering its ragged fingers, in the form of quays and the mess of boatyards, into the saltings and the mud. There on the dropping tide the swans clean their bellies, the oystercatchers peep and the water slides away in the trickling of rivulets and the bursting of little bubbles. The yachts that are absent have left wet nests in the mud, and in the big boatyard, Whisstocks, the men weld the sheets of an aluminium hull. At the Anchor, at the bottom of Quay Street, they talk about genoas and the effects of salt on fibreglass; in the Bull, on Market Hill, the price of houses.

The whole shape and history of Woodbridge has been governed by this uptown-downtown transition, by this meeting of Suffolk and the sea. These are the twin worlds between which Woodbridge has led its existence. Long roads lead in from Suffolk, from the west and the north, to the triangular market place at the top; at the bottom they become the long fingers of the quayside, trailing out towards the sea. The town is utterly compact in the commercial centre—in the tight, almost clenched atmosphere of Church and New Streets, and in the one great cross-artery of Cumberland Street turning into Thoroughfare.
But Woodbridge is essentially and wonderfully ragged at both ends, a place both reaching out and sucking in, a place for exchange, somewhere that has drawn its energies from the world beyond it and thrived on them.

The double focus, the up-down polarity, happens even within the space of one building. The Shire Hall, moored at the bottom end of Market Hill, is the flagship of the town. It was built in 1575 by Sir Thomas Seckford, an Elizabethan lawyer and courtier, and Woodbridge's greatest patron. He moved the County Sessions here from Melton and built the Hall to house them. It is at the same time the most solid and flamboyant of buildings. It has been greatly messed about with since it was built (the arcades on the ground floor were originally open to the air for a corn market)

On the crown-wheel floor of the 1793 tide-mill. It is possible in this building, where the structure and mechanisms are made almost entirely of wood, to come closer to the world of seventeenth and eighteenth-century shipwrights than in any other.

The lower end of the Shire Hall, built in 1575 to house the County Sessions Court. Prisoners were incarcerated behind the little cell doors at the foot of the stairs, which led up to the court-room above.

but in the big tent of its hipped roof, the great blazon of the Seckford crest, the embracing arms of the double staircases descending at both ends from doorways on the first floor and, above all, in the extravagance of the moustachioed and curlicued copings on the gable-ends—more Chinese than Dutch—it still embodies the civic swank and dignity of the upper town. Until recently it was used as the Magistrates' and Juvenile Court, where drunken inhabitants were fined and admonished for their wilder excesses behind the wheel of a car. At the upper, western (and, in this scheme of things, *smarter*) end, a notice is still fixed to the little iron gate at the bottom of the staircase, saying 'Magistrates Only'. At the other end of the building, the relative slum end, there is no gate on the staircase. The offenders had to go in from this ignominious side to their judgement. A wreck of a rowing boat sits here rather forlornly, filled with earth and planted with a few desultory flowers. Tucked in beside the main doorway, facing not the market but the port, are two grim little metal doors, with iron straps criss-crossing them. Not, it must be said, in use now, these are the doors of two small cells for the prisoners. Any horrible effluvia from there could safely trickle off downhill.

The sea is ten miles away down the winding reaches of the Deben (pronounced with the first *e* long). Its invitation away to the south west from the Ferry Quay is one of the most entrancing aspects of the town. There can be no doubt that this was the way the Saxons came, in their shallow-draft boats, first invited by the Romans in the fourth century to defend this eastern shore as mercenaries and then remaining, thriving after the Empire collapsed and eventually reaching their peak of power and wealth in the seventh century under the Wuffing dynasty, their palace four miles upstream from Woodbridge at Rendlesham. Almost certainly it was these kings who were buried in the great Saxon cemetery at Sutton Hoo, just across the Deben from Woodbridge.

There was a settlement on the Woodbridge side too, probably up on the hill around the site of the church, with an uncluttered view down to the river and the boats drawn up on the Deben mud. The name of the town is itself Saxon—a corruption of *Woden brigg*, Woden's town.

The Saxon church and the manor of Woodbridge are mentioned in the Domesday Book, but otherwise the early medieval history of Woodbridge is something of a blank. It was not a very particular place. In the twelfth century a small Augustinian Priory was founded here and the canons, against the bitter opposition of the Ipswich merchants, managed in 1171 to acquire the rights (or at least half of them) to a small weekly Wednesday market here. It was not a great success. Half of the market dues had to be paid to Ipswich to mollify the burgesses and the residue was scarcely enough to maintain the poorly endowed Priory. Appeals from the Prior to the townsmen in 1296 for some extra funds ended in riot. To increase their earnings, the monks almost certainly built a tide-mill down on the saltings, probably in about 1170. It was driven quite simply by ponding the high tide in a large pool and then, on the ebb, releasing the water through a sluice into which a wheel was suspended. A tide-mill has stood on the site ever since (the present one, heavily restored and altered, was built in 1793) and is a source of pride to the town. But the sad fact is that a tide-mill is greatly inferior to a mill on a running stream. It is a testament, in a sense, to the poverty of Woodbridge's site—on a river which can provide no fresh water, which is extraordinarily difficult to sail up at most states of the tide, whose distant mouth is blocked at low tide by a treacherous and impassable bar, and in the whole length of which the problems of silting are chronic. The tide-mill focuses all of this. The old pool of about seven acres (now converted into a yachting marina) provided enough head of water for about four hours work. The time at which this window occurred was dictated, of course, by the tides themselves. As often as not, for one of his two daily shifts, separated by over eight hours, the miller had to work at night.

In the Middle Ages the Deben was an unregulated river. There were no river walls and, unchannelled and unbuoyed, the water slopped seawards in the most unreliable of ways. Any trade or shipping from this part of the coast was far more likely to choose Aldeburgh, Dunwich, Ipswich or even the tiny muddy creek known as Goseford, just above the mouth of the Deben near Felixstowe Ferry. There was never a town there, but Goseford had the one advantage of being close to the royal manor of Walton. It was in this unlikely place, for example, that in 1346 Edward III chose to gather his fleet of thirteen East Anglian ships and three hundred-odd sailors before setting off for the siege of Calais. Goseford men, however few of them there might have been, were also later granted the right to supply beer and victuals to the town of Calais itself. Meanwhile, ten miles away up the river, Woodbridge, like an immature eel, continued to bide its rather boring time, doing nothing, being nothing, producing nothing beyond a little salt from pans down on the water's edge and a squabble here and there over market dues.

The great transformation of Woodbridge comes towards the end of the Middle Ages. It coincides, to a great extent, with the rise of towns all over East Anglia, the richest and most urbanized part of England until the end of the eighteenth century. The growth of the cloth trade with northern Europe had stimulated both weaving (there were twill-weavers in fifteenth-century Woodbridge) and shipping, together with all the ancillary trades in their wake. Woodbridge had been able to afford the new Church of St Mary the Virgin in the middle of the fifteenth century, crowned by a tower over a hundred feet high. The whole building is wrapped, as if in a thick suit of chain mail, in knapped flints, imported all the way from the Wash. Every stone has been chipped open to reveal its glossy black core. This dense, dark and knitted surface to the building is relieved around the base of the tower and in the north porch with elaborate flushwork panels. Here the flints are fitted like *petit point* into the nooks and crevices of limestone frames, all of which play variations on the capital letter M, the badge of the Virgin. It is this smartness of the church which makes it a fitting bride

Woodbridge's smart end, the fifteenth-century church of St Mary and the Shire Hall on Market Hill beyond it. Most of the town's business was conducted in the churchyard. The table tombs were used as benches and desks and a large urinal was built against the church tower for common relief.

to the very masculine Shire Hall, just a hundred yards away and about a hundred years younger.

It was a marriage across the great divide in Woodbridge's history. Little more than a century separates its great religious and great secular monuments. One is medieval, the other essentially modern. One is decorated with the symbols of the Virgin Mary, the other with the coat of arms of Woodbridge's most distinguished benefactor. What had happened? What had suddenly brought Woodbridge alive?

The simple, probably far too simple, answer is that Woodbridge had become a port. New forces were operating throughout East Anglia, England and Europe—a surge in population, a boom in trade, the profound cultural change reflected in the break-up of the medieval order, the growth of independent nation states, the dissolution of the monasteries. Woodbridge's Augustinian Priory was one of the first to go in 1536; Thomas Seckford bought the manor of Woodbridge (late Priory) for £764 8s.4d. in 1564. Along with most of East Anglia, Woodbridge became fiercely Protestant. In the religious terror of Mary Tudor's reign, Alexander Gooch, a weaver from the town, and Alice Driver from Grundisburgh, a small village three miles away, were both burnt for heresy on Rushmore Heath. Alice—and it takes some effort to visualize the nastiness of this—had her ears cut off because she had compared the Queen to Jezebel. A traveller in the middle of the seventeenth century arrived at Woodbridge to find that 'the inhabitants are more miserably divided in their religious notions than at Framlingham. About one half of them are Orthodox, the rest heterodox, with sectaries of almost all denominations, as Presbyterians, Independents, Anabaptists, Sabbatarians, Jews, and what are worse Quakers in great plenty. Nothing seems omitted that the great enemy of mankind [Satan] can invent to gratify itching ears for the destruction of their souls.' Dervishes and Turkish priests, the writer went on to claim, had been brought from abroad to assuage the constant tickle in Woodbridge ears.

To look now at the elegant puritan restraint of the Friends' Meeting House in Turn Lane does not conjure up pictures of fanatical radicalism and, in modern-day terms, this multifarious splintering of religious opinion is not miserable in itself but evidence of an astonishing new vitality in the town. This period, from the middle of the sixteenth century until the beginning of the eighteenth when, in Daniel Defoe's words, Ipswich, and even more London, had 'sucked the vitals of trade in this island to itself', was the great time for Woodbridge. For 150 years it escaped the dullness of being nowhere, of the constant drift, inherent in the place, towards backwater muddiness. No one in that exciting period could have written as casually and contemptuously as Edward Fitzgerald, the poet, did, relaxing in the middle of the nineteenth century on his yacht *Scandal*, floating in the Deben, of 'this Woodbridge, with its capital Air and self-contented Stupidity (which you know is conducive to long Life)'. In the sixteenth and seventeenth centuries Woodbridge was a place of short lives and adventures, of failures and brutality, of rivalry and triumph, of noise, filth, stink and movement, of elaborate ceremony and massive drinking, of few rich and many poor, of disease, enterprise, fire, witch hunts and piracy, of expansion, disaster and eventually of decline.

Imagine yourself for a moment in this other town, in what can truly be called Renaissance Woodbridge. It has more people in it than ever before, just over 900 in 1520, 1,100 by 1603 and 1,450 by 1670. By 1600 there are weavers, tailors, carpenters, shoemakers, blacksmiths, grocers, glovers, tanners, brewers, innholders, drapers, mercers, a goldsmith, a clothier, bricklayers, joiners, sailors, merchants, haberdashers and chandlers all living in the town. By 1650 the list has grown to include butchers, bakers, an apothecary, a barber, a cooper, a linen weaver, shipbuilders, fishermen, glaziers and cutlers. By the end of the century a doctor, locksmith, feltmaker, hosier and pipemaker have all started businesses here. It is a picture of compressed variety, of an urban compactness, but one with an extraordinarily large throughput, a fat trunk of energy feeding through this transformer of a town, increasing tension, accelerating the rhythms of men's lives. It is not, on the whole, a world of *horizontal* differentiation. There are no smart areas and poor areas. The grand brick house built on the site of the Priory, still called the Abbey and now a school, was lived in by the Seckfords from 1564 until 1674, and is set apart in the large priory grounds. That is an exception. The merchants (the Woodbridge grandees)—the Kempes, the Beales, the Smythes, the Basses, the Coles, the Redgraves and the Angels—would have lived hugger-mugger with their servants, dependants and employees. The separation would have been vertical—the poorer the person the higher, the more atticky and confined the accommodation. It is difficult in a way to get the sense of meanness and poverty of much of the sixteenth-century town. The big, Georgian shop-fronts slapped on to Tudor buildings have given most of the streets a more wide-eyed, ingenuous air. But if you go into the little back alley called Glovers Yard, just off the north-western corner of Market Hill, something of the earlier atmosphere remains. The windows are tight and pinched, barred over with close-spaced wooden mullions to prevent theft, if nothing else.

The London ship has docked. It is Wednesday, market day in the early seventeenth century. At some time in the sixteenth century the river walls have been extended as far as Woodbridge. The river now runs in a good if tortuous channel. It is probably buoyed. Pilots at Bawdsey have guided the merchantman in over the bar and it has made its way upstream on the previous tide. Just below Kyson Point, a little downstream of the dock, lighters have literally lightened it as it waits there settled on the mud for the next tide and the last reach through the Pool and into the quays. There are boats already there. Wool is being loaded on to one moored in Jessup's dock. The customs dues on wool alone, payable at the Customs House in Quay Street (built in 1589), are running at £600 to £700 a year. Lengths of sisal are being stretched on the ropewalk. Salt is going into another at Basse's Quay next to the Tide Mill, carried there in carts from Basse's warehouse just across the quayside road from the Ship at the bottom of Quay Street. The London ship is hauled the last few yards into the Town Dock by an eight-oared Woodbridge-built longboat. It was built just upriver at the Lime Kiln Quay yard of good straight Framlingham oak, the best in England, vast quantities of which were shipped out of here. In 1636 alone four hundred loads of timber were carted from seven miles inland and then carried by ship around the coast to the yards in Deptford and Woolwich. There are fourteen ships registered here in all, twelve of under fifty tons and two of over a hundred.

The London ship is an emporium in itself. It carries Flemish onions and the interlocking Dutch pantiles which will soon cover every roof in the town, German and French wines, perhaps coal shipped from Newcastle (there is a coal warehouse just up from the Town dock), specialist timbers, and salted fish. Timber—principally pine for the masts and spars—flax, tar and potash from the Baltic would all be delivered. Lighters are taking out the last loads of malt, rye, butter, cheese, grain and saffron to another coasting schooner waiting down at Kyson Point for the dropping tide to carry her out to Bawdsey.

Some of the inbound goods are stored on the quay-side warehouses. (All the old ones are gone now from the Town Dock and Ferry Quay, but go along the Riverside Path to the site of the Lime Kiln Quay. Almost everything has changed here too. Pine bedsteads are churned out by the million and in the nineteenth century a swimming pool *for women only* was constructed out of part of the old dock. But here, in a quiet, run-down sort of way are the last of the old warehouses, with stepped Dutch gables in beautiful, dark, rather roughly made bricks, and with blackened, tar-soaked weatherboarding on the walls. Holland is inescapable on this muddy waterfront—the mixture of water and the de Hooch sense of smallness and clarity. Here alone can you get a feeling for the intimate, hand-made quality of this early modern enterprise.)

Many of the smaller goods are taken up to the market, either up Quay Street and then Church Street or up the New Street, which was cut through to the market at some time in the sixteenth century to improve access. Here you can still see one of the most extra-ordinary pieces of machinery to have survived from the seventeenth century. Almost at the top of the street is an inn called the Bell and Steelyard. It was probably built at the time the street itself was made, a classic timber-framed Suffolk house, with the upper storey jettied out a foot or so beyond the lower, and the 'studs'—the upright timbers in the face of the wall—closely spaced. This was for show because, for structural purposes, the building would not have needed so many timbers. In a small-scale way it repeats what is done so well throughout Woodbridge: the cramming of luxury details into the confined space. In the eighteenth century, as in so many of Woodbridge's Tudor buildings, large picture windows were cut in the ground floor walls. Hanging out from the face of the building at the level of the eaves is a metal contraption, like an iron gallows, roofed over with its own little mid-air porch. This is the steelyard itself. Carts coming up from the quayside fully laden would be brought to a stop underneath it. Metal slings were passed under the belly of the cart. A heavy lead counterpoise was then pushed along the steelyard by the operator at the top until the leverage lifted the entire wagon off the ground. Anything up to two and a half tons could be weighed on these giant scales. The weight of each local wagon would be known and the weight of the load could be easily calculated.

From there it is a short climb to the market. This may either have been in what is now called Market Hill or just beyond it, in the space between the back of the King's Head pub (which may have originally been called either the 'Ocean Monarch' or, in the classic Woodbridge juxtaposition, the 'Plough and Sail') and Queen's Head Lane. The inn itself would have been more than a drinking place. It was hotel, bank, warehouse, exchange, scrivener's office, and, on occasion, auction room.

The right to have a market stall was itself a valuable thing. One of the sixteenth-century grandees of Woodbridge, Lionel Tyler, in his will of 1569, lists his 'good ship *Erasmus*' in the same breath as his two 'fish stalls (17 feet by 9 feet) extending south from the *fishestalls*'. This can only mean that the market was expanding. Beside the stalls was the pillory into which miscreants were locked for the day and at its foot a '*putrefactum*' where anyone who fancied could deposit their nastinesses to make the humiliation worse. You could only do so when the pillory was occupied. Heavy fines were imposed for dumping foetid rubbish there.

Glover's Yard off Market Hill, tight and cramped, the close-spaced density of early Woodbridge.

This is where the countryside most obviously invaded the town. But to understand the texture and feel of a seventeenth-century town one must abandon the rather rigid distinction between urban and rural that exists in our modern minds. Even in the nineteenth century rural folk cures were applied in Woodbridge—a sapling ash for the rickety child, a Good Friday bun for the rheumatics, a live fish dying on the body for whooping cough, the scattered ashes of a mouse to scare away more general ills. The town was utterly bound in with the countryside. The citizens would have been heavily involved with the work of the land. At harvest and even at ploughing time, Woodbridge would have come to a virtual stop. A visitor in the late summer would have found it almost empty, all the people out working in the fields. This is not as difficult to recollect in Woodbridge as in other places. Behind the tightness of the streets, unseen by the casual visitor or glimpsed only in the form of tree-tops beyond high walls, are large open spaces, now gardens, that were once fields and orchards. There is a lady in Cumberland Street who still keeps a cow in the ground beyond her Georgian façade. In Ship Meadow, the allotments, with their cabbages and beans and flaccid lettuces, are the direct descendants of the smallholdings on which the vulnerable commercial structure of Renaissance Woodbridge must also have relied.

If this gives a picture of settled coherence and contentment, that would be wrong. There is an air of wildness and naughtiness, a certain marginality to the life of Woodbridge in the flood tide of its existence. Woodbridge men were regularly arraigned for conniving at the escape of pirates. John Flicke was arrested in 1577 for receiving pirated goods at the town dock. One of the Seckford brothers had to pay the enormous fine of £12,000 for capturing a Venetian merchantman, the *Uggera Salvagina*, 'by mistake'.

A fuzzy line between new enterprise and illegality colours the whole period. The market and its dues were regularly bypassed even by the quality of the town. In 1585 Sir Humphrey Seckford and several others were fined for selling cattle and pigs in the churchyard, twopence a beast. The churchyard, in fact, seems to have been the great meeting-place. The inns of Market Hill at that time faced *in* towards the churchyard. Debts were paid, bequests received and bargains struck in the porch.

The tombs themselves were used as seats and tables.

The Porter's Lodge of the 1842 Seckford Almshouses. The matron now lives here.

So much drinking went on there that a large urinal, twenty-six feet long and six feet wide, was constructed next to the tower, only demolished with revisionist disgust in 1863. A sort of rugger was played in the Campinge Close next to the churchyard, probably with something like a cricket ball, in which nine 'snotches' had to be scored by the winning team. It usually took most of the day. Everyone joined in, including the minister and churchwardens, who also thought it appropriate to pay two shillings and twopence for decorating the town's archery butts with flags and boughs of gorse. A traveller in Suffolk in 1634 found a party of Woodbridge men enjoying a picnic down at Bawdsey Ferry where they had arrived after a morning sail down the Deben. On Perambulation Day, which seemed to have happened as often as people felt like it, the bounds of the parish were beaten. There was always some sort of party, starting with a 'cheering' at Widow Spalding's next to the churchyard, then a quick walk round the town, more drinks on the common, and then a social division of the fun, with the 'Honestie' going to the Ship (now Burkitt House at the bottom of Angel Lane) or the Crown (still there on the corner of Thoroughfare and Quay Street) for beef and wine, and the men and boys going to the King's Head for beer, bread and cheese. The two guilds, of Our Lady and of St Eloi, the first missionary to Flanders, were the focus for further processions and entertainment.

There was of course a darker side. In 1596, as the Churchwardens Accounts record, John Henlington was paid threepence 'for making a place upon the Pillarie for the witches to stand on'. In 1633, at Old Goody Carre's trial in Bury, four of her Woodbridge neighbours identified her as a witch. And in July 1651 Margery Ebbes and Thomas Horsman were both ducked in the old witchpit in a field north of the Bredfield Road. Both drowned and were thus proved innocent.

What lay behind this retributive viciousness? It can be seen, perhaps, as a pustule breaking out on the skin of seventeenth-century Woodbridge, as an outlet for shared tension, releasing through a scapegoat some of the anxiety that poverty, crop failure and unexplainable disease caused to accumulate within the town.

Fire, in thatched houses with chimneys lined in a mixture of mud and dung, was an ever-present hazard until the first widespread use of brick in the eighteenth century. The cramped living conditions, the inadequate diet of the poor, the general lack of hygiene, and the uselessness of folk medicine all made this town, like others, a classic breeding ground for disease. The streets were unpaved except for the sort of cobbles in the gutters you can still see in Angel Lane and epidemics visited the town throughout the century. There were 84 burials in 1604 (compared with 26 the

Lime Kiln Quay, where some early and very Dutch warehouses survive on the edge of the silty Deben. Unlikely as it might appear, Woodbridge's greatest warships and merchantmen were launched from this quay.

previous year). The Churchwardens spent eightpence on a 'Book of Prayer for the Sickness to be read in the Church'. Another 72 died in 1605 and in 1612 an unprecedented 178. None of this, however, could compare with the swathe cut though Woodbridge by the great plague in 1665. It had reached Harwich by the middle of June and by 10 July was in the town.
It spread quickly and, within three weeks, 173 people had died. Another 149 succumbed in August. No services apart from burial were held in the parish between July and September. Virtually all of the plague victims were buried in pits on Bearman's Hill, which was probably the area of the town now known as Mill Hills. In 1710 an outbreak of smallpox killed 148 people, most dying within a day or two of contracting the disease.

This intense vulnerability of human life, in an era before adequate medicine, before state welfare, before any form of insurance or government assistance, makes the achievements of a place like Woodbridge even more remarkable. It is now a town which looks after itself, restoring cottages, diverting traffic, rightly preening its charming unpretentious self. A quarter of the population in the centre are now retired. It is in part a place for poodles on the elasticated lead and televisions turned up loud for the slightly deaf. And it thrives on the shopping needs of about 20,000 people from the area to the east known as the Sandlings.
A conscious effort is needed to remove this modern gloss of comfort and settledness and to envisage the conditions in Woodbridge's great centuries as a market port. This was not a place made in comfort but in fierce adversity. Nevertheless, even apart from the charity set up by Sir Thomas Seckford which funded some alms-houses through the income of property in Clerkenwell, the parish constantly gave to the poor and to itinerant

beggars. There was a never-ending stream of 'maimed soldiers and mariners', 'a poor man that had great losses at sea', 'Robert Gray which lost his ship with merchandise', 'two Scotty's men', 'a poor man which had the King's broad seal [to beg]', 'two Grecians', and many other pitiable cases. All received charity from the parish and then, more often than not, were given a lump sum to clear off.

Against this background, Woodbridge not only survived but flourished. Between 1625 and 1638 eleven merchant ships were built in the Lime Kiln Yard which at that time stretched all the way from the river up to the Thoroughfare. Some, like the *Levant Merchant* and the *Muscovy Merchant*, were big international trading ships of four hundred tons' burden, whose plain and epic names embody precisely the air of seventeenth-century puritan enterprise. Almost certainly they would have been launched without either their spars or rigging—so as not to ground on the shallows in the Deben—and either towed or sailed under jury rig to the Thames where they would have been masted and fitted out. Before the end of the century fifteen men-of-war were built here too, most of them doing convoy duty for the Royal Navy in the East or West Indies, but others fighting both the privateers out of Dunkirk who harried this coast and the Dutch in the long struggle for supremacy of the seas.

Some of these warships too were enormous. The largest was probably the *Prosperous*, demanded of the town by royal writ as a form of taxation in October 1634. Under threat of gaol for the principal citizens, Woodbridge was forced to construct, equip, man and victual for six months a ship of seven hundred tons, with a complement of 250 men. A meeting in the churchyard decided reluctantly to comply, if only to stay in with the crown, whose controlling influence on shipping made its goodwill necessary. More enthusiastically, it is certain, two fourth-rate battleships, the *Advice* and the *Reserve*, of forty-eight guns and just over 500 tons each, were built here in 1650 for the Commonwealth Navy. A few years later the *Preston* and the *Maidstone* were added to the Republican fleet. After the Restoration, the Royal Navy continued to commission Woodbridge ships and the *Albermarle*, the *Kingfisher*, the *Hastings* and the *Ludlow* all went out from these yards before the end of the century.

No image of Woodbridge is more striking in the mind's eye than one of these finished ships, the Framlingham oak new and clean, being towed out on the flood-tide, away from the quays and then down the first reaches of the Deben to the sea. It is the unlikeliest of pictures—the scale is hardly right—and in the end likelihood won. Smaller craft have continued to be built here until this day, but after the end of the seventeenth century nothing on the earlier scale was attempted. The yard below the Common Quay, where the 663-ton *Kingfisher* was built, had silted up within thirty years. The superior situation of Ipswich on the Orwell and of the Kent ports meant in the end that the great scale of things ebbed away from Woodbridge. It continued as a port until the early years of this century. Brigs and schooners continued to be built here, but the trade was almost entirely coastal. There was a settling of the mind and the idea of Muscovy or the Levant became again as foreign as they had been in the Middle Ages.

Meanwhile, Woodbridge received its polish. The officers of the large garrison housed outside the town between 1803 and 1815 built themselves—or more often rebuilt—the lovely Georgian houses on Cumberland Street. These are like a series of Chippendale bureaux, each with the refinement of a boot-scraper outside the front door. A small theatre was built for the officers in Theatre Street. It is now an auction room. Edward Fitzgerald, the translator of the 'Rubaiyat of Omar Khayyam' came to live here and deplored the ordinariness around him. The first of many gifted artists and illustrators, their charming wives and importunate dogs moved in and began to make Woodbridge what it is today. The Seckford property in Clerkenwell became immensely valuable and Seckford buildings began to spring up all over town—a dispensary for the poor and sick, a lending library, a public pump named 'Victoria', and a huge palace of a 'hospital' for the old. The school boomed, the railway arrived and the town spread. A Zeppelin bombed it, killing six. In 1926 the last barge unloaded 500 quarters of wheat for grinding at the Tide Mill. A one-way system was inaugurated and the Deben Yacht Club blackballed another candidate. The life-blood of gossip coursed through the streets as it had always done. Conservation zones were decided on, car parks built and the town was twinned with a place called Mussidan, somewhere in France. Ghosts appeared in Cumberland Street, smelling of fish, and in the Mariners' Arms the decline of Woodbridge tea-rooms was discussed, as ever, with undisguised relish.

BLANDFORD FORUM
Dorset

ABOUT TWO in the afternoon on 4th June 1731, in a house at the corner of Bryanston Street in BLANDFORD FORUM, a tallow chandler's apprentice was working at the furnace under a cauldron of boiling animal fat, which he was clarifying to make soap. By mistake, he stoked the fire too high. He panicked and started to rake out the burning sticks of gorse from the mouth of the furnace to reduce the heat. The sticks continued to burn after he had dragged them away and the flames caught the dry boughs of spare fuel stacked behind and beside him. The room was immediately on fire. Within minutes the flames had spread to the roof and from there across the width of the narrow streets to the adjoining blocks of houses. The crowded town was built of timber and largely roofed in thatch. Almost every building had its own woodshed in the back yard, filled with combustibles. A strong wind was blowing from the northwest.

The Great Fire of Blandford lasted almost exactly twelve hours. The Rev. Malachi Blake, the Congregational Minister in the town, has left an extraordinarily graphic account of the disaster. It is larded with his vigorous Puritan relish at the evidence, as he puts it, 'of God's *rebuking Hand*', but despite this near-rejoicing tone, there can be no doubt from what he says that a big fire in a wooden town was—in its suddenness, its unstoppability, the totality of its destruction and the hopeless terror and disorientation it brought to the people—the exact equivalent of a comprehensive and indiscriminate air raid.

As soon as the 'dismal Cry of Fire' was heard in the streets, the three pitiable fire engines—hand pumps on wheels—were brought up to the junction of Bryanston Street, White Cliff Mill Street and Salisbury Street, 'but to no Purpose; for in little more than half an Hour they were either all burnt or render'd unfit for Service.' The wind drove the flames southeast towards the middle of the town, near the church. All the houses immediately north of the churchyard were on fire within fifteen minutes of the first alarm. 'The *Fire* spread it self with that *speed* and *fury*, that every Thing was soon devoured before it. Not a Piece of *Timber* but what was burnt to a *Coal*. The *Pewter* in many Houses was not only melted, but reduced to *Ashes* by the fervent Heat. Our *Silver*,' and here is the Rev. Blake's delight at material disaster, 'in a literal Sense, became Dross! And if any made *fine* Gold their *Confidence*, what a sad proof had they before their Eyes, of their extreme Folly, and its utter insufficiency to make them *happy!*'

The wind soon shifted to the north, driving the flames into the southern part of the town and throwing enough burning embers into the air for them to be carried a quarter of a mile across flood meadows and the River Stour to the hamlets of Blandford St Mary and Bryanston, where the thatched roofs soon caught, and where the houses were also soon utterly destroyed.

The speed of the wind and the way in which the town was planned—with a second avenue of attack for the fire formed by the rows of small service buildings in the gardens at the rear of the main houses—combined against the inhabitants. Another contemporary witness, a William Jeanes, in a letter written a few days later describes how 'the fire spread itself into different parts of the town with such fury, that severall of the poor people who were labouring to putt the fire out where it first began, had their own houses consumed before they got home; and many of their houses were so encompassed with the fire by its getting first to the back houses, that they saved little or no goods, but were glad to escape with their own Lives. . . .'

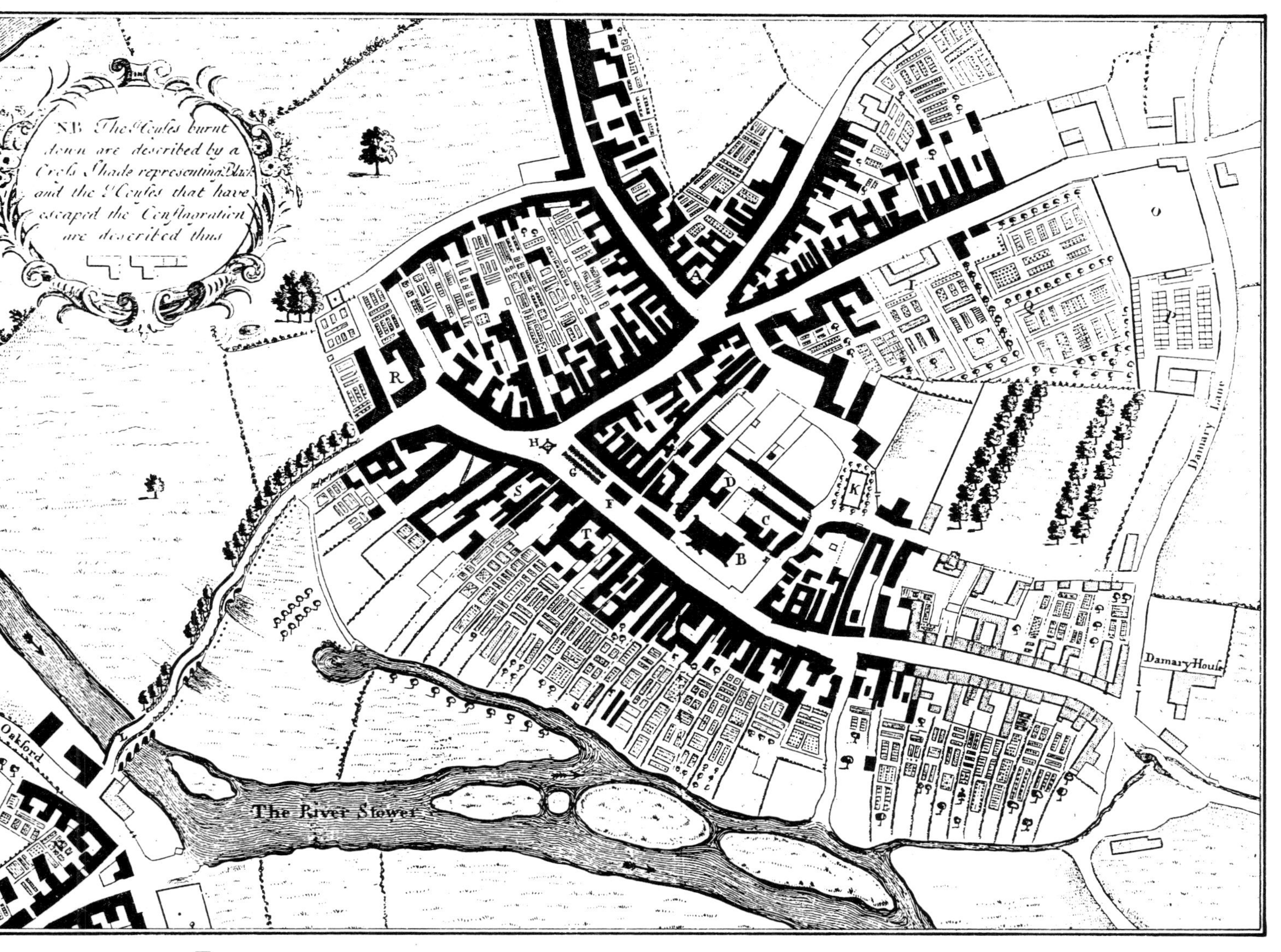

The map of Blandford measured and drawn by the Bastard Brothers and sold in London, a sort of eighteenth-century disaster movie, after the fire of 4th June 1731. The town was rebuilt on almost exactly the same plan. The only real changes were made in The Market Place, where the cross, stalls and butchers' shambles were removed to create a grander space in the town centre.

Nothing could be done. People moved their possessions to other houses, further away, but they too in time were caught. By seven o'clock in the evening the whole town was burning or burnt, except for a few houses at the northern edge and at the east end of East Street, which had been rebuilt—and all-importantly roofed in tiles not thatch—after an earlier fire in 1713. Other families simply put everything valuable in the street, but a firestorm seems to have developed and great gusts of flame blew the length of the thoroughfares burning everything over which they passed. The only way in which people could breathe was with wettened handkerchiefs over their mouths; the streets were so hot that the soles of people's feet running over them were scorched. Walls and chimneys, deprived of the beams that supported them, crashed down, some on people trying to escape the flames. So fierce was the fire that huddled families 'were glad to lie down behind the Tomb-Stones, which were a *Shadow* to them from the fervent Heat.' And as tangible as the flames was the fear. 'I shall never forget,' Malachi Blake wrote, 'the Horror and *Affrightment* that appeared in every Countenance, rendered yet more *frightful* by the labour and Toil of the Day. Many were scarce known even to their *nearest Neighbours*, so disfigured were they with Sorrow and Smoke.'

Many parents lost sight of their children for a time and sat weeping over their deaths, but in fact none of them had died, and all were later rediscovered and reunited. In a reaction to trauma that became familiar in the wars of this century, many of the people simply went to sleep wherever they could, in barns and outhouses, others under the arches of the bridge over the flood meadows by the Stour, others in hayricks and under hedges while their homes burnt.

'The Church held out against the Fury of the Flames a long time, not having any House joining to it. At length the Steeple took Fire, and that more than once; but by the great Care and Diligence of some Persons it was quenched again. However, about *Twelve of the clock at Night*, the Fire was seen afresh in the *Middle* of the *Roof*. This also might have stopped at first had they had *Engines*, or could they have got *Ladders* and *Vessels* to carry Water: But these were all burnt. It was towards *Two of the Clock in the Morning* before it broke through the Roof into a *Flame*. Then the *Fire roared* dreadfully, the *Lead melted*, the *Stones split and flew*; nay, so fervent and irresistible was the Heat, that the *Bells* themselves *dissolved* and ran *down in Streams*.

'Man is born unto Trouble, as the Sparks fly upward,' Malachi Blake gloomily concluded. And it would be difficult to conceive of a more heartbreaking set of circumstances than in Blandford on the morning of 5th June. There were sixteen people dead—perhaps surprisingly few—many of them to be found 'burnt black as an Hearth' when the rubble was picked away. The scorched survivors were suffering torturing pain and the bewilderment of loss. Before the end of July there were to be fifty-two burials in the churchyard, many dead from the smallpox that was already in the town before the fire. (The normal burial rate in Blandford was two or three a month.) Four hundred and eighty families were entirely or partly homeless, sixty of them suffering from smallpox.

The fires continued to burn, suddenly erupting now and then as they came across a coal bunker or a winter fuel store. The only food was some bread that had been in the oven as the fire took hold; the black and rigid

47 *& 49 East Street. Originally one merchant's house built soon after the fire, now* Cards & Things *and* Blandford Saddlery, *with the earliest Victorian shopfront in Blandford.*

51 *East Street. A pair of small artisans' houses, 1730s, now* Music Forum *for records and* The Sapling, *a gift shop.*

53 *East Street. The old Star Inn, remodelled in the nineteenth century, recently closed and deeply missed. Now* Temptress Fashions.

55 *East Street. Originally a mid-eighteenth-century shop, now* Collier's *the butchers with 1957 black-tile fascia.*

57 *& 59 East Street. A pair of mid-eighteenth-century artisans' dwellings with central passageway; now* The Treasure Box, *jewellers and* The Gorge, *a café*

loaves were dug out of the rubble surrounding them for the people to eat. From this moment and from this blackened scene begins the creation, in an extraordinary triumph of will, of the most perfect small Georgian town in England.

Help began to arrive immediately. Bread, beer and beef came in waggons from neighbouring towns, money from Dorset gentlemen and, as the news of the fire spread, contributions too from all over the country. George II gave £1,000, his Queen Caroline another £200, the City of London over £2,000. A play was put on at Drury Lane Theatre 'for the unhappy sufferers from the late fire'. The total collected came to £16,152. An Act of Parliament was passed to ensure that the disaster would never happen again and that the money given to relieve the town was fairly distributed. A Court of Record was set up, manned by a string of local worthies, and this Court became, in effect, the emergency government of Blandford. Wooden shelters for sixty families were erected in a garden at the north-eastern edge of Blandford. A makeshift church, called the Tabernacle, paid for by £300 of the King's money, was built in the little square still bearing that name. The Court had power to make rules to ensure 'the better security and ornament of the Town, and all sorts and conditions of people'. Never again, the Court decided, would a distiller, candlemaker, soapmaker, common baker or common brewer pursue his business (they all involved the use of fire) in the Market Place without being found guilty of being a common nuisance. The use of thatch was forbidden; all houses were to be of brick, with a slate or tile roof.

For the distribution of the collection money to be fair, an assessment had to be made of the damage done by the fire. The Blandford *Fire Survey*, as it is called, is in effect a complete picture of the town on the morning of 5th June 1731. It is preserved as a tall and narrow manuscript accounts book in Dorset County Record Office. Like a destruction layer discovered in an archaeological dig, it gives a fascinating and precise description of the physical, economic and social structure of a small country town at the beginning of the 1730s. It is not quite a complete description, since those few buildings not burnt or damaged are not included. The 571 separate claims, however, do represent those made by a little over 90 per cent of the population of the town.

The most striking part of the survey is the

East Street. A large shop-er's house from 1730s, now ice Appliances, *electrical goods.* *se originally entered through* *ageway on left-hand side,* *'Georgian Passage', a high-* *fancy-goods arcade.*

63 *& 65 East Street. A pair of mid-eighteenth-century artisans' houses, now* Frickers *the bakers and* Macnally's *decorators.*

67 *& 69 East Street. A similar pair to 63 & 65, with the original entrances from the passageway between them. Now* Ottoman Kebab *and the incomparable* Dorset Bookshop.

71 *& 73 East Street. Originally only two storeys high but carefully heightened to four in the nineteenth century. Now* Solitaire *jewellers and* Pitmans *fish, poultry and game.*

astonishing differential between the rich and the poor. The bottom 45 per cent of the population (259 claimants) owned just over 4 per cent of the wealth in the town; the top 7 per cent of the people (40 households) put in claims that represented over 52 per cent of the whole. But even those figures obscure the nature of things at the social extremes. Over a quarter of the town, more than 150 households, claimed less than £10 each for the loss they had suffered (often everything they had), some putting in for—or at least being assessed at—no more than a single guinea. These were the very poor, often living in the back houses—described as 'very old and bad'—that were built at the rear of the medieval burgage plots. They formed the wide foundation of a social pyramid which narrowed rapidly above them eventually to reach the inconceivably distant pinnacle of the town's very rich. The top 10 families claimed £20,697, the bottom 150 less than £1,000 between them. At the absolute summit, claiming £4,652—over £1,700 more than its nearest rival—was the family that was to hold the town in its grip for the next three decades, eventually becoming so rich that they could withdraw from town life and take up the easier existence of country gentlemen: the Bastards of Blandford. (You should say the family name as it reads; only the most delicate of inhabitants puts the accent on the second syllable.)

The Bastards were master-builders. They had ridden in on the boom in country house building which had swept Dorset in the early decades of the century, usually building and equipping houses designed by other architects. By the time of the fire they owned several properties in Blandford, including the Greyhound Inn at the west end of the Market Place, some houses in Salisbury Street and their own house and shop at 75 East Street, opposite the church. The founder of the firm, Thomas, had died in about 1720, leaving six sons. The three youngest left to work

75 East Street. John Bastard's House, put up soon after the fire for £704 10s. Now Southern Electricity *with the most monstrous shop front in Blandford.*

26 The Market Place. Two houses, one in front of the other, built by the Bastards at the same time as 75 East St for £420. Late nineteenth-century shopfront now Howard Hall *estate agents.*

24 & 22 The Market Place. Originally one late eighteenth-century house, now the Oxfam *shop and* E.H. Jeans *newsagents.*

elsewhere, one to be a ship modeller for the Navy in Gosport, the others to work as independent builders. The eldest son, also called Thomas, died in Blandford in 1731, shortly after the fire and perhaps because of it. John and William Bastard, both in their early forties, vigorous if rather dough-faced men, were therefore left in charge of the business and effectively of the town. John, as the slightly older, was undoubtedly the guiding spirit of the two; he became Bailiff or Mayor six times, while his younger brother managed only twice.

It was John, together with Thomas Gardener and Benjamin Byles, the loss adjustors from the Sun Fire Insurance Office in London (where the Bastard goods and property were insured), who drew up the *Fire Survey*. It bears the imprint of John's meticulously material mind, nowhere more so than in the descriptions of the goods belonging to Bastard and Co. destroyed in the fire. These represent a large proportion, £3709 10s. 4d., of the total Bastard family claim and the *Survey* furnishes, room after crowded room, garret by garret, the Bastards' house-cum-shop at 75 East Street.

This was a large and high-quality business, spreading its tentacles into every corner of men's material lives. The effect is cumulative, and it is worth detailing some of the mass of it. 'In the shop next the Strete', for example, there were on sale: 2 bedsteads, 6 oval tables, 1 napkin press, 1 chest of drawers, 6 yards of material, 6 good chairs, 3 small tables, Dutch fashion, 5 large hanging glasses, 4 pairs of large glass sconces, 8 coffee mills, 18 hand tea tables, 'some japann'd, some Walnut', 50 snuff boxes, some good, some plain, 20 essence and salt bottles, some in cases, some not, 2 dozen punch ladles, several Dogg Calls and other little things, 4 setts of castors for Lignum Vitae [an eighteenth-century cure-all in the form of grated tree-resin], 8 good picture frames, 2 tea kettle

20 *& 18 The Market Place.*
The original Red Lion Inn built by the Bastards soon after the fire and their most sophisticated exercise in English baroque, much smoother than their own house down the street. Converted to three houses before 1802 and now Curry's *electrical goods and the* Prudential *insurance office.*

16 *The Market Place.*
Late eighteenth-century red brick, with later Doric columns surrounding the door.
Now John Farmer *shoes.*

14 *The Market Place.*
A largish shop-cum-house with beautiful brickwork from the 1730s. A mid-nineteenth-century shopfront now houses Roberts Electrical Ltd *and* Dikes Bakery Shop.

stands, 4 book desks, 10 glovė sticks, 10 large dressing glasses, the best make, 1 marble monument (£3 10s.), 12 pairs of brass compasses, boxes of candles and 2 dozen flambeaux, 10 black porter slaves, 8 ditto shorter Slaves for helmets, shields and banners, a Cafoy [imported French fabric] lining for a coach. In the cellar below there were barrels of beer, wine, cider and brandy as well buckets and lamps. In the chamber upstairs, looking out on to the Market Place, an amazing 'new walnut settle covered with red Silk', as well as a mass of ribbons, silks, pillows, curtains, canvas and linen sheets, two marble tables for monuments, and bed quilts . . . The list goes on—clock cases, one oak, one walnut, one japann'd, 3 pairs of black bags for funeral work and '6 black horse cloths for mourning Coach horses' (the funeral coach itself was stored—and burnt—in a barn behind the parsonage). The attic contained a minutely described jungle of hinges, dovetails, clockpins, 20,000 tacks (£1 10s. 0d.), waistcoats, hats, yards of green velvet, a large calico quilt, glue, lead moulds, curtain hooks, cravats, Holland handkerchiefs and '7 pairs of new piazzas'—whatever they might be. We would know about none of this if it had not been destroyed in the fire and one has to ask: how on earth did they remember it all?

Any hint of crudity among the eighteenth-century provincial rich is immediately banished by this

12 The Market Place. A pair of early post-fire houses now Barclays Bank.

A nineteenth-century bridge over the carriageway to the back of No. 12.

6 The Market Place. Lloyds Bank, *c.1925, the biggest, the only non-Georgian and the only stone building in the street.*

inventory. It would be tedious to go on too long—the Bastard possessions cover pages—but to take one small example, the furnishing of John Bastard's own bedroom destroys any idea that these men were country builders blundering towards a sense of style. It is the private place (he and his brother remained bachelors throughout their lives) of an educated and sophisticated man. Around his bed (worth £15 0s. 0d.) stood: a pair of globes and stands, a small globe, a chest of drawers, a glass cupboard for books, 3 plaster statues, 1 looking glass, 1 table, 3 cane chairs, 2 stools, 3 gilded picture frames, 1 new coat and waistcoat, 2 pairs of breeches, 5 pairs of stockings, 2 of silk, '1 Dimaly [?] waistcoat', 1 new peruke, 'one good sett of Instruments for land measuring', a great many other fine instruments for drawing, 1 pair of shoe buckles of old silver, 2 fine fans, 1 weather glass, a collection of fine prints, maps and drawings, '2 setts of small skails and waits', black lead and pencils of different sorts, 2 fine pocket books, a perspective portfolio, surveying drawings, a book on heraldry, 6 books on 'Building and parts of building', one pair of pistols and a carbine. (Total worth: £84 10s. 0d.)

From this crowded room—or at least its successor—with its utterly material and ambitious culture, its books on architecture, its measuring instruments and knowledge of finesse, the new Blandford was to emerge. It is the town you see today, in its essentials unchanged since the great Bastard period after the fire—a rebuilt, re-envisaged Georgian town. The part played by the Bastards is not clear in every detail—there is no way in which they can have rebuilt the whole town themselves—but it is at least certain that the new church and the little Tuscan fountain house next to it, the new Town Hall in Portland stone, their own new house at 75 East Street and its neighbour, the

The Market Place. mid-eighteenth-ntury shopkeeper's ·use in red brick, · years the ·wn printer and ·w W.H. Smith.

2 The Market Place. The Old Greyhound Inn. The Bastards' third major building in the square put up soon after the fire and the only one in stucco—white pilasters on a pale green façade and a greyhound in the yellow space below the pediment. Now Humberts *estate agents and* Traill and Co. *solicitors.*

1 West Street. A small mid-eighteenth-century shop over a carriageway to the back of the Greyhound. Now Trisha Fashions.

The Market Place in BLANDFO

new Red Lion and Greyhound inns both fronting on to the Market Place—in short, everything important in the new Blandford—was their work.

These buildings, on which the pediments are sometimes broken, the quoins deeply rusticated and enlarged, the cornices and window frames enriched, and the pilasters made giant, create a street scene that stretches the fabric of its own Englishness. Pushed into the relative normality of the brick façades around them, the Bastard work just seems to verge on the baroque side of the strict Palladian fashion of the time. The Bastard buildings, like the family itself, are part of the town but exaggerate their importance within it. As a result, whether by accident or not, Blandford town centre is a marvellous and subtle game, playing with the balance between the formal and the expansive, the symmetrical and the off-centre, the Palladian gravity—of the Town Hall, for example—and what Robert Adam

ORUM looking towards East Street

called 'movement' in architecture, that slightly unsettled and pleasurable dancing of the eye from element to element within the whole.

Almost nothing of the town plan was changed. The butchers' shambles and the market cross were removed to open up the Market Place and to give the new façades some air-room, but schemes to regularize and broaden other streets ran not only out of money but also into resistance from those whose house-plots were to be affected. In another fascinating way but perhaps one which was to be expected, Blandford remained the town it had been before the fire. At the height of the disaster, as the Rev. Pitt described in a poem written soon after,

> The Scarlet rob'd, who late on Dainties fed,
> With their own Slaves, partook the Gift of bread

but within days of the fire's cooling, the order of Blandford society had begun to reassert itself. Fire had levelled the town, both physically and socially, only for a moment. In John Bastard's *Fire Survey*, there is some fascinating evidence which would suggest that this surely rather ruthless man helped the reassertion of the social order by adjusting figures to his own advantage. Where valuations are altered in the notebook, as several are, it is almost always downwards. When it comes to one of the Bastard houses in Salisbury Street, however, the initial valuation of £200 is adroitly changed, with two careful strokes of the pen, to £400. Despite his close involvement with the rationale behind the distribution of the collection money, John added a sour and grumbling note at the back of his *Fire Survey* in 1734, claiming that the Commissioners had 'Made an unEqual Distribution, and gave Sum More and Sum less than there true proportion of there Lost, and this turned out a bad thing. . . . Every one had a just Rite to his Share [and] it was not in the power of men to Judg who was Proper Objects, nor who was poor, nor who was Rich.' (Charity was not close to the Bastards' heart.)

The new town, as you can see today as you walk along the streets, re-established the social hierarchy that is revealed in Bastard's *Survey*. In an area no more than three or four hundred yards across in any direction, you will find a tiny mid-eighteenth-century social landscape preserved in brick.

To begin at the top end, there is immediately a lesson in the deceptiveness of appearances. One might expect the Bastards to have had one of the most impressive houses in town. And indeed, from the outside, the single building covering the eastern end of the Market Place and the western end of East Street, known as the Bastards' House, looks like a palace: it is penetrated by a great carriageway in the very centre, above which a pair of pilasters, capped with the so-called 'Bastard capital'—a baroque invention derived in the end from Borromini—rise to the grandeur of the pediment above. But this is a face not a function, and this is not one house, but three. To the right of the arch were two tenements, let to a brazier and an apothecary. The Bastards lived only in the relatively cramped left-hand half. (It is now occupied by Southern Electricity who have obliterated everything that should not have been obliterated on the ground floor.) Your expectations sink—did the Bastards live in mean-minded ordinariness, hoarding their money for things other than personal delight? Not quite. If you plead with the lady downstairs who is trying to sell you a fridge that you are a scholar and student of English social history who needs to see more of the house for your own peace of mind, you might be allowed upstairs. On the mezzanine floor at the back, now filled with empty Toshiba boxes, you will find—only partly hidden by the cardboard—one of the prettiest small rooms you will ever have seen, probably built in the years soon after the fire. It is painted a beautiful, smoky blue, the same colour perhaps as they used on the ceiling of the church across the road. Above a plain dado there is wooden panelling decorated with leaf-and-dart moulding and, above that, a wonderful hanging swaggy plaster frieze of oak leaves and acorns strung between human masks. On the two end walls, there are three richly decorated doors, two of them there simply for effect. One leads into a cupboard six inches deep, the other into a blank wall. You will now think of the Bastards as impresarios, businessmen-showmen: perhaps this was literally a showroom—to persuade clients to use the services of the firm. Or perhaps, given the state of their previous house on this site, it was a sort of boxroom.

That is the exception, as one would expect from such a family. The pattern in the rest of the town is far clearer and you will soon discover the class-zoning of eighteenth-century Blandford. North of the church and around the small irregular square called The Plocks is a cluster of some of the smartest houses in town. One of the best, on the west side of Church Lane, has been demolished and all you can see now is the ugly back of Woolworths; the others have now been taken over by solicitors, the British Legion and council offices, but it is still worth standing in front of Lime Tree House on the Plocks, drinking in the simple prettiness of a good-to-middling house built in the 1730s for a family worth perhaps £800 or £900. It is very straight—no baroque games here—with many aspects contributing to its elegance: its plainness, then the shallow cove of the white canopy over the door, and finally the decorative brickwork, with bands of lip-red bricks running around each window and down to the matching window on the floor below. Coupar House, diagonally opposite, is far more pretentious, with its Portland stone facings, broken pediment and—to be honest—its ugliness. No one knows the architect of this house, but it looks like a Bastard idea gone slightly wrong.

This group of houses, sited well away from the mess and smell of the Market Place, up on the hill, with a view over the beautiful woods on the far bank of the

Stour, represents the core of smartness. But they are not the only good houses in the town. In fact, the houses of the professionals and leading merchants are scattered quite casually around Blandford, really only avoiding the Market Place and tending towards the old edges of the town, perhaps because those parts had on the whole escaped the fire. Both the beautiful Eastway House, towards the eastern end of East Street, and Eagle House, in White Cliff Mill Street, for example, existed quite happily despite being situated amidst a high concentration of the very poorest artisans' houses which were not entered by a front door but through a passage that often still runs through the middle of each pair. In this way, there were the purely working-class districts in the eighteenth-century town. To the modern mind, this coexistence has a very odd feel to it; it was an easy mixture of rich and poor. Not surprisingly, this has not survived until today. Of the two streets in the town which had this class mixture, one has gone each way. The bottom of White Cliff Mill Street is now dirty, broken and horrible, with many empty lots, a degraded air and—currently—several abandoned buildings. Eagle House, at heart as elegant as anything in The Plocks, stands here as a shored-up and maltreated wreck, almost opposite the Half Moon Inn, the most soulless pub in the town's most soulless street. Eastway House, by contrast, with its lovely, curving rococo parapet, its urns and ironwork, presides over its end of East Street in a queenly way. The 1713 cottages next to it are all prettified and boutiqued, gentrified almost in sympathy with their grander neighbour.

The middle-ranking shops-cum-houses are all concentrated in the Market Place and in the openings off it. They are the glory of Blandford and together they explode one myth about the beauty of English towns—the 'accretion theory', which maintains that only by the slow addition of different styles over many centuries can any form of urban beauty be achieved. It is nonsense. The Court of Record ruled that owners of property fronting on to the Market Place should at least start rebuilding before 25th March 1736 or lose both their share of the collection money and the land itself, which would be compulsorily purchased from them. The idea was to prevent trade slipping away from the town to other markets but the effect was been to make this uniquely beautiful place all of one moment.

As this was not a green-field site, but a redevelopment with many separate property owners, there was no opportunity for terraces in the new style. Each man rebuilt his own place, with his own ideas of commodity and delight, but the materials to hand were the same, above all the brick in all its variations. It is this simultaneous sameness and difference that makes the shop-houses of the Blandford Forum Market Place so wonderful a whole. The bricks vary in all sorts of ways but, above all, in their colour: the metallic sheen of burnt 'blue' bricks, used by the Bastards to make a solid steely skin for the central bay of their own house; others elsewhere making *chainages* between the windows, either red on blue or blue on red; the corners of grey pilasters picked out in plummy red; the aprons to windowsills in softer, yellower red than the darker frames of the windows above them; the façades sparkling with white keystones above the windows, or slashed across with a broad white stuccoed band. Many of the bricks are laid in what became known for a while as 'Bastard bond', in which nothing but 'headers'—the narrow ends rather than the long sides of the bricks—are revealed. Some houses use black mortar, others the calmer, less dramatic, creamy white. You could spend two hours here reading nothing but the bricks.

I have left the best of the Bastards' buildings until last. The church, apart from the Town Hall, or Corn Exchange as it is now known, is the only stone building they made.

It is not the outside, however, that is so good. Walk in through the large doors under the tower at the west end and you will find yourself in a space which is as near as a church will ever come to a drawing room. Flowery ribs trace the shallow, smoky blue vaults across the nave and aisles, coming to rest at either side on a row of tall, Ionic columns, painted off-white. It is relaxed, warm and worldly. Three-quarters of the way up on the right-hand side is the Corporation Pew, also designed by the Bastards. It is the most contented piece of church furniture in the country. The vicar describes it as a first-class railway carriage. The pew is turned sideways on to the altar, and at its head is a large and sumptuous hooded throne belonging to the Bailiff, dripping with flowered ribbons and hung with fruit and wheat, all carved in the Bastard workshops across the road, and upholstered—like the seats for the Burgesses which run up to it on either side—in lush and receptive red velvet. This was the chair occupied for years on end after the great disaster by the Bastard Brothers, the makers of Blandford, the Kings of their time.

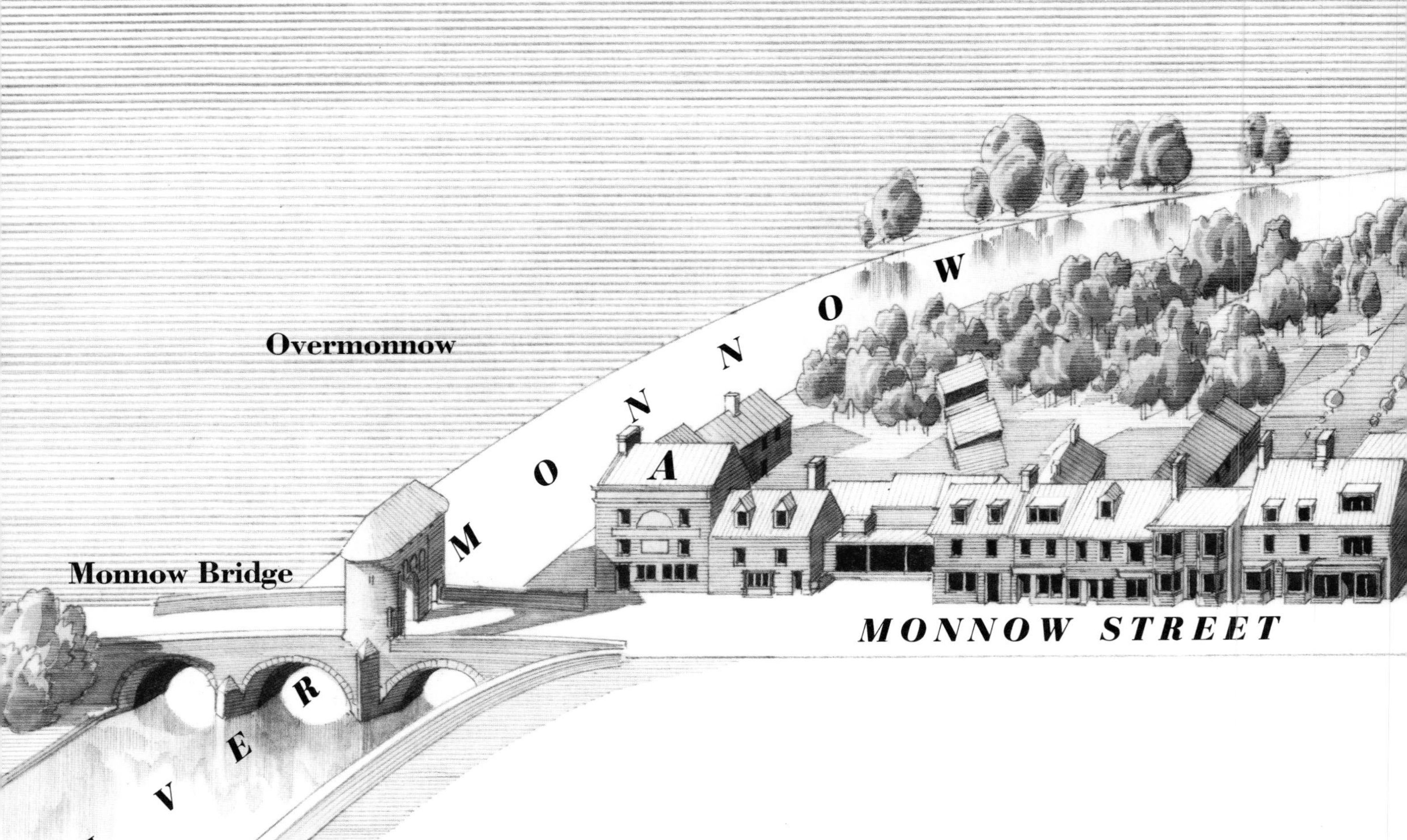

MONMOUTH
Gwent

TO INCLUDE MONMOUTH in a book about English towns will, in some quarters, bring a shriek of indignation. Now in the county of Gwent—very much part of Wales—the town is overseen from very Welsh planning departments outside Pontypool and is, ecclesiastically, legally, governmentally and economically, part of Wales. This was not always the case. Until the re-organization of local government in 1974, Monmouth was the county town of its own English county, Monmouthshire, which had been created in 1536 when Henry VIII had annexed Wales to England. It sent two knights to Parliament (Welsh counties only sent one), was subject to the English courts in Westminster and to the judges on the Oxford circuit. The town itself was part of the diocese of Hereford in England and the licensing laws—at first, anyway—were as liberal as those in the English counties to the east.

But it was a muddle. This is a borderland, a place of cultural mixing and confusion. Throughout the Middle Ages, Welshmen had regularly murdered Englishmen in these streets and had been murdered in return. There had been a bloody Welsh-English battle in the meadow just outside the town wall and many Welsh-

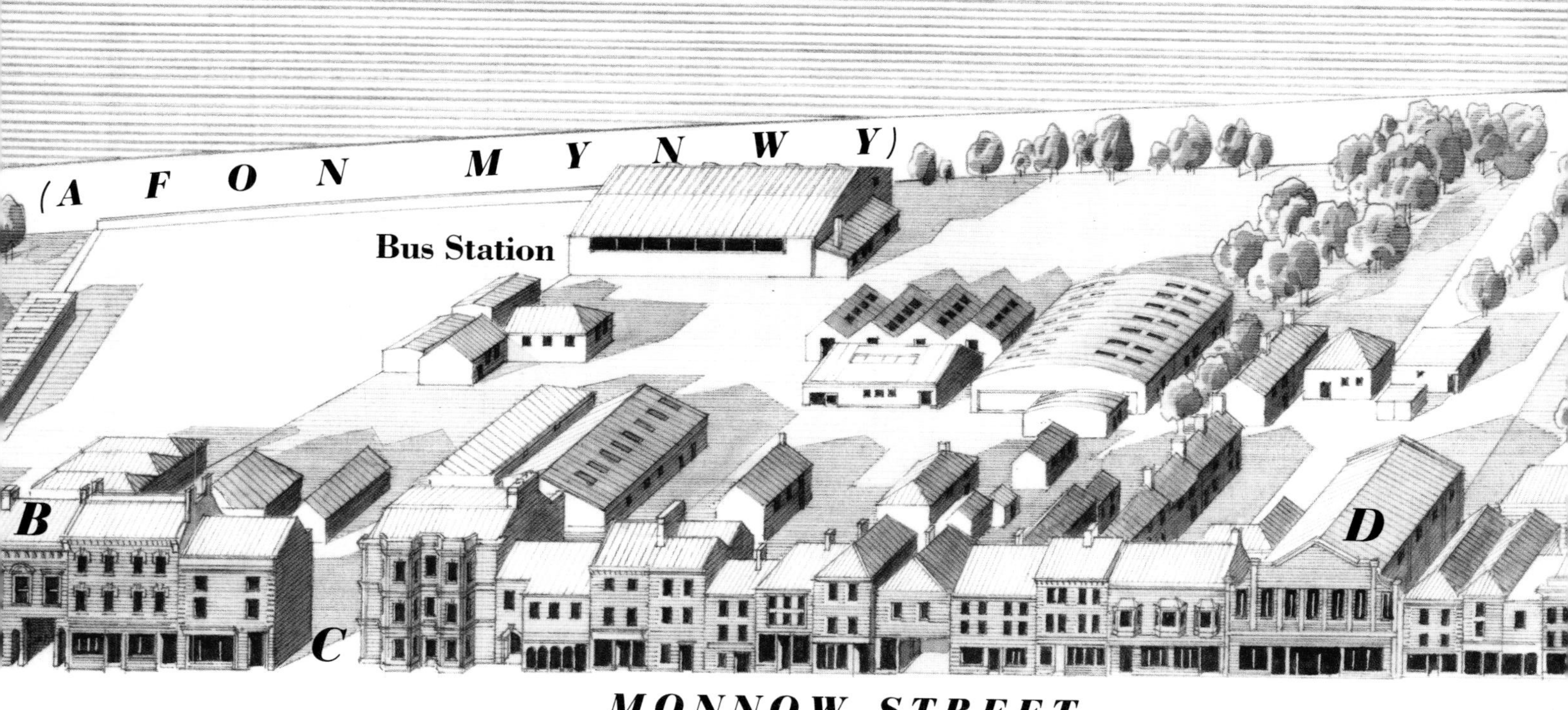

EXPLANATION
A The Barley Mow Public House
B The Oldway Shopping Centre
C The site of 83–85 Monnow Street, recently demolished
D Peacock's Drapers

English marriages inside it. Some of the official arrangements too reflected this part-Welshness. Apart from the town of Monmouth itself, most of the rest of the county was in the Welsh diocese of Llandaff. For a while the pubs in Monmouthshire were forced to close on a Sunday, like those in Wales, though this was later changed back again. Monmouthshire sportsmen can play for Welsh national teams, although there is a great mixture of enthusiasms here for Welsh rugby and English soccer. When a choice had to be made in 1974, I have heard it said that the only reason Monmouth opted for inclusion in the Welsh county of Gwent and not in Hereford & Worcester—as its new English neighbour is called—is that the rates were likely to be lower in Wales.

There was, it is true, a time in the early 1970s when the Welsh Nationalist candidate received more votes than anyone else in local elections, but that was more to do with the character of the man—a dynamic, passionate tribune of the people—than what he actually stood for. In truth, the town is divided over this issue, and there is a simple and immediate way here, when talking to someone in the street, of telling on which side of the border he stands. If he pronounces the place *Munmuth*, with the first syllable rich and caky, and the second slurred away, his sympathies are probably Tory and English; if *Monmouth*—narrower, more precise—he's likely to be Welsh and mildly democratic.

I once sat at a table here with a rich woman on one side, and a working-class woman on the other, both of them deeply concerned for the conservation of the town, which was coming under new and severe commercial pressures. Each blithely pronounced their different versions of the name and discreetly failed to mention that my own vowel sounds were wavering uncertainly and ingratiatingly between the two. When asked, *Munmuth* said there were no class distinctions here; *Monmouth* said there were. We were in the suburb of Overmonnow, in the housing estate called King's Fee. I asked them if there was any distinct name for the other end of town—almost certainly the oldest part—between the Castle, the Church and the Haberdashers' School. It has always been the better

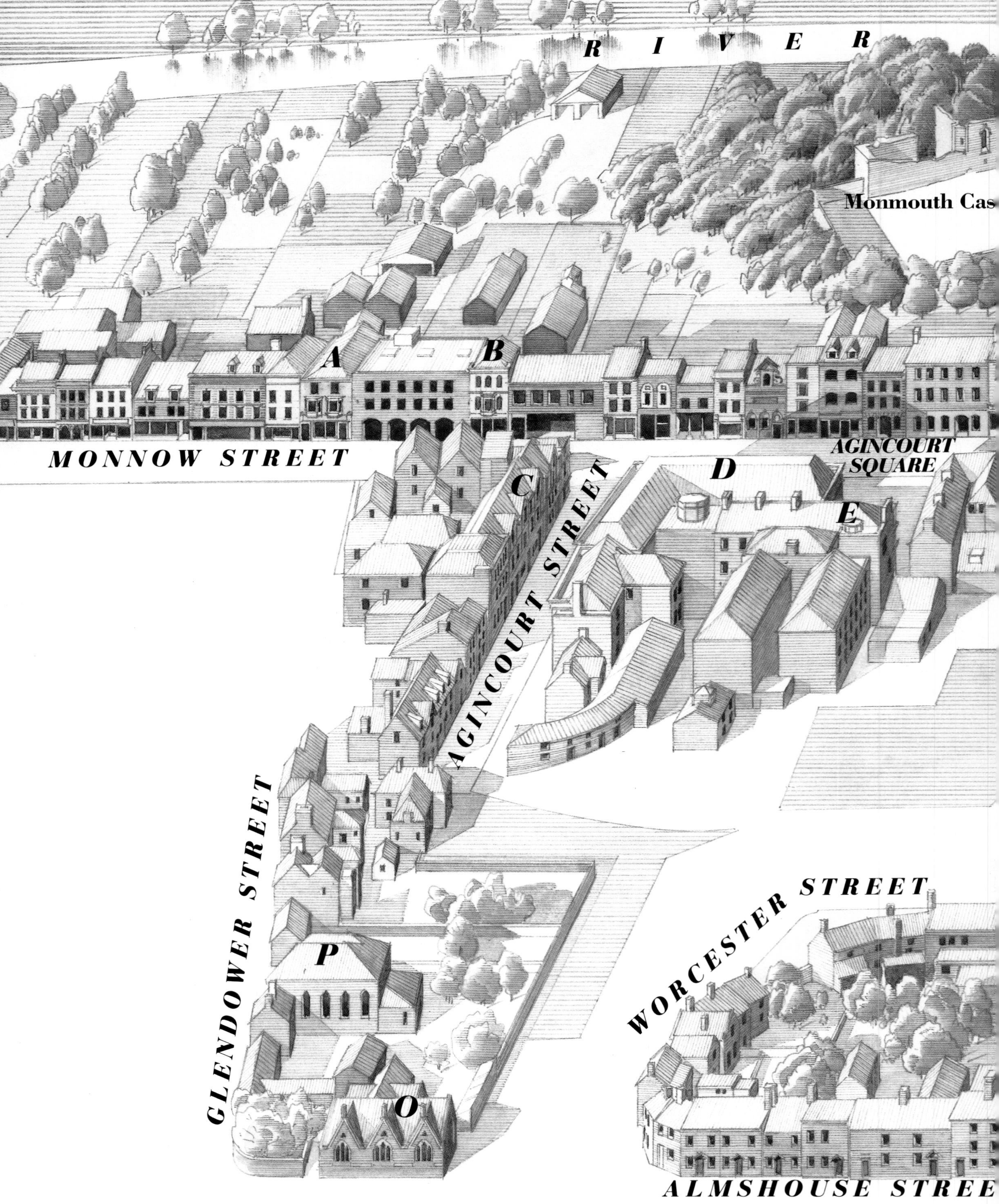
R I V E R
Monmouth Cas
A
B
MONNOW STREET
C
D
AGINCOURT SQUARE
E
AGINCOURT STREET
GLENDOWER STREET
WORCESTER STREET
P
O
ALMSHOUSE STREE

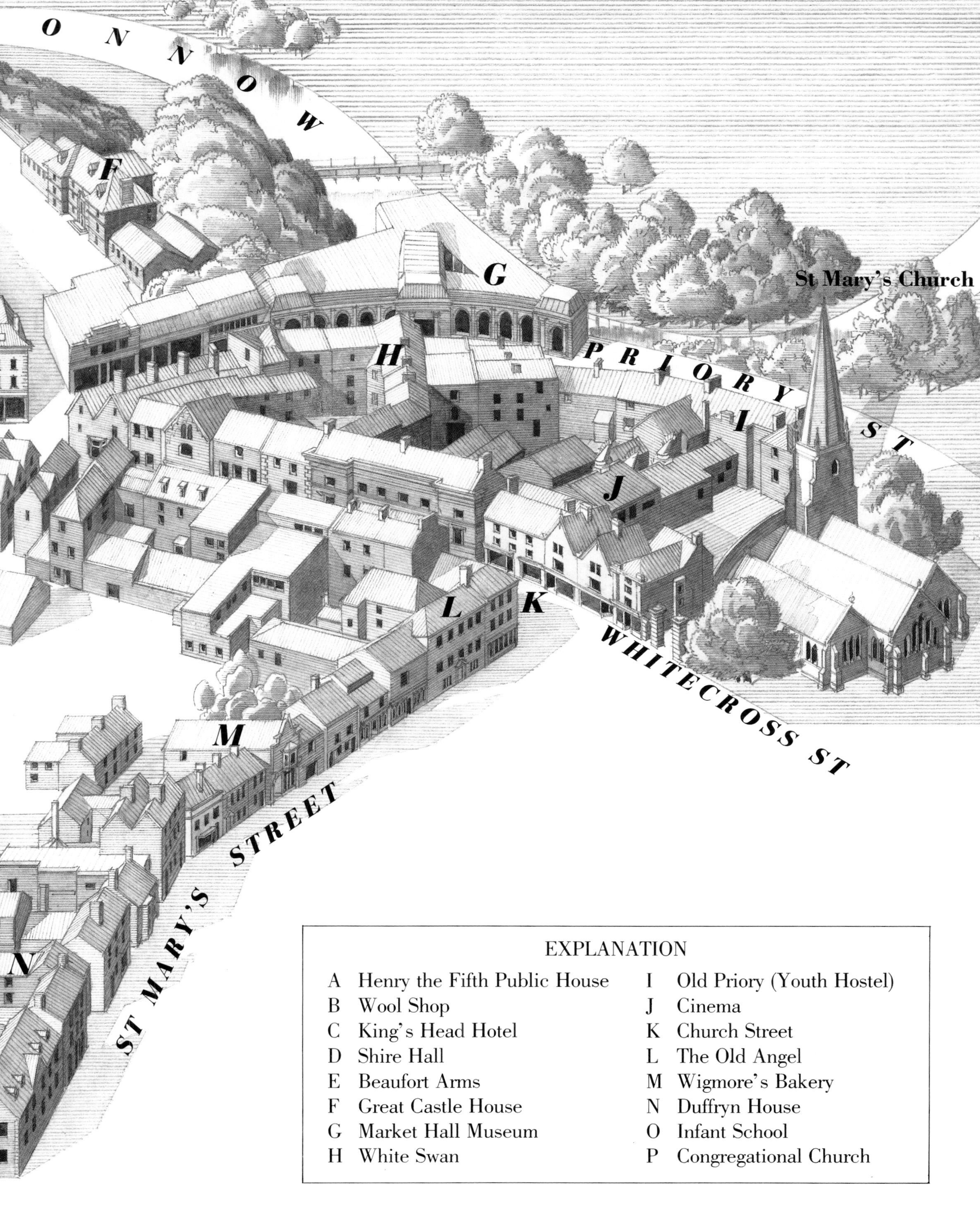
ONNOW
F
G
H
I
J
K
L
M
N
St Mary's Church
PRIORY ST
WHITECROSS ST
ST MARY'S STREET
EXPLANATION
A Henry the Fifth Public House
B Wool Shop
C King's Head Hotel
D Shire Hall
E Beaufort Arms
F Great Castle House
G Market Hall Museum
H White Swan
I Old Priory (Youth Hostel)
J Cinema
K Church Street
L The Old Angel
M Wigmore's Bakery
N Duffryn House
O Infant School
P Congregational Church

part of town, standing up out of the floods from the River Monnow. Was there a name for it? They answered at the same time: 'No, not really' (*Munmuth*), 'Yes: posh' (*Monmouth*).

This has always been a halfway house and, of all the towns in this book, it is the one with the least definable air. Most of the town occupies that rise of highish ground between the two rivers, the Monnow, from which it takes its name, and the Wye, into which the Monnow flows. The tall, woody hills of the Wye valley surround it on all sides. In the eighteenth and nineteenth centuries tourists used to come here on boat trips down the River Wye, regarding Monmouth as the most accessible version they could find of Wild Wales, the roughness of the local manners sending a frisson of delight through the over-bred travellers. If you come here now, however, there is not, at first, a single element of wildness (if you can discount Welsh Nationalist enthusiasms) to be found. It is a place, or so you might imagine, buried in the depths of its provincial charm. This is the birthplace both of Henry V and Charles Rolls, one of the founders of Rolls-Royce. Statues of this famous pair stand opposite each other in Agincourt Square: Henry a little misshapen on the Shire Hall, Charles more nobly cast, on his own plinth. What better representatives could you ask for to embody the rich self-congratulatory Englishness of England than these two? And with that sort of thought in mind Monmouth can lead you a long way up the (wrong) path to a vision of itself as settled and content.

Go to the middle of the town, to the marketplace, which is filled with stalls on Saturdays. Previously known as the Market Place, it is now called Agincourt Square, renamed in the early nineteenth century, as was Glendower Street running off it, to gratify the Wye tourists with a reminder of Henry V. It is a fascinating and charming piece of half-planned half-provinciality. Dominating the square is the Shire Hall, a distinctly odd building put up in 1724 on the site of the Elizabethan Market Hall and far too big for the site. It eats into the cobbled space in front of it, cutting off the view of its neighbouring buildings—a sort of shouted and half-grammatical claim by the county town to importance and status. The most significant role this building played was as the Assize Court, which was held here until 1939. Monmouth, as the county town, thrived for centuries on the regular business from the court. The lawyers' fees earned at the court paid for many of the large Georgian houses that are peculiar to this part of the country and which are scattered around the town. The habit of argument engendered at the Assizes also entered the town's soul.

The pubs and hotels crowd up against the Shire Hall. Nice little dress shops stand opposite, behind their fine and fluted Corinthian shop fronts. Everything here is working as it is meant to do in a market town. The buildings are prettily painted, there are baskets of hanging flowers; nothing is rigorously planned, but there is a visual concordance. It is a proper place, the quoins and cornices are carefully picked out in complementary colours. The wide flat faces of the big houses convey an air of comfort and relaxation. There is no real striving here. Everything is slotted into the familiar grammatical hierarchy of a market town. Here is the Shire Hall; the good hotel, the King's Head, is next to it. Another, the Beaufort, across the way, has—sadly—been turned into flats and shops, but the planning department has insisted that the developers keep the black-and-white ionic façade as it was. Along Church Street, now pedestrianized, the old Angel Hotel is now a Swiss kitchen shop, but the outside looks fine. In the streets spreading out beyond there is a flat calm, with as little going on, and as little tension as in the regular symmetry of a Georgian façade.

On beyond the church, at the bottom of Whitecross Street, in St James's Square, a beautiful tree, a catalpa, stands in the middle of the street. The tree hangs its limbs out towards you, draped with its large pale handkerchief leaves like the hands of a fop. How very like Monmouth this tree is: the relaxed confidence of the truly content. But come a little closer and you will see something more. Very discreetly, and invisible from a distance, the branches of the catalpa have been bolted together with iron rods.

Look at Monmouth again in the light of its hidden structure. I was sitting in Agincourt Square not long ago. Women with baskets were pausing to talk. Men outside the Punch House were reading the *Beacon* in the sunshine. I was on the steps of the Shire Hall. There was a boy next to me. As I watched him, he spat on the stone flags and then leant over to one side, putting his lips to the spout of a small yellow can from which he sucked—I could not see what it was. He then looked at me and his eyes were rolling upwards. He moved his face from side to side, like a horse frustrated in its stable. I took the yellow tin from his hand; it was lighter fuel and this boy was high on it. He did not

Part of Monmouth School, originally founded in 1614 on a bequest from William Jones, a native of the town, who had made his fortune selling Welsh cottons in Hamburg. These buildings were put up between 1865 and 1895.

know where he was. I took him to the hospital on the edge of town. Monmouth was happily continuing on its way while this boy was destroying his mind.

There is another scene that comes as a surprise. On Christmas Eve 1985 Monmouth had a riot. There had been a party in Rolls Hall on Whitecross Street. One hundred and fifty people, aged between seventeen and twenty-five, had come out of the Hall and had apparently spontaneously rampaged through the town. A police van was overturned and the blue light on top smashed. The police station was stoned and another police car kicked in. The crowd ran down St Mary's Street and Worcester Street, smashing the windows of Shirley Smith Soft Furnishings and Wigmore's Bakery. Police reinforcements from other parts of Wales arrived and arrested eight of the rioters, seven of whom were charged with criminal damage.

This town is not all it appears to be. These incidents might be seen as no more than momentary deviations from the norm, the sort of thing that might happen anywhere; but throughout Monmouth's history, which has always been one of division and rather tense conflict, this sort of paroxysm has regularly occurred. Even now, there is a current in the town which, after you have been there a while, comes to dominate all others. After many decades of backwater existence, during which Monmouth did little more than rise to the weekly excitement of the cattle market down by the river—the day when the pubs stayed open longer—and subside after it to a marginal quiet, new pressures are impinging on the town.

Monnow Street has long been its main shopping area. It is probably an ancient trackway, and is lined with the burgage plots that were laid out by the lords of the Norman castle at the end of the eleventh century. It was never, and is not today, the best part of the town. It was protected by the fortified bridge across the Monnow but was outside the main walls of the town that ringed the high ground to the east. Monnow Street was often flooded. The houses slumped into the wet land beneath them and the foundations had to be re-constructed at regular intervals with the cinders from the ironworks in their backyards.

This long but really quite ordinary street—bulging in places to accommodate the market stalls and animals—is now under pressure, as the large multiple chains jostle for outlets in the town. Monmouth is divided over this issue too and, in a new but quite intelligible alignment of forces, the radical conservationists are lined up against the conservative entrepreneurs. Both the local council and the local newspaper are conservative in their sympathies and have managed the incursion of developers into the town almost as smoothly as these things have always been handled. However, with one supermarket chain in particular, called Kwiksave, there have been problems. Kwiksave applied late in 1986 to redevelop the site of 83-85 Monnow Street, which at the time was one of Monmouth's finest buildings, a Georgian, Grade II listed house with a classical porch, stone quoins and an impressive cornice. The supermarket needed listed building consent to alter the house but they never applied for it. Instead they put scaffolding up on the front of the building, had the whole structure declared unsafe by the Council (Kwiksave had already made internal alterations, including the removal of load-bearing walls and a staircase, which may have reduced its stability) and had it demolished. At the moment the site is a hole in the street, waiting for Kwiksave's replacement. There is nothing the Borough Council can do to make them rebuild on the site. Nevertheless, Kwiksave does have permission to erect a fake Georgian house, four storeys high but—and this is the bizarre part—without any internal structures above the shop ceiling on the ground floor. This is a truly Baroque solution to the problem of inserting a supermarket into an old town: a pastiche house with regular Georgian windows and doors, whose steel-framed interior is an utter void, and with a large extension at the back, like a cassette halfway out of a video-recorder. Is this what planning legislation is for?

That kind of story, if not quite so extreme, is common enough nowadays. Throughout the country developers are moving into small towns—especially those within reach of a motorway—with an eye on the extra money that people there now have, on the poor condition of much prime-site property, and on the actual inability of local authorities to interfere very much with their commercial interests. What makes Monmouth different from most towns is the ferocity of the local reaction to such goings-on. In most places there is a sliding and apathetic acceptance of the decisions taken far above people's heads. Not here. Monmouth, and the countryside around, is plastered with dayglo pink notices saying simply 'Prosecute Kwiksave'. The message is unavoidable. A stream of leaflets, newsletters and posters in shops (most of the small shops are friendly to the cause) and in the hands of supporters on the street, all urge Monmouth not to be indifferent to its own fate. Other issues are introduced to heighten the emotional atmosphere of the campaign: the neglect and destruction by other developers of the archaeological evidence under the floors of the Monnow Street houses; the fate of the Royal George, an ex-hotel in the old part of the town, which has been in a poor, half-improved state for too long; the Council's plans in the mid-1960s (abandoned because there was not enough money at the time, but not to be forgotten) for a 'spine road' that was to be driven through the centre of the great open space of Chippenham Meadow and the heart of the medieval town, all for improved traffic-flow; the astonishing scheme for Monmouth Police Station which was to have had its own helicopter landing-pad. Listen for a while to the conservationist advocacy and you will begin to doubt if authority and sanity can co-exist.

In all of these ways Monmouth is a wildly contentious place. Despite that initial air of calm, you will soon realize that it froths with dispute. And in the light of that, and of the long history of its disputatiousness, you will come to realize that what might have seemed a muddled, borderland atmosphere, the co-existence of opposites, does in fact represent the reality of the place itself. It is a town founded on argument and on the shuffling, shifting interests of different power-groups. And here, for a moment, in a way that is more dramatic than in any other town I know, you get the feeling that a town presents itself as a place of stability and rightness (I am thinking of the look of the houses, the order of a street) as a counterpull to the realities of its commercial and political life. The life of a town, which at heart is a commercial thing, is involved in constant negotiation. It is not like the life of the countryside, where the land and its workings can be relied on as an essentially repetitive process. A town cannot be expected to be repetitive. A town is a place founded on change, or at least with the threat of change close to the surface. The building of a town in many ways fixes, and even denies that process of change. It makes status into property; it makes people into buildings. Perhaps the roots of small-town classicism are to be looked for in psychology; as you will see, the period when Monmouth was acquiring its contented style was one of its most gripping moments of political and social struggle.

No one is quite sure how old Monmouth is. There was a Roman camp nearby but it did not form the nucleus of the town as it is today. There was probably some sort of Celtic farm or even hamlet here, but they are all irrelevant to the town. Essentially, this is a Norman plantation in a borderland. The castle, on a highpoint commanding crossings of the Monnow and the Wye, was established here in 1068, at first built in timber and then gradually replaced in stone over the succeeding centuries. Little of it is now left—a few lumpen walls—but it still plays its part in the drama of the town's topography. It dominates the street plan, which is much as it was in the fifteenth century. The plan reveals Monmouth as a castle-cum-market town, with the addition of a Benedictine priory as the dominant ecclesiastical element. The lords of Monmouth—for the first two hundred years a Breton family—encouraged settlers to come here by offering them low rents, good sites for town houses and, by the end of the thirteenth century, the protection of the town walls. By then, too, the town had become one of the lordships of the Duke of Lancaster, one of the titles held by the Kings of England. It was this royal connection, made even stronger after Henry V was born in the castle in 1387, that confirmed Monmouth as an English rather than a Welsh place. The town and its authorities became the object of Welsh hatred, and its fortunes suffered terribly during the rebellion of Owain Glendower early in the fifteenth century. When Henry VI granted Monmouth its first charter in 1447, he guaranteed that the burgesses of the town should be tried within the lordship 'only by Englishmen of the

The Wesleyan Methodist Chapel, in St James's Street, like almost every other nonconformist chapel in the town, was set back behind the houses fronting the street. Nonconformity was strongly identified with radicalism and this discreet siting of chapels may, perhaps, represent an effort to placate the dominant Anglican authorities. This—nonetheless—gloriously theatrical building was designed by the local architect G.V. Maddox in 1837.

said borough and not by any Welshmen for ever'.

Many hundreds of years later in 1792 this outpost of Englishness paid its tribute to Henry V, the 'gleaming King' as he was called at the time, in the form of the statue on the Shire Hall. But there is another memorial to him in the town which is far more beautiful. In 1673 the Marquis of Worcester, soon to be Duke of Beaufort and by that time Lord of the Manor, erected a new house on the site of the old castle a new house, the Great Castle House, so that his daughter-in-law could 'lie in of her first child near that spot of ground and space where our great hero, Henry the Fifth, was born'. This romantic idea gave rise to the most attractive house in Monmouth, a tall building with a big-hipped roof and a giant-coved cornice, with the walls built of old and rather flaky pink sandstone blocks, probably plundered from the castle gatehouse nearby. It is now the headquarters of the local Territorial Army unit, but you may, on request, look inside at the extraordinarily rich plaster ceilings, flowered and swagged above the slightly wobbly panelling, and the many portraits of red-jacketed colonels. The people of Monmouth are, I was told here, only quite enthusiastic about the idea of part-time military service.

An outpost of Englishness it may officially have been, but in no way was the town a single political unit. During Glendower's rebellion, many Monmouth people sided with the Welsh and were later prosecuted. Many tenants had failed to pay their rents to the Duchy while rebellion was in the air and a special Assize was held in 1413 'to hear and determine divers treasons, insurrections, and rebellions within the lordship of Monmouth'. Most were pardoned, as by that time the crown was anxious to mend its fences with the Welsh.

At the very moment Monmouth emerges into the modern era, its people are found fighting among themselves. A report made to Henry VIII in 1519 blamed the terrible state to which the town had sunk on the incorrigible habits of its people. There had been 'of long time great variances, strifes and debates . . . great Riots, affrays and unlawful assemblies . . . in the said Town, both to the great unquietness and disturbance of the mayor, burgesses and inhabitants, [and] to the great hindrance and loss of goods'. You have only to go to the town today to know exactly what they were complaining about. Monmouth will argue about anything. In the sixteenth century it was weirs on the Wye and the Monnow and the freedom to have corn ground wherever one wanted. Today it is planning acts and the preservation of the past. And you only have to talk to some of the officers in the planning department to hear a modern version of the exasperation with Monmouth's disputatiousness that has been a constant element throughout its history. It is not exactly an aggressiveness; it is more simply the love of argument. In a town which for four hundred years housed the Assizes and which was packed with lawyers both professional and amateur, one should perhaps expect nothing else.

The most fascinating aspect of Monmouth's argumentativeness is the way in which the streets of the town can be seen as the theatre for its disputes. In the seventeenth and eighteenth centuries these disputes had been formalized into the political manoeuvring of a small group of seven or eight families, the focus of whose political attention was the Duke of Beaufort and his agent. In the sixteenth century things were not quite so smoothly managed. As the historian of Monmouth, Keith Kissack, has described, the parliamentary election of 1572 was a wild affair. Usually two families, the Somersets and the Morgans,

Wigmore's Bakery in St Mary's Street, one of the victims of the 1985 riot.

dominated the election, each having one of their sons elected as a Knight of the Shire. This particular year, however, the Sheriff of the county, Thomas Herbert, decided to put up his son Henry as a candidate for a seat.

The electors of the county (about nine hundred men) turned up at the Castle on the morning of election day; while waiting in the Castle Yard they started playing some rather boisterous games during which a door and one or two windows were broken. Thomas Herbert then put into effect what was probably a pre-meditated plan. He left the Castle and the noisy crowd of opponents, went out through the marketplace, down the length of Monnow Street and over the bridge to the Church of St Thomas in Overmonnow where he had arranged for his son, and their supporters, to be waiting. There, outside an alehouse opposite the church, the Sheriff asked the assembled crowd: 'Are you content that Mr Charles Somerset [whom he had previously squared] and my son, Henry Herbert, shall be Knights of the Shire?' The crowd then shouted, as they were meant to do, 'A Somerset' and 'A Herbert', with only one or two dissenters shouting 'A Morgan'. The noise was so loud that it could be heard at the other end of town where Morgan's great crowd of supporters were still waiting in the Castle Yard for the election to begin. In raging panic all nine hundred of them stormed down the length of Monnow Street and over the Monnow Bridge shouting 'William Morgan, William Morgan!' They were too late. By the time they got across into Overmonnow the Sheriff had declared his son and Charles Somerset elected and was galloping off home towards Wonastow. The Morgan faction caught up with him and demanded justice but he stood firm: his son remained MP and his very Monmouthian coup remained valid.

This freelance corruption gradually evolved over the following two hundred and fifty years into an altogether more rigid affair, indissoluably wedded to the figure of the Duke of Beaufort. The Duke was only rarely present in the town, as he spent most of the time at Badminton in Gloucestershire, but he had a house outside Monmouth called Troy, and his agent was an all-powerful presence in the town. From the early

The Wool Shop in Monnow Street.

Duffryn House in St Mary's Street.

The two façades of Cornwall House in Monnow Street: (bottom) *the earlier, built about 1700, looks on to the garden and Chippenham Meadow while* (top) *facing the street, is a less satisfactory composition, made late in the eighteenth century. This was the powerhouse of Georgian Monmouth, the home and office of the Duke of Beaufort's agent.*

eighteenth century onwards the agent lived in the beautiful Cornwall House on Monnow Street, a double-fronted building with perhaps its finer façade at the back, looking onto the open expanse of Chippenham Meadow.

The town oligarchy, equally amenable to the Duke's and its own wellbeing, enjoyed a life of luxury and extravagance in which elections were manipulated, all attempts to extend the franchise resisted; in which corporate property was often pilfered; and which paid little attention to the welfare of the town as a whole. This was the group of people who endowed Monmouth with so many of its fine Georgian houses. One town clerk, when the Council decided to look into his whereabouts, was discovered to have been living in the West Indies for many years, from where he somehow continued to draw his salary. Offices moved slickly around those in the inner circle. One Rev. Thomas Prosser, for example, began in 1779 as an usher at the Haberdashers' School (founded in 1615 and still here today, buying up ever more property in the town), was Headmaster in 1780, a member of the Common Council in 1802, Vicar of St Mary's, Monmouth in 1815, and mayor and chief magistrate in 1806, 1813, 1816 and 1818. Sycophancy and self-serving were the only necessary qualifications for office and the Duke made every effort to keep it that way.

By 1818, just as Prosser was oiling his way towards the last of his triumphs, those burgesses who were excluded from the inner circle felt that they had had enough. For many years Monmouth was now to be convulsed with a paroxysm of litigation and canvassing, of debate and violence over its political future. The matter at issue was whether the mayor and the burgesses could be elected only after nomination by the common council (manned by the inner circle of oligarchs) or whether the electing and nominating body should be the whole body of existing burgesses. It was essentially a struggle between the narrow, conservative, ducal party and the broader, radical town party. The Duke's agent Wyatt, after a weak start, ended in bullish humour. 'Now nothing but the Strong Arm of the Law', he wrote to his master, 'will put down the abominable spirit that prevails in the town. . . . Punch the rascals as you can.' Those tenants who held Beaufort property and sided with the radicals were given notice to quit. At the various part-triumphs enjoyed by each party along the way, the town was decked in flags, and giant celebratory dinners were held. No trick was left untried by the Duke's party: 'money was offered in profusion; houses, farms, lands, premises etc. for the same purpose . . . the fair sex connected with that party was put in requisition . . . the sacred pulpit [was] prostituted to hold [the town party] up to obloquy and execration.' The Duke was thought to have spent between £7,000 and £8,000 on one mayoral election. Vicious stories were written and printed, members of the town were imprisoned for debt, others (including Prosser) went mad. The only ones to benefit were the lawyers retained by the two sides, who ate and drank heartily and charged their clients a fortune. By 1826 the body politic of Monmouth had actually split in two, with two mayors, four bailiffs and two town criers announcing conflicting messages. Eventually the radical party divided into opposing factions and left the way open for the old ducal guard to resume its place.

As one can still see today, some measure of the old Monmouth radical spirit remained, even after their defeat. At the 1831 parliamentary election for example, some of the burgesses were thought to be defecting to the other side and planning to vote for the Duke's son, the Marquess of Worcester, who was standing as a parliamentary candidate. 'Is this true?' asked one radical pamphleteer, 'Are there men in Monmouth so debased, so lost to their every sense of dignity as men? What! crawling round the foot that spurned you? Kissing the hand that inflicted the death blow to your independence? Tell it not in Gath. . . . If such a degraded being presents himself at the hustings, if he disgraces his lips by polling for the Marquess of Worcester, I trust the men of Monmouth will do their duty, and give expression to their insulted feelings and never permit such a man to mingle in your company without a sample of the treatment due to apostates.' Modern elections are anodyne by comparison.

This is a strange town. It has all the attributes of its mixed component parts. It is English but Welsh. It is sub-ducal but it is radical. It is smart and snobbish in places and full, as one woman said to me, of 'little ticky-tacky how d'y'does'. But it does not have the smooth sheen of other towns on the make in southern England. There is something angular and uncomfortable about it, as though the attempts to incorporate the various elements at play here are actually too much. Monmouth, perhaps, has some doubts over its own identity. Of all the towns in this book it is the one least certain about where it is going.

WEYMOUTH
Dorset

THE YACHTS ease across the water in the bay; the teenagers thump the side of the Coin-o-matix in Slotsa-fun on Royal Terrace; the Directors of Devenish's Brewery, leaning back in the Old Rooms on Trinity Street, contemplate with satisfaction the sales figures for their range of 'Newquay Steam' beers; the old women queue, in threes, for the Thursday Thé Dansant in the Royal Hotel on the Esplanade (£1.20, tea, sandwich and a cake); the Harbour Master in his office by the Sealink terminal watches a bass boat coming in off the Shambles; the helicopters from the naval base in Portland hammer out over the bay towards the Lulworth ranges; the teller in the Kentucky Bingo on the Esplanade mouths numbers into the microphone while his eyes slew sideways at the television on his desk; the Range Safety launch oozes into the harbour; and water is added to whisky aboard the yachts parked five deep against the Custom House Quay.

WEYMOUTH, on the Dorset coast, is well. The Cherbourg ferry is in, its height and whiteness extending the buildings, just as, in the Georgian prospects of the town, the masts and rigging of ships in the harbour peer over the rooflines of new terraces. As night comes on, the dark length of Dorset curves out to the east, spotted with the lights of Osmington and Lulworth. Behind the foreground screen of yellow bulbs, strung in loops from post to post for a thousand yards around the curve of Weymouth Bay, the shapes of naval frigates and their auxiliaries manoeuvre in the dark.

The windows of the Town Crier are open—the best pub in Weymouth, run by the Town Crier herself—and the seven-piece jazz band inside plays out across the bay, while the girls in white high heels clip out along the concrete pavement, and the Weymouth whiff of vinegar and chips is sharp and heavy on the air. Above the lacy iron edges of the Victorian shelters on the Esplanade all the flags of Europe blow out to sea in the mild westerly, and pairs of biddies arm in arm walk slowly home towards 'Beachview', 'Southview', 'South Sands' or 'Sandview', as the breathy honk of the ferry's horn announces it is leaving for France.

But Weymouth goes on into the night. The Naval Police cruise the pedestrianized medieval streets in a van. In Verdi's, the downmarket nightclub in Maiden Street near the harbour, without the chic of Malibu or the Steering Wheel, the sailors in leather jackets dance alone or with each other, turn now and then to the pretty local girl in her black cotton halter neck and ask politely for a dance. She looks seriously into the middle distance, shakes her head half-smilingly and then gives a straight look meaning NO.

Late at night the wealthy return to their yachts in the harbour; the rest to the little hotels into which the terraces on the Esplanade are now divided, where 50p in the meter in the room will turn on the electric fire, where dinner is at 6pm and breakfast at 8.30am, both sharp, and where the plumbing is so arranged that when someone empties the basin in his room every basin in the building chokes and gurgles in sympathy. The last moments of each resident's day are in this way telegraphed to every other.

This holiday town, lively in the season, hardly alive out of it, is three towns sewn more or less neatly together. The geography of the site explains them: an inlet of the sea pushes into south Dorset between a hilly promontory on the southern side and a low sand spit on the northern. The tiny River Wey runs down into the head of the inlet. Medieval *Weymouth*, which was probably the earliest settlement here, was a narrow strip of houses along the southern edge of this excellent

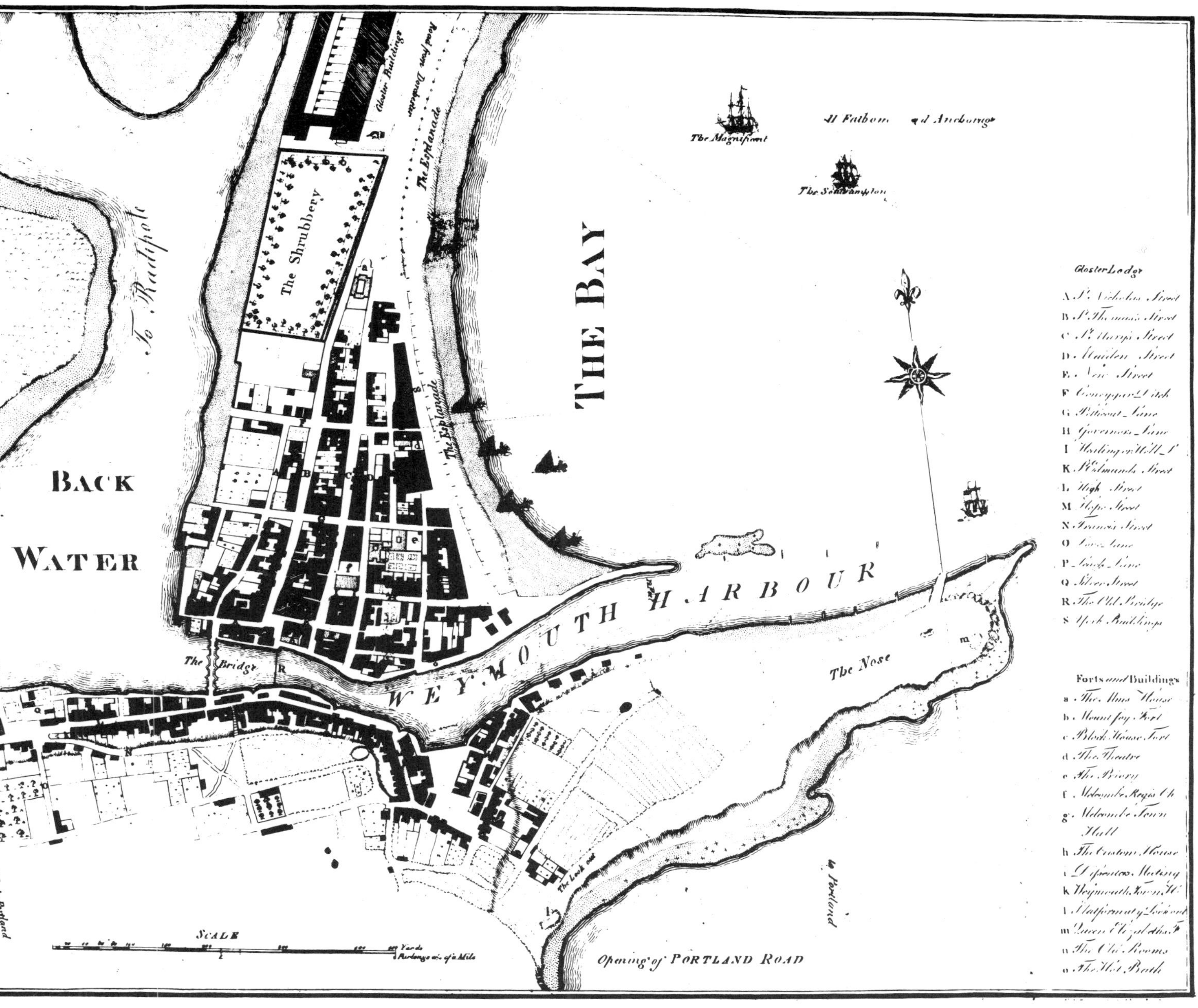

A plan of the town sold at Mr Delamotte's Library on the Esplanade in about 1790, just as Weymouth was being transformed from a pair of medieval boroughs on either side of the harbour to a royal seaside resort. The bathing machines are shown on the sands, the royal frigate Southampton, and its escort the Magnificent, lie waiting in the bay. A gesturing hand points out Gloucester Lodge, the royal residence. As yet, the sweep of terraces, lining the Esplanade from the harbour mouth to the far end of the sands, is not complete.

all-weather harbour. Although some damage was done to its fabric by German bombs in the war and by redevelopment in the 1960s and 1970s, you can still grasp something of its original style. It is essentially a small place, cramped between the hill and the harbour, its streets contoured across the slope like those in Welsh mining villages. There is a neatness about them. Two sixteenth-century houses survive in Trinity Street. One is the Devenish head office, the other is looked after by the Civic Society and is occasionally open to the public. Both are in white Portland stone, from quarries a few miles away to the south. They are local, workmanlike buildings, nothing particularly remarkable about them except their age; they are simply the town houses of some fairly small-scale merchants. There are warehouses down these streets too, made of the same white Portland rubblestone, and a boatyard is still working on the site of one of the slips that has probably been there since the Middle Ages.

If this had been all there was, the harbour might never have become anything more than Polperro in Cornwall or Robin Hood's Bay on the Yorkshire coast. But old Weymouth has been left behind by its upstart rival across the other side. As the sand spit thickened and solidified in the early Middle Ages, a separate town, *Melcombe Regis*, developed over there. There was real loathing across this narrow stretch of water. Until 1832 both towns sent their own members to Parliament and, in both, the elections were utterly corrupt. The two towns squabbled over harbour dues and regulations, over ownership of the water between them, the right to erect quays abutting on to it and —at heart—the relative status of their two sides. Ships were sunk and men drowned. Even when by order of the Privy Council the two boroughs were amalgamated in 1571, the arguments continued. Mayors were threatened, quays demolished, honour upheld. During the Civil War the two towns were for a time occupied by the different sides. In February 1645 an intense and destructive cannonade was fired across the harbour by the Royalists on the Weymouth side into Parliamentarian Melcombe. The Royalists put their shot in a furnace before firing it and it set fire to any Melcombe houses on which it landed. In return the Roundheads sent fireships across the narrow width of the harbour into the gathered boats on the far side. It was a peculiarly vicious episode in the town's history. There is a (replica) cannonball stuck in the gable of a house in Maiden Street in Melcombe which is said to have been there ever since the Royalist cannonade. (It is somehow typical of Melcombe that this, one of the oldest houses in the town, at the back of the famous Ship Inn, made of beautiful Portland stone and with its historic memorial in the gable, should now be a public loo on the ground floor. There is another loo on the corner of Bond Street and the Esplanade, occupying the ground floor of a wonderful miniature Renaissance château in apricot brick with creamy stone facings, built in 1883 as a bank. Can this be borough policy?)

Melcombe has more swank about it than its smaller rival. The blocks and streets are on a small scale but there is nothing villagy about them. They were laid out on a grid, probably in the thirteenth century, perhaps arranged by the small priory that was here until the Reformation. The straight streets and regular blocks remain as they were designed. Melcombe was the new place, the coming town, a licensed wool port or 'staple' from 1310. There is no hint here of the burgage plot, with land attached, that is so prominent a part of the design of more agriculturally based towns. From the start Melcombe (with the suffix 'Regis' from 1336) was a commercial place and its design is expertly fitted to its purpose: multiple access from the quays up into the body of the town; warehousing in the 'dockland' strip just in from the quay; the Custom House originally near the site of the bridge but in the nineteenth century moved to the elegant and substantial merchant's house (c. 1800) which now bears the name; and several inns lining the quayside. One sixteenth-century building survives, the Ship, then as now the ideal forum for the life and business that is hinged to the harbour. It was near here in July 1348, off a ship landing merchandise from the continent, that the Black Death first arrived in England.

There is no trace of rivalry now between the north and south sides of the harbour. But each of the original towns has in a sense won a victory. Both Melcombe Regis and Weymouth are now known jointly as 'Weymouth' but it is the old middle of *Melcombe* which people who live there now refer to as 'the Town'. That is where you can find the Guildhall and the church of St Mary, both elegant and gracious Regency buildings in Portland stone on the sites of their clumsier predecessors. This is the old municipal core of 'the Town'. The way in which people use the phrase is still exact and oddly pedantic. I asked directions from someone to a shop which turned out to be just beyond the Black Dog in St Mary Street in Melcombe. 'Go to the end of Town,' she said. 'It is only five minutes' walk.' The twentieth-century end of town is two miles away, but until the eighteenth century the Black Dog was one of the last buildings on the road north. Beyond it lay the almost naked sand spit, with the town rubbish heap on the eastern sands and, on the other side, nothing but a windmill and a large rabbit warren called the Cunigar. The Town still ends where it did 300 years ago.

The locals, in the way that locals have in a holiday place, ignore the reality of the tourists' world. To the north and east of the medieval streets you will find the

The Cherbourg ferry docks next to Devonshire Buildings, one of Weymouth's most billowy pieces of holiday architecture, built in about 1805 at the southern end of the Esplanade.

third town in Weymouth, the one which has taken over from the other two, which has made the Guildhall and the municipal church of St Mary seem no longer the focus of the place, its triumphant centre, but oddly tucked away and unimportant. This third town is the seaside resort. Its mile-long front is a marvel, best seen from the southern end where it curves out on to the harbour wall. It is a long, smooth slide of a street, an open, bowed ellipse, brought to sharpness in the level brows of the Georgian terraces that line it for a mile, and backed, in the far distance, by the undulating horizon of Dorset hills. The ending of façades in rounded pavilion-like stubs, as if sandpapered for comfort, the billowing out of those façades in shallow conversational bow windows, the pretty wrought-iron balconies on the first floor, all this facing the morning

Off Hope Square in old Weymouth, south of the harbour, a part of town left behind by the glamorous new building projects on the Esplanade.

sun, the blond width of the sands, the people on the beach, their striped wind-shelters, raffia mats, the Punch and Judy show, the electronic fortune teller and the melting vanilla cones: this is architecture and town-planning on holiday, the most civilized place in England. From the application and business of the port, and the clotted commercial density of medieval Melcombe, this architectural bay extends an open hand away from the town. If one imagines it for a moment made not of terraces but of individual villas, with their mutual isolation and their perky, peaking little roofs interrupting the dominant and fluid horizontal of the bay, one can be thankful that here at least the architecture has matched the place.

By the middle of the eighteenth century, Weymouth and Melcombe had been in long decline. The Civil War had left a bill of £20,000 for which Parliament would grant only £2,000. The silting of the harbour mouth had restricted the size of vessels that could use it and Poole had taken over most of the French and Newfoundland trades. The politics of the town and the election of the four MPs were frankly fraudulent and openly venal. Commerce was indolent enough for coaling ships to remain for months berthed on the Melcombe quay, casually unloading a single cargo as the town needed it. The Town Corporation scarcely met more than once a year. The place was defunct.

The revival started slowly and in the wrong place. In 1750 Ralph Allen, millionaire, owner of quarries, the great promoter and Mayor of Bath, bought a house in Trinity Road on the Weymouth side of the harbour. Until his death in 1764, he brought fashionable friends down here for the summer season. There was a salt-water bath on the other side of the harbour and a cramped little sixteenth-century house near Allen's in Trinity Street served as the Assembly Rooms. It fell out of use in about 1790 and is now known as the Old Rooms. This was the beginning of the resort, referred to in the *Sherborne Mercury* as lacking the 'genteel accommodation' such a place required. Until the early 1770s, no great change had been made to the fabric of the town. The resort had squeezed itself into the structures of an earlier age. In the fifty years that followed all that was to change.

The first break was made by a speculative developer from Bath, Andrew Sproule, who in 1773 opened a hotel and Assembly Rooms far out beyond the limits of the old town. They were 250 yards up the beach, in the middle of nowhere and—the first building in Weymouth to do so—*facing the sea*. (The original hotel no longer exists. It was replaced in 1897–9 by Weymouth's most pompous spectacular, a red brick palace with fat pepperpot towers at the corners and five floors of sea-view rooms. This superbly intrusive presence in its Georgian surroundings is now owned by a bus company from Wigan in Lancashire and is full every night of the season with customers brought down from the north.)

In 1776 an Act of Parliament was passed to improve the Weymouth environment. The streets were to be paved, guttered, cleaned, watched and lit. A five-shilling fine could be imposed on anyone leaving his waggon, cart, dray or carriage too long in the street. Thatch was banned and any obstruction—projecting windows, porches or signs—was to be removed from the pavements. This law has had a great effect on the appearance of the town. The bow windows in the streets of old Melcombe never come down to pavement level; they are sheared off below the first floor, creating the charming, jettied effect of repeated oriels just above eye level along East Street, for example, or St Alban's Street. On the Esplanade, where the builders were not confined by the limits of medieval houseplots, the entire building could be set back slightly so that the shallow bow could come down to ground level and still not impinge on the pavement.

The improvements were extended throughout the town. The old inlet known as the Ope (on the south side of the harbour behind the Old Rooms) was filled in and new houses built there. The water supply was improved and cattle were banned from walking on the pavements. In 1780 the Duke of Gloucester, George III's younger brother, commissioned the building of a house between the new hotel and the northern edge of old Melcombe. This straightforward red-brick building, with two large Venetian windows framing the façade (disfigured now by a hideous aluminium greenhouse attached to it) is the key to the moment of Weymouth's most glorious success.

It was in June 1789. The Revolution was coming to the boil in France, and until earlier that year the English court had been turned upside down by the sight of a mad George III, who was terrifying and imperious in his madness, impossible to deal with, instantly angry, confused and intolerant; a distraught Queen who burst into tears at unexpected moments; and the prospect of an uncertain Regency. As the King began to recover in March, salubrious sea-bathing was suggested to speed the convalescence. His son, the Prince of Wales, was already spending time in Brighton, but the King and the Prince hated each other, and could not have borne a summer holiday together. Weymouth was the obvious place. The King's younger brother already had a comfortable if not very large house there, and anyway, according to a contemporary account-cum-advertisement, 'as a Watering Place . . . Weymouth stands unrivalled with any other on the coast. The general tranquillity of the bay, the Clearness of the Water, the Softness and almost imperceptible Descent of its Shore, are highly favourable for the purpose of Bathing.' That gives the right tone: calm and ease, the horizontal air.

Not that the town itself was calm. How could it be, when it was about to strike the eighteenth-century equivalent of oil? Workmen were down from London refurbishing Gloucester Lodge and the houses next to it, which were to accommodate lesser parts of the approaching Royal Household. The King, Queen Charlotte and the Princesses Charlotte, Augusta and Elizabeth ('The Royals', as Fanny Burney, then Keeper of The Queen's Robes, called them) took six days from Windsor on a progress through the south of England. Everyone was delighted. Only Sir Charles Mills was apprehensive. He held the Manor of Langley in Hampshire on the direct road from Windsor to Weymouth, on condition that he presented 'His Majesty, whenever he passes that way, with a brace of white greyhounds in silver collars led on a silken cord and coupled in a gold chain'. For the next fifteen years he was to spend a great deal of time waiting at the side of the road with a new set of these expensive and irrelevant beasts.

Weymouth was hysterical with excitement. On 30th June the Mayor, Aldermen and Common Council waited on the outskirts of the town until four o'clock in the afternoon, their colours flying and the town band repeatedly practising *God save the King*. The whole town had gone mad on decorations. 'The preparations of festive loyalty were universal,' Fanny Burney later wrote in her journal. 'Not a child could we meet that had not a bandeau round its head, cap, or hat, of "God save the King"; all the bargemen wore it in cockades; and even the bathing women had it in large coarse girdles round their waists. It is printed in golden letters upon most of the bathing-machines, and in various scrolls and devices it adorns almost every shop and almost every house in the two towns.'

At last the royal party arrived. The men-of-war lying in Weymouth Bay fired a 21-gun salute. They were answered by the royal battery on the Esplanade. Flags were everywhere and thousands of Dorsetmen crowded the Esplanade. It was the happiest moment in the history of the town. The King looked fine; the court, in attendance, only mildly patronizing. 'The most violent gusts of joy and huzzas' echoed to Portland and back, none more violent than those from the people either too small or too far away to see anything. 'Is this not a charming trait of provincial popularity?' Fanny Burney asked her diary. But what did the King think? The Mayor and Common Council strained to hear his verdict. The ugliest man ever to have sat on the English throne looked at the bay. He paused for a moment and then, according to the *Gentleman's Magazine*, 'in terms of real satisfaction', uttered the most valuable sentence ever heard in Weymouth: 'I never enjoyed a sight so pleasing.' It was going to be a bonanza.

From the start, the royal visit followed the outlines of what is still the ideal family holiday; the only difference lay in the excited attitude of Weymouth itself. The whole family goes for a walk in the evening on the sands. Beautiful, restful, you might think, but 'an immense crowd attended them—sailors, bargemen, mechanics, countrymen; and all united in so vociferous a volley of "God save the King," that the noise was stunning.' The next day, being wet, they stay in Gloucester Lodge, where 'domestic pleasures took place'—literary conversation, select parties at cards. Crowds gather on the Esplanade outside the windows, shouting the national anthem whenever they catch a glimpse of the King or a footman who might be him. For the first week, as a gentle introduction, the King has a regular warm salt bath. On 7th July the King is allowed to take his first sea-bathe. Everyone is cleared from the water. His bathing machine, a giant cart with a little octagonal summerhouse on top and a royal coat of arms over the door (in regular use by the public until 1916 but now preserved in the Town Museum) was drawn out by a horse until axle-deep in the water when the bather could step out in all modesty to swim. The King took to the water at about half-past seven in the morning. (Bathing later in the day was said to 'occasion great depression of spirits.') It went very well. But again Weymouth was a little over-enthusiastic: 'Think but of the surprise of His Majesty,' Fanny Burney wrote to a friend, 'when the first time of bathing, he had no sooner popped his royal head under water than a band of

The most flamboyant loo in England; an 1883 bank, now a public convenience.

music, concealed in a neighbouring machine, struck up "God save great George our King." '

In France events were moving to the climax of 14th July. In Weymouth, 'uninterrupted jollity and universal joy pervaded the breasts of the vast multitude.' The princesses bought books at Mr Delamotte's library. Portland fishermen presented Their Majesties with a live porpoise which was sent to be placed alive in the St James's Park canal. In the evening the Royals went to the theatre, where the party sat under a crimson silk canopy on a platform raised above the crowd. But 'its entertainment was quite in the barn style; a mere medley—songs, dances, imitations—and all very bad.' This was near the beginning of the holiday. Towards the end the dramatic quality was intended to improve: Mrs Siddons, the greatest tragic actress of the age, arrived and hopes lifted. But she decided to play pastoral comedy, not her forte. 'She looked too large for that shepherd's dress,' was Fanny Burney's verdict.

As an alternative, for the young princesses anyway, there was dancing either in Gloucester Lodge itself or in the Long Room at Stacie's Hotel, where a coffee room, card room, billiard room and shops could all provide their extra diversions. It was here in 1798 that the news of Nelson's victory over the French Mediterranean fleet on the Nile was announced to the Master of Ceremonies Ball: one hundred and fifty of the nobility and gentry gave three cheers. The following day the garrisons of Weymouth and Portland were drawn up on the sands, stretching the entire length of the beach and together they fired off three tremendous victory volleys. The King walked up and down the Esplanade reading excerpts from the dispatch to the different noblemen he met. Sailors danced reels on the deck of the St Fiorenzo and Mr Fisher gave an address at the Theatre:

> Such prowess every tribute justly craves,
> 'E'en Arabs shout "Britannia rules the waves"

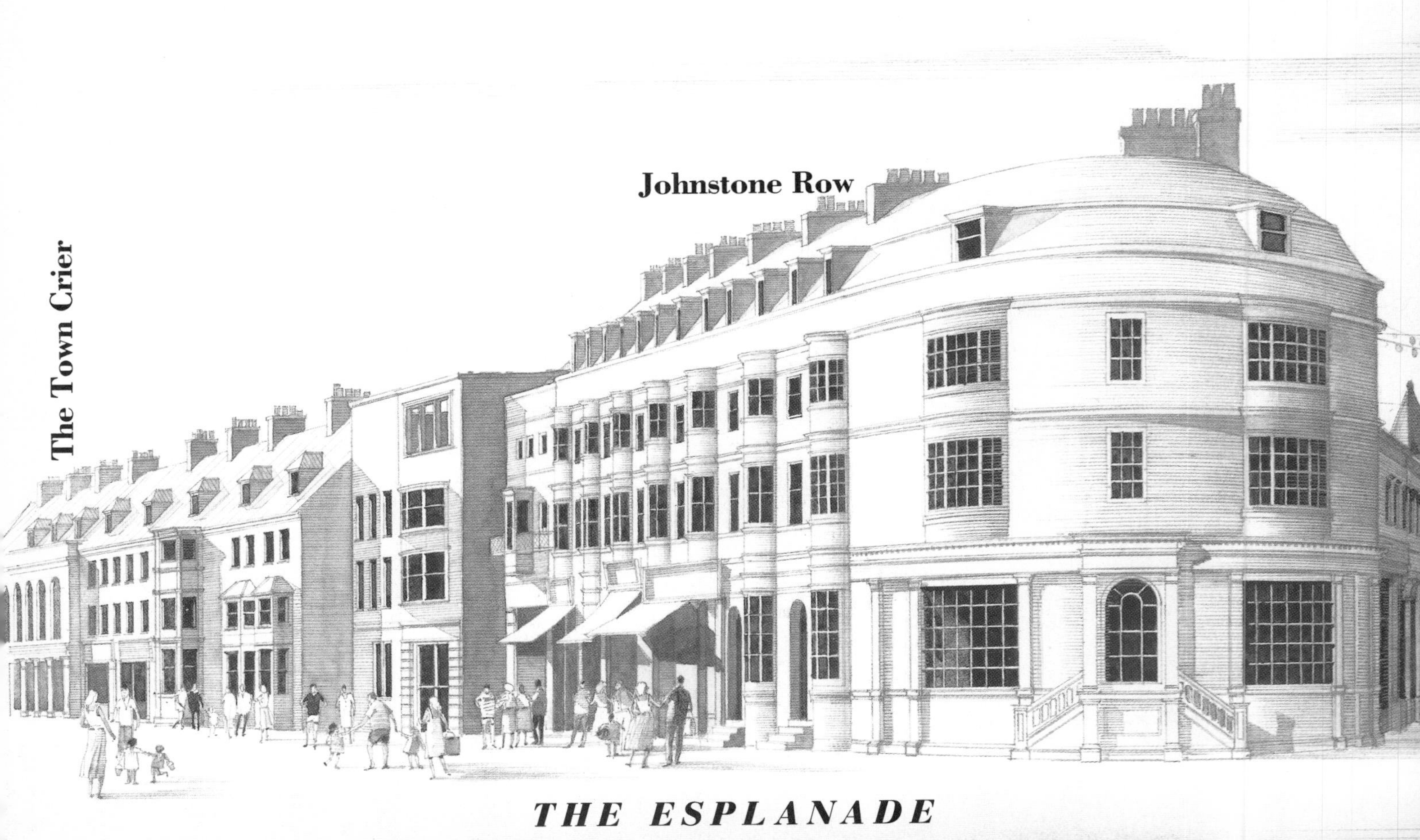

Part of WEYMOUTH in Dorset with the statue

In the daytime there were expeditions into the surrounding country but far more exciting was sailing in the bay. A 74-gun ship-of-the-line, the *Magnificent*, and—much faster and more fun—a frigate, the *Southampton*, stood by every day, one for royal protection, the other for nothing but pleasure. The Queen was usually sick, the princesses displayed astonishing firmness and the King was ecstatic as day after day they went out sailing: the court could not quite understand it. In later years they would themselves take to yachts in a little flotilla that clustered around the royal frigate, but in the early days they were left behind and forced to take refuge in bad jokes about sea-sickness and being *sick* of the *sea*. Meanwhile, far offshore, the captains of the warships were showing off to their sovereign. One day an American packet failed to lower her top-gallant sails—the usual mark of respect—for the royal pennant on the *Southampton*. The *Magnificent* immediately 'altered her course to take a slap at her, as the sea phrase is,

orge III erected by the grateful inhabitants in 1809

with an 18-pounder.' She immediately lowered most of her sails. This exercise in holiday imperialism was fun, but the favourite game was for the *Magnificent* and the *Southampton* to approach each other under full sail on opposite tacks, with a combined speed of twenty knots or more, and to rush past one another, almost brushing sides. At the moment of climax, when the gun-ports of the two ships were inches apart, the entire crew of the *Magnificent* would cheer the rapidly passing Royals. The experience was said to have 'had a charming effect on the whole party . . .'. At the end of the holiday, Captain Douglas of the *Southampton* was knighted.

The King continued to come here every summer until 1805 with only one or two interruptions. Weymouth was something of a boom town in these years. It was so expensive that for a while even the Royal Household had supplies brought down from Windsor. By the end of the century Royal Crescent, just north of the Royal Hotel, was begun, and buildings all along the southern end of the Esplanade were

beginning to establish a continuous front, where before there had been nothing but the back gardens of houses in old Melcombe. York Buildings, the first terrace built facing the sea and now so altered as to be unrecognisable, was completed in 1783. Nearby, Harvey's Library and Card Assembly, now the Town Crier—with its Reading Room downstairs and Card Room above—was there by 1800. Devonshire Buildings, at the very southern end, was up by 1805. The Borough at the time insisted, to conform to the architectural taste then sweeping the English seaside, that this building should come to a round end and not be shorn off square. The prettiest terrace in Weymouth, Johnstone Row, was complete by 1811, with the 'roundhouses' at the end of both this and Coburg Place incorporated later. The rest of the seafront grew piece by piece throughout the first half of the century: Royal Terrace 1816–18; Belvidere, very slow in the building, 1818–50s; Brunswick Terrace finished 1827; Waterloo Place at the northern end was not complete until about 1835. The rather out-of-place Victoria Terrace, faced in Portland stone (which is leaden compared to the brick and stucco of the others) was built in 1855–6.

Throughout the time these prestige blocks were going up, the streets behind them were also being transformed into miniature versions of the Esplanade, with their bow windows, fanlights and moulded door-cases. Here was a straightforward class hierarchy: the grander and larger apartments on the front for the smartest families; those behind for their poorer inferiors. This relationship has, ironically, now been reversed. The little Georgian cottages are among the most expensive houses that come on the Weymouth market; the terraces on the front are devoted either to cheap Bed and Breakfasts or, at ground level, to Bingo, amusement arcades and vinegary chips.

At the King's Golden Jubilee, in 1809, the people of Weymouth made their most charming gesture to the town's increasingly mad patron. They paid two hundred guineas for a statue of the King standing next to a table on which rested the crown and the books of the Constitution. A lion and a unicorn were included in the price. It is this statue which now stands at the crucial juncture of the town, just at the point where the Esplanade joins the streets of old Melcombe, the hinge of the old and the new. Since 1949 the statue, made in Lambeth of the artificial Coade stone, has been painted

A minor triumph of Victorian jollity crowns the southern end of the Esplanade as it turns around the sands.

with great success like a fairground toy. Nothing could be better; it is an image of monarchy on holiday. With giant letters the plinth on which he stands is inscribed:

The *grateful* Inhabitants
TO GEORGE THE THIRD
On His entering the 50th Year
Of his REIGN

The King died in 1820: Royal Lodge, as it had been called since 1801, when he had bought it off the Duke of Gloucester, was sold up. Two thousand lots were bought at prices made enormous by their sentimental associations with royalty. The slowness with which the new terraces along the Esplanade were completed is a measure of how the energy had gone out of Weymouth. George IV never came here. The air of effortless and delighted success gave way to one of nostalgia. The Hussars in Thomas Hardy's epic drama *The Dynasts* remembered the best days in Royal 'Budmouth', that wonderful, lustful, holiday time

When we lay where Budmouth Beach is,
O the girls were fresh as peaches,
With their tall and tossing figures and their eyes of blue
and brown!
And our hearts would ache with longing
As we paced from our sing-songing,
With a smart *Clink! Clink!* up the Esplanade and down.

At last the railway arrived in 1857 and Weymouth entered the expansive phase of mass holidays which lasted until the coming of cheap flights abroad. It now has 4,500 hotel beds and the holiday business is stable, if not expanding. The Gloucester Hotel has recently been closed. It was the most prestigious in Weymouth, the very building in which George III and his family stayed; it is now to be cut up and sold off by Devenish Brewery as private flats. This is an unpopular move in the town as it leaves a vacuum in the most important part of the Esplanade, but it is symptomatic of Weymouth's condition. The resort is savagely seasonal, dependent on high-volume cheap holidays. It cannot support a large luxury hotel because high-class tourists do not go there. Devenish has recently spent £1.5 million on a hotel in Dorchester because the Thomas Hardy trade can support it. The romance of Weymouth, which really is no more than a charming and sentimental story of an old King feeling happy by the sea, does not have the same pull.

The harbour still supports a fleet of about thirty fishing boats, most of them catching scallops, crabs and lobsters. A small wholesale business now operates out of the very pretty Victorian fish market on Custom House Quay. There are several other outlets for the shellfish, including French hauliers who bring their trucks over on the Cherbourg ferry. On the Weymouth side, Devenish no longer brew beer in the Hope Square brewery: this large, confident red-brick building, with all its outliers of maltings and warehouses, is likely to be converted into some form of leisure complex. On the other side of the harbour a company from Essex is well advanced in a massive plan to redevelop the western side of Melcombe. The Backwater is to be renamed the Inner Harbour and its stink of sewage removed. Luxury flats will ring the new quayside there and a giant new shopping centre with food hall and on-roof car park are to be built over the medieval plan. Some listed buildings are to be demolished and others 'façaded' —a taxidermist's job of evisceration and restuffing within the preserved skin. But that side of town is already heavily degraded and there is no doubt that both its environment and Weymouth's economy needs something done. One must hope that what results is not as cheap and charmless as the newish Colwell Centre that adjoins the site. Only then will the twentieth century not have failed a town where the medieval core and the long, langorous limbs of its eighteenth- and nineteenth-century extensions make its Victorian claim as the 'Naples of England' not quite absurd.

BUXTON
Derbyshire

Duke of Devonshire between 1780 and 1784

THERE IS a fragrance of aristocracy in the very air of this Spa,' wrote Augustus Bozzi Granville, the fashionable London doctor and Fellow of the Royal Society, on arriving at BUXTON in Derbyshire in 1841. 'The very first *coup-d'oeil* at the "Grand Hotel", as I surveyed the interior of that large building, showed me that I must take some pains with my toilet.' The Grand Hotel, at the eastern end of the Crescent, is now the municipal library, Buxton is no longer a spa and the fragrance of aristocracy has all but evaporated on the winds of the High Peak. But in some ways little has changed since 1841. Dr Granville had chosen his words carefully. He found a *fragrance* of aristocracy, nothing more, and in conversation that evening with the 'handsome' manageress of the Grand he forced her 'to admit that Buxton wanted more society . . . The sojourning of the Duke, the sovereign lord of the place, with three or four more leading people of *ton*, . . . would in every way improve its standing.'

Buxton is a town where nothing has ever mattered more than the improvement of standing, where pains must always be taken with toilets, and the degrees of *ton* can be precisely measured. It is a preened place, where the maintenance of 'class', in all its meanings, is the business of life. In the shape of the town the social structure could not be clearer. There are three layers: middle-class substantial; public would-be aristocratic (the showplaces); and, in Upper Buxton, the oldest part, which long preceded any of the eighteenth- and nineteenth-century spa-based invasions, the service end, the working-class housing, the cheap cafés, the Chinese takeaway and the unattractive pizza place, the nightclub where teenagers get drunk at night, and over which the other end of town shakes its head, the Kwiksave superstore (cheaper than the Spring Gardens Gateway in the middle), the District Council sheltered housing on the site of a demolished hotel, the everyday substructure, the unvisited basement of any town.

If you walk quickly from one end of Buxton to the other, the experience is curiously like a tour through a large country house: the immense comfort and ease of the private apartments; the arrangement for display of the public rooms; and the utilitarian meanness, cheapness and grittiness of the back quarters. All is precisely defined and well-regulated. The smart end, the reservoir of class, overflowing with *ton*, is in The Park, a circular drive on the northern edge of town. It was laid out in 1852 by Joseph Paxton, employed by the Duke of Devonshire, who by then owned three-quarters of Buxton. Here, secure in what Vera Brittain later called 'the unfathomable depths of provincial self-satisfaction', the Buxton families that counted for something in the late nineteenth century built themselves their immensely solid, tree-shaded piles, each guarded from the other, each surveying its own small estate. Paxton had consciously modelled the scheme on Nash's Regent's Park in London, but in the distance between the Regency emphasis on openness and the mid-Victorian on substance, the charm had gone.

Walk around The Park now. It is a clotted world, the heavyweight ballast of Buxton, each house a self-protective clump of municipal virtue. But it is a fascinating place, not least for the presence here of a few houses designed by the young Barry Parker and Raymond Unwin, the future creators of Letchworth. 'Longford', in The Park, and 'Greenmoor', in Carlisle Road next to it, both date from around the turn of the century and show the beginnings of those playful and inventive quirks—outside balconies, bay windows canted out to catch the late sun, a juggling with volumes, clustering chimneys, shallow strip-dormers in the roof—that break the restrictions of solidified self-importance to which so many of these houses are devoted.

It is not difficult to measure the social distance between the large middle-class houses here and the traditionally poorer and more cramped streets in the upper, older part of the town. 'Tuppence ha'penny toffs', I've heard the grandees from one end called at the other, 'the *crème de la crème*'—those French vowels given a quiveringly ironic Derbyshire vibrato—'or at least they think they are'. 'Do you remember that darling little manageress, that vision in brown at Hargreaves in Spring Gardens? She thought she was everybody, didn't she, the day she was serving out fresh orange juice—with ice—"*At Home*" in Carlisle Road. The ice, that was just it. All gone now, of course. You don't hear any "Dust your front off, clean your brasses" nowadays. And look what they've done to Spring Gardens; it's a shame.'

Vera Brittain, the socialist and feminist, was brought up here between 1910 and 1919. Her family controlled the wholesale provision trade in the town and they lived in 'Melrose' in The Park. 'I hated Buxton', she later wrote quite calmly, 'with a detestation that I have never felt since for any set of circumstances:' She does not usually feature in the promotional literature produced by the town. The only memorial is a small plaque outside 'The Paxton Suite' in the conference centre. Even its sad little presence shows considerable generosity from Buxton towards its most famous daughter. Her considered verdict was that Buxton and its provincialism 'stood, and stands, for the sum-total of all false values . . . the estimation of people for what they have or pretend to have, and not for what they are. Artificial classifications, rigid lines of demarkation that bear no relation whatsoever to intrinsic merit, seem to belong to its very essence, while contempt for intelligence, suspicion and fear of independent thought, appear to be necessary passports to provincial popularity. . . . Social snobbery and unreal values seem to reach their height in towns with between ten and twenty thousand inhabitants. Buxton, which my father used to describe as "a little box of social strife lying at the bottom of a basin", must have had a population of about twelve thousand. . . .'

This is probably unfair (you have only to think of Eric Gill on Chichester or the enthusiasms of the Garden Cityists to see that there is another way of looking at these things) but there may be something in it. Rumour and gossip still lead a spirited life here—this hotel is to be prosecuted for the squalor of its kitchens, that councillor did very well thank you out of the new developments—and the mere history of Buxton as a showplace, a place that has always needed to be attractive to survive, guarantees that 'The Maintenance of Standards' against 'The Lowering of Tone' will often seem more important than what Vera Brittain might have called 'real values'.

She may have been wrong in thinking that it was the size of Buxton that made it so aware of *ton*. The battle-hardened smile of the professional landlady, and the smooth promotion of the Mountain Spa, are of course the product of its need to be 'a high class resort'. The whole town is not really a country house; it's a hotel.

It all begins with the water. The old village of Buxton was up on the hill on the southern side of the River Wye valley. Down near the river was a series of springs, one cold but several distinctly warm, with a temperature, as William Worcester wrote in 1460, 'even as honeyed milk'. (This particular comparison persisted into nineteenth-century descriptions of Buxton's water, variations being worked on mother's milk, calf's milk and so on; only the coolly realist Celia Fiennes demurred. 'Its not so warme as milk from a cow', she wrote blandly in 1690. It is in fact a constant eighty-one degrees and is still used, at its natural temperature, to heat the town swimming baths and to fill the radiators of the Devonshire Royal Hospital.)

In England, only the springs at Bath—much hotter—and at Bristol—a little cooler—shared this miraculous property of natural heating. Still nobody knows precisely where the water comes from, although the reservoir must be at least 20,000 feet deep to be warmed by the heat of the earth's mantle. If you stand around for a few minutes next to its only public outlet now, the little fountain called St Anne's Well, put up in 1940 on the south side of the Crescent, you will find a steady queue of Buxtonians coming to fetch water there. Why? There are the ecologists—the spring is pure, not polluted by the Water Board with chlorine or fluoride; the sentimentalists—the water itself is old (fifty years was the best estimate I heard) and when it fell as rain the world was a better place; the superstitious—it was marvellous for rheumatism and arthritis; the gourmets—it made the most delicious tea; and the mercenary—people were willing to buy it for 60p a bottle in the Tourist Information Centre on the other side of the road (in the building which contains the natural spring and the now neglected natural baths) and anything anyone was willing to buy must be worth having for free.

In these little plastic bottle rituals, seriously undertaken, not to be joked at, you are witnessing the residue of this town's original cause for existence. What these people are doing now supported almost the entire economy of Buxton from at least the fifteenth century until the Second World War. As you stand by this dribbling spring of tepid, tasteless, unfizzy water, it is a little difficult to realize that everything around you stemmed from its existence. Without St Anne's Well, Buxton would be an ill-considered village above the unnoticed valley of a small Peak District stream. As it is, the centre of Buxton is one of the most comprehensive Georgian and Victorian pleasure landscapes in England.

In the Middle Ages, it was a curative well. In 1538, as Glastonbury too was approaching its demise, 'the bathys and welles' in Buxton were 'lokkyd upp and sealyd'. Crutches and other testimonials, which had been left there by those whose ailments had been cured, were all removed, so that there 'schullde no more idolatre and supersticion be there usyd'. But it did not remain closed for long. By 1553, with the accession of Catholic Mary to the throne, it was back in use. A year or two later, the Earl of Pembroke was having Buxton water put in barrels and delivered to his home. In 1572, George Talbot, Earl of Shrewsbury, built New Hall—in effect a hotel—on the site of what is now the Old Hall Hotel, just to the west of the Crescent and with a bath house (on the site of the Tourist Information Office) attached. Talbot had been entrusted with the custody of Mary Queen of Scots, whom he had housed in the decrepit and draughty castle at Tutbury in Staffordshire. The pain in the Queen's left side, of which she continually complained, was probably rheumatic. The Buxton spring was known to be good for rheumatism, and—to the everlasting benefit of the town, as helpful a move as George III's visits to Weymouth—Mary Queen of Scots came to take the waters here.

Fashion followed her and the Earls of Leicester, Warwick and Sussex, Lord Burleigh and Robert Cecil all came for various unspecified cures to Buxton. This may well have been its most glittering period. It produced Buxton's first effective propagandist, a Dr John Jones. The arrangements for bathing, as he described them, were perfectly civilized. The baths were 'bravely beautified with seats round about: defended from the ambyent ayre: and chimneys for fyre, to ayre your garmintes in the Bathes syde, and other necessaries most decent'. The women could walk in the long gallery of the hall, where there was a form of indoor bowls. For men there were outdoor bowls, shooting with a long bow, ball games of various kinds and, particularly to be recommended, running up and down stairs or in the galleries, carrying weights. It might almost be California.

Only when you come to the section dealing with the water's effects does the image of a modern health farm evaporate. Jones lists the following ailments for which it would be worth coming to Buxton: 'Rheumes, Crampes, Fevers, Numnes, Headaches, Itchinges, Weak Sinewes, Shrinkings, Old Scabbes, Ringwormes, Ulcers and Apostemes [abscesses]'. This list is followed by an even more graphic picture of what those who were here for a cure might be afflicted with:

> Women that by reason of overmuch moisture, or contrary distemperature bee unapt to conceave.
> Al such as have their whites [of the eyes] too abundant and that be overwatry.
> Item, weake men that bee unfrutefull.
> Likewise for all that have *Priapismus* and that be perboyled in *Venus Gulf.*
> Profitable for such as have the consumption of the Lungs.
> Beneficiall for such as vomit blood, as hath bin well proved.
> Very good for the inflammation of the Liver.
> Excellent for overmuch heat, and stopping of the veins.
> Beneficiall for all such as be disquieted with burning of urine.
> Unordinary desire of going to the stoole, dooing nothing or very little with great payne, it cureth.
> It stayeth wasting of mans seede, the Hemoroydes and Pyles, it soon amendeth.
> Against the overflowing of womens months, it much avayleth.
> It taketh away the Ricket.
> Overmuch vomiting it easeth.

And so on. This partly obsessive, partly random list of afflictions represents—with all the unfussiness of the Elizabethan mind—the sort of fascinated anxiety over the body, its innards and orifices that led people to come here for the next three centuries and more. Jones recommended that his patients should stay in the bath for one or two hours and then go to a warm bed, with hot water bladders tucked in under the armpits and groin. Some rubbing of the flesh until it was red was recommended but no drinking of the water. He included a long prayer in his book, to be said at every bathing.

Nothing of the fabric of sixteenth-century Buxton survives. Over the next two centuries the New Hall and the bath buildings were occasionally restored, improved or replaced. A new well-head was built by a grateful patient, and the gospel of Sir John Floyer, the apostle of cold bathing, arrived to add another ripple to the *frisson* of Buxton. Nothing, according to a postscript added to his *Essay on Cold Bathing* (1702), was more effective than cold water in restoring, among other things, 'lost *Erection* . . . When all other Remedies have failed, nay and after some Years standing (cry Mercy, not standing, I mean) when the case has been old . . . and the Clock-weights of their hearts sunk and hung low, &c, there I say, in more than Twenty such cases the Cold Water has wound up their watch and set their Pendulum *in statu quo*, &c.' Can anyone have believed him? This, as one example of the water-madness promoted by spa enthusiasts (hydropathomaniacs in the grip of hydropsycholepsy), was the treatment recommended to the sufferer. He should 'go into the country, out of the sight of any Women, and find out some very *Cold Spring* or *River*, where he should first plunge overhead, then put on his Hat and Dublet, to prevent catching Cold from the Wind and Air, and sit up to the Wast for an Hour at least, Night and Morning, and for a Month drink nothing but new Milk, twice a day sweeten'd with Sugar of Roses; at Noon eat well-roasted Mutton with Cold Salets, as *Cucumbers*, *Lettice*, *Purslane*, &c. and drink nothing but Spring-Water with a little Claret-Wine, and at night wrap up his *Whore-Tackle* in a Linnen-Cloath, and so to sleep.' It was said to be foolproof.

In retrospect, these visions and revisions are nothing much in the history of Buxton. The place had become slightly run down. Sir Thomas Browne's son, Edward, suspected that the mutton he was served in a low, rattish lodging house here in 1662 was probably dog. A generation later Celia Fiennes found the town and baths squalid, overcrowded, inconvenient, ill-maintained and extortionate. Conditions improved after 1705, when the Duke of Devonshire hired a London hotelier to run the Old Hall, first in 1712 when new baths were built, and again after 1750 when they and the accommodation were both refurbished. But this tinkering was not enough. The success of Bath, the rival spa, its growing number of visitors and rising *ton*, its elegant and inventive new town planning—all this was throwing Buxton even deeper into the shade.

William Cavendish, fifth Duke of Devonshire, the grandson of the great Lord Burlington, suddenly and massively wealthy on the income from his copper mines (said to be £30,000 in both 1779 and 1780, primarily due to the Royal Navy contract by which the bottoms of the men-of-war were sheathed in Derbyshire copper for the first time)—this was the man who was to make Buxton great. His original scheme—to lay out colonnaded streets and spacious squares around the springs—was thwarted by a local man who owned two crucial acres in the middle of the site. Under normal circumstances he would have been lucky to get £100 for them. He asked for £2,000. The Duke offered £1,200, was refused and negotiations were broken off. The space available for the Duke and his architect, John Carr of York, became cramped and the birth of New Buxton was in some ways spoiled.

The new scheme had a double centrepiece—the great Crescent, which had to be built over the bed of the River Wye itself, which now flows in a culvert beneath it; and, on the far side of the valley, the huge stables, now the Devonshire Royal Hospital. Carr probably also designed Hall Bank, the row of houses and shops climbing up the west side of the hill to Upper

Hall Bank from The Slopes, Buxton's prettiest row of houses, designed by John Carr soon after the Crescent and from the start intended as lodging houses for families coming to take the waters.

Buxton, still the town's prettiest street.

Compared with Bath, it must be said that there is something sadly inarticulate about these Derbyshire buildings. Carr's Crescent is, in the end, a rather clumpy thing. Unlike the relaxed and open half-ellipse of the Royal Crescent in Bath, this is a semi-circle, a shape too constrained for elegance, too tall for its width and in visual need of its other half for perfection. The arcade which rings the ground floor is too narrow and produced many contemporary complaints about its meanness. Nor is the setting properly arranged. Nowhere here do you find the miraculous sequencing of perspective and constraint, of invitation and arrival so perfectly achieved by the Woods in Bath. John Carr was a lesser artist and despite the expenditure of over £60,000 on the Crescent and the Stables by the time they were finished in 1790, Buxton still has the air of a botched job. The relationship of the Crescent to the bath building next door is awkward. The steep hill opposite, landscaped by Sir Jeffrey Wyatville and Joseph Paxton into gardens known as The Slopes, shuts off the sky, blocks in the Crescent, and makes the space in front of it claustrophobic. At the back and side is a jumble of half-confused buildings and semi-streets with no more organization about them than sheds on a construction site. Finally, the great Stables are inconveniently far away from the three hotels in the Crescent—St Ann's at the western end, the Great or Grand at the eastern, and the Centre, originally the Duke's own town house, in the middle.

By its own standards of rationality, decorum, elegance and utility, Buxton's proudest monument is a piece of appalling town planning. It does have its conscious beauties—its colour, described by one visitor in 1796 as 'a golden half-moon'; the large Corinthian salon at the eastern end, on the first floor, which was the Assembly Room for the spa; and the rear elevation of the block itself, four plain stories on a wide convex curve, as dignified and austerely Roman as any of the great palaces of the Italian Renaissance. But more interesting than any of these is the one virtue which the Crescent has by accident. In going off half-cock, the Cavendish-Carr scheme for Buxton is peculiarly evocative of its time. As a model of the grand idea dumped in the wrong place, it is an entirely appropriate monument to its setting. The pretensions of Buxton are effortlessly revealed by the half-failure of its architecture.

Imagine yourself in Georgian Buxton at the height of the season. You will have bought in advance a guidebook, *A Description of Buxton and the Adjacent Country or the New Guide For Ladies and Gentlemen resorting to that Place of Health and Amusement where for the convenience of the public His Grace the Duke of Devonshire has magnificently provided such very handsome and ample ACCOMMODATIONS. Compiled by W. Bott, Buxton 1798.* The book's relentless boosterism extends the season from April to November. You should be warned, however, that Buxton is a thousand feet above sea level, that it rains, snows or sleets on at least 260 days a year and that June to September is a more realistic proposal. Almost the only warning Mr Bott gives is that Buxton water 'when drank in considerable quantity . . . is found to possess a binding and heating quality'. Nevertheless, it is superior to Bath (too hot) and Bristol (too cold) and if taken with rhubarb all problems are averted.

You will find, in 1800, say, that 'The Mountain Spa' is no longer quite the Alpine remoteness it was in Celia Fiennes's day and most of the roads have been turnpiked forty years or more. The London coach drops you outside the Grove, where a chaise for hire will carry your gouty uncle and rheumatic aunt to the accommodation in St Ann's Hotel at the western end of the Crescent. There is room for about seven hundred to stay in the town and 'though its buildings do not possess uniformity, it may boast what is of infinitely more advantage to invalids, of lodgings suited to every conditions of visitors.' What this means is that lodging houses and hotels outside the Crescent and its immediate area can still descend to the truly squalid, particularly in the upper part of town. Residents at St Ann's, perhaps the second most prestigious hotel after the Great, have the privilege of taking the waters first, from 6 a.m. onwards. Those in lesser establishments, not the property of His Grace, must wait until after 9 a.m.

On arrival, as a girl staying in Hall Bank wrote home to her sister in August 1810, 'we spent the remainder of the day as most travellers in our situation would have done, or as most of the visitors of Buxton do,—that is, we took possession of our apartments, made tea, sent for one of the resident physicians to consult him on the case of my uncle and aunt, enquired what families were then in the village, lolled an hour or two, took an early supper and went to bed.'

How sinkingly familiar this sensation is, the opening moments of a holiday which is not of your choosing, the arrival in sterile rooms, the peering out sideways at the rainy view, the looking in cupboards, the temptation to cause an upset and the prospect ahead of bored and enforced politeness, of enveloping *ennui*.

Across the other side of the Crescent, in the Great, another quite different sort of traveller has arrived. A young aristocrat, the Hon. John Byng, a conservative, witty and sardonic man, who doesn't much like other people and prefers solitary travel, has come to Buxton under a misapprehension: 'Buxton strikes me as a good excuse for hurrying from London,' he writes in his journal, 'to relieve a set of nerves nearly worn out . . . hoping that, even yet, there must exist in the country, by the want of baneful intercourse, somewhat more purity, and civility; where you may escape eternal insult, and viewing the ill-treatment of every animal who cannot resist:—Besides, the uproar of a small London house, with stairs like Jacob's Ladder, makes my blood to boil; in every sense of the word. . . .' But Buxton does not fulfil his dream of Rousseauesque escape. It turns out to be 'a most uncomfortable, dreary place', as he wrote the next day; 'and The Grand Crescent might be better named The Devonshire Infirmary; "The whole a labor'd quarry above ground". —Snug lodging houses, with adjoining small stables were more necessary and comfortable than useless, ill-contrived grandeurs: but the Duke, I suppose, was made prey of by some architect, a contrast of his Grace, as having some genius, and no fortune.'

Worst of all, in Byng's view, were the Ducal Stables. They are certainly the grandest stables ever built in England—a vast construction, an equine palace, with a circular exercise colonnade of Doric columns one tenth of a mile around, occupying the entire centre. They were converted into a hospital 'for the use of the sick poor' in 1859 and the central exercising yard was covered over with an iron dome, then—at 165 feet across—the biggest in the world. (You must visit the hospital today, not least for the wonderful example of architectural lettering, over 500 feet long, in the dedicatory inscription that encircles the dome.) Byng, however, was not to be impressed: 'Up early to find my cavalry; who are lodged in a most ill-contrived, magnificent mews, where all things are in common; and where they and their furniture must be hourly watched; nothing like a quiet stable to be call'd your own!' He quickly resolved to leave: 'I spy'd about for some time, unknowing and unknown; till I returned to our coffee room [now part of the library], where I subscribed, and breakfasted . . . To people obliged to fly hither for relief, Buxton, as furnishing hope or health, may be tolerable; but it will not do for my plan . . .' He left to find the guileless common man living and working in the Derbyshire countryside.

The more patient and less contemptuous visitors made the best of what was on offer. There was the water to be drunk from St Anne's Well across the gravel from the Crescent. Some years later Dr Granville described how 'A nearly decrepit old woman, seated before the scanty stream, with her shrivelled hands distributes it to the applicants as they approach her. Now it is one of the great attractions of the German Spas that smart female attendants are provided, and ever ready to supply the limpid and sparkling waters in crystal or china beakers.' But here the conditions were too 'generalizing' for the superior class of visitor to come down to the well and they sent their servants to collect the water and bring it to their lodgings.

And of course there were the baths themselves. Some of these were scarcely more salubrious. Dr Granville went to have a look at the public bath. It had a scum on the surface of the water which an attendant raked off from time to time with a broom. 'Altogether the bathing in such a *piscina* was not such as to please my fancy; and when I beheld the class of persons, too, who kept coming in (for the access is free and the bath always open), and their dress and appearance—when I saw the pot-bellied farmer of sixty, half palsied, and the lame artisan with his black and callous hands, and the many who suffered from cutaneous disorders—all plunging together, or one after another in quick succession—some of whom would set about scrubbing from their hardened cuticles the congregated perspiration of ages, with a hairbrush kept *pro bono publico* on the margin of the bath;—I say, when I beheld all these things, I confess my courage failed me.' He bathed instead in the private gentlemen's bath, which was pleasant enough, but he missed the '*satinization*' of the skin he had experienced at Wiesbaden.

Hypochondriacs—'large, lean and yellow'—stalked apart from the company but were always attended by a valet and a footman. Lunatic quacks dispensed blithely universal cures: 'A cough. Drink a pint and a half of cold water lying down in bed. An inveterate cough. Use the cold bath. It seldom fails. Deafness. Use the cold bath. Blindness. Is often cured by cold bathing. Raging Madness. Keep on the head a cap filled with

Pavilion Gardens, Buxton's great Victorian fun palace, built between 1871 and 1875 by Edward Milner as a diversion from the rigours of hydropathy and an escape from the rain.

snow for two or three weeks. Or set the patient with his head under a great waterfall as long as his strength will bear.'

There were also more prosaic diversions—enchanting promenades, a pack of harriers, shooting for partridge, hare, woodcock and snipe on a moor next to the Macclesfield Road and 'Also the romantic hills adjoining thereto'. Chatsworth, Haddon Hall and Kedleston were all open to visitors and within easy touring distance. The natural miracles of the Peak District—caves, ebbing and flowing pools, the odd-shaped rocks and declivities of Matlock Dale, all these sights 'propt round with *Peasants*', as one chronicler put it—gave almost infinite scope to the geology bores. 'A gentleman obliged us by explaining the action of a *siphon* concealed naturally within the mountain, by which the heated waters of the sea are brought under *hydrostatic pressure* most violently towards the surface. I cannot, I confess, exactly comprehend what he means.' The other hazard was the landscape expert: 'Charles, who last summer visited Bath and Cheltenham, finds fault with the cascade. He says it would yet bear much improvement and thereby add greatly to the beauty of the whole.'

In the town itself there was shopping in the Crescent and, increasingly, along Spring Gardens. Despite

Byng's predictable contempt, the shopping was quite good. There were three hairdressers and tailors in 1790, two cabinet makers, jewellers, linen drapers, milliners and petrifactioners, who sold souvenirs made of local semi-precious stones. (These were quite pretty; there are some examples in the museum.) A breeches maker, confectioner, haberdasher and toyman all catered to the holiday trade. A circulating library in the office now occupied by the Registrar of Births and Deaths in the Crescent lent out travel literature and other excellent, amusing works, although the people of Buxton itself never borrowed anything and were considered philistine: 'The constant bustle in which they live during the bathing season leaves them but little time or inclination for the culture of the mind.' There was a theatre, although it was small and shoddy, and the only bowling green was at The Cheshire Cheese, right up at the other, worst, end of town and not highly to be recommended. Mr Billing's billiard table, near the Old Hall, was a better proposition.

Byng returned now and then for the night, entering acid condemnations in his journal. '*Tuesday*. Buxton, the vilest of all spots. *Wednesday*. The sick and lame, who come to bathing places shou'd live in lower floors, in private lodgings; and shou'd not be hoisted up in great noisy hotels.'

Buxton's crowning bauble, the 1905 Opera house by Frank Matcham; nothing but marble and Edwardian cherubs.

He reserved his worst remark for the Dress Ball, which took place in the Assembly Room in the Great Hotel on Wednesday nights. It was the highpoint of the Buxton week. The subscription at the turn of the century was a guinea, which admitted you not only to every Wednesday Ball but to every Monday and Friday Undress Ball too. There was also a family subscription—'one guinea the first, half a guinea each after'. By the 1840s these prices had been halved. The balls began on the first Wednesday in June 'precisely at *eight o'clock*, and close without reserve at *eleven*'. Gloves were required and were sold at the door for those who came without.

Byng's reaction could be guessed at. 'Last night was the first dress'd ball; (much good may it do them) But, from the generally crippled appearance of the company, little dancing can be expected.' Others were less knowing: 'Buxton having within these few days had a number of arrivals of the first fashion, the Assembly Room appeared to me uncommonly brilliant.' And none was more crushing than the cosmopolitan, half-Italian Dr Granville. The Buxton assemblies, he had heard, 'are "dull work" to go through, as the two besetting sins of the English, shyness *cum* stiffness, are said to prevail on such occasions more than usual. . . . It is either dull gaiety or gay dulness with them all, whether "at home", or at "quadrilles", or at a "*soirée musicale*", or at a "*déjeuner dinatoire*"; in fact, at a funeral, *tout comme* at a wedding:—and "*voilà la société dans ce pays-ci; où le plaisir ressemble tant à l'ennui . . .*".'

Remember, when you come here, the stiff, shy, crippled ghosts hobbling between the baths and the coffee room and the deadening assemblies, for whom boredom was always a form of pleasure. Buxton never became what it wanted to be nor what at times it thought it was. But there is no need to be too harsh on it. Buxton is not an eighteenth-century failure; it is a Victorian success. The arrival of the railway in 1863 brought large numbers of people here for a water cure which towards the end of the century developed baroque idiocies of treatment of which earlier quacks could never have dreamed. Mist atomization of volcanically warmed *water*, later chilled on glacier ice and passed through the rays of an *electric* lamp (this in particular was of immense glamour around the turn of the century) and played in needle sprays on the supine body of the patient *from below* (known technically as *douche ascendante*) would be guaranteed to cure whatever the charlatan hero of the day might choose. Fortunes were spent on this and many other forms of 'hydropathy' in the nineteenth century and Buxton throbbed on the profit. Enormous hotels like the Palace (1868) and 'Hydros' (such as the building in Terrace Road now housing the Museum) were erected and heavily patronized.

People bathed in peat, soup and meat extract. Thermal Baths were erected next to the Crescent. They are now an upmarket shopping arcade, but visit them anyway for the beautiful Eton-blue glazed tiles that still line the walls. In 1871 a Winter Garden was erected by Edward Milner, Paxton's assistant at the Crystal Palace, and this, as The Pavilion, now forms part of the conference centre on which much of the town's economy depends. A great domed Octagon was added to it in 1875. In 1905 the complex was crowned with, of all things, a miniature Opera House, a chubby and exuberant exercise in the sumptuously small. It is now the headquarters of the yearly Buxton Festival.

Buxton failed to realize the ambitions of classical coherence which the fifth Duke and his architect had envisaged. Instead, it became almost a pastiche of the grand-picturesque town centre, in which large and self-sufficient buildings like these stand about as casually as models on a drawing-room table. The idea, as it emerged, is not coherence but delight—an *ah!* at turning the corner, as though this were a collection of eye-catchers all rather densely sited in a park. I met a woman in Buxton who had recently moved from Barnsley. She told me that she had spent the first month looking for the middle of the town before she realized that what was in front of her was all there was. It is, in the end, this slightly confused inconsequentiality of Buxton, mixed in with its self-importance, that gives it its charm.

Apart from a truly heartless modern shopping development in Spring Gardens, which makes the Berlin Wall look like a cottage by Lutyens and Jekyll, Buxton is in good shape. But there is one real and easily rectified mistake. The Devonshires gave a Pump Room to the town in 1894. It stands opposite the Crescent. This building, shamefully, is now occupied by a sort of mini Science Museum called a Micrarium, which is nothing to do with either Buxton or its spring water. It means, absurdly, that there is nowhere in the town where one can see a water establishment of any kind in anything like its original condition. This, as William Stukeley warned the people of Glastonbury who were dismantling their abbey to make piggeries, is not right. However weird the water business now seems, the town should not disown its source:

> Come ye cripples, rich and naked,
> Lame and limping, stiff and sore;
> If your bones have ever ached,
> Dip and they will ache no more;
> Come to Buxton
> Come to Buxton
> Here the healing waters pour!

A Prospect of WHITBY from the south-east show

WHITBY
North Yorkshire

Town on the banks of the River Esk

EXPLANATION

A Bridge End
B St Ann's Staith
C Marine Parade
D Captain Cook's House in Grape Lane
E The cupola of Sir Nathaniel Cholmley's Market Tollbooth

ON THE COAST of North Yorkshire, the harbour at WHITBY lies embedded in the heights that surround it, a habitable niche on a difficult shore. In all except a northerly gale, when the swell can roll in past the long and elaborate breakwaters at its mouth, swilling the shipping that is gathered there, this is a calm place, the only safe haven for a sizeable vessel in a stretch of cliffed sea-coast, over a hundred miles long, that lies between the Tees and the Humber.

This is the mouth of the River Esk. Unlike those other rivers, the Esk does not drain a wide and prosperous flat land conspicuous for its farms and money. Whitby is backed by the moors, which are high, dark and unprofitable. They begin within a few miles of the town and are not the sort of hinterland a port could ever have depended on. The valleys are narrow and steep, the roads difficult and winding, the farms small and little more than self-sufficient. This is not Woodbridge, where the sea is ten comfortable miles away down the meanders of a drowsy river and where the luxury of Suffolk has cossetted the town into self-contented ease. Here the sea, and the harbour's shelter from it, has been the one significant influence. This is the central fact about the place: Whitby has always lived by the thing from which it is a refuge.

The waters beyond the harbour mouth have always been a busy shipping route. It was quite possible in the eighteenth century to see four hundred sail, or more, from the cliffs on either side. Even today you will never find the North Sea empty, but dotted with the coasting ships on their way from Newcastle to Harwich or to the ports in Europe. In the days of sail, when a northerly or north-easterly wind was blowing hard, this was an extremely dangerous coast, when ship after ship, unable to hold up against the wind, was driven ashore, in the way that a school of whales will sometimes be washed up to die in numbers on the sand.

One weekend early in February 1861 may well have been the worst. The wind got up on the Friday evening and increased all night until it was blowing a hurricane from the north-east. Everyone in Whitby knew that a catastrophe was in the offing. At eight o'clock on the Saturday morning the brig *John and Ann*, of Sunderland, 'came ashore', as they said, at Sandsend, about two miles down the beach from Whitby. The local men put out through the surf in a *coble*, one of their high-stemmed, flat-bottomed fishing boats designed to cope with a shelterless shore. (You can still see many of them gathered at the New Quay in the Upper Harbour.) The coble saved the crew of five. At ten o'clock, the schooner *Gamma*, a collier from Newcastle, hit the sand, and the Whitby lifeboat —little more than a large coble itself—took off the crew of four. Next was the *Clara*, en route from Newcastle to Madeira. Again the twelve seamen were rescued by the lifeboat, the last man only a moment before the ship suddenly disintegrated. That same morning the lifeboat rescued the crews of the *Utility* and the *Roe*, both driven ashore in the groaning surf.

Almost the entire population of the town was now either on the cliffs or the sands watching the disaster as it happened. At two in the afternoon the brigantine *Flora* succeeded in making her way between the piers bounding the narrow entrance at the habour mouth, but the sea and wind were driving straight in behind her and she ran aground on Collier Hope in the Lower Harbour, a sandy beach where today, at low tide, you can wander, crushing the mussel shells underfoot.

The *Merchant*, a schooner, bound with its cargo of coal from the Tyne to its home port of Maldon in Essex, had left Sunderland the previous day. Early on Saturday morning her boats had been smashed and her bulwarks carried away by the sea. She was now adrift, with only a jib and a scrap of a fore trysail hoisted. At three o'clock the crew was exhausted and were unable to prevent the ship's running aground any longer. They decided to make for Whitby. As they approached the narrow opening of the harbour mouth—made even narrower by improvements throughout the previous century, precisely to make it a better haven in this sort of wind—three heavy seas struck the ship and carried her through towards the sands. She hit land and the crew took to the rigging where the seas continued to break clean over them. Within twenty minutes the lifeboat, its crew already exhausted from five rescues, had launched again and had come so close to the stern of the *Merchant* that one of the lifeboatmen had managed to get a boathook on to it. The mate of the *Merchant* was at the ready with a coiled rope to throw to the lifeboat, but the coxswain decided it would be easier to take the crew off forward of the main rigging. The master of the *Merchant* and the mate then advanced with the rope but when they reached the bows they found the lifeboat had capsized and the crew were struggling in the water.

Everyone on shore could see exactly what was happening. Lifebuoys were thrown in and rockets with lines attached were fired, but none of them did any good. One of the men managed to get on to the capsized lifeboat but was washed off again. Gradually the Whitby men drowned. Only one of them, Henry Freeman, was wearing a cork jacket and he was seen to be slowly fighting his way towards the shore. Men waded into the surf, holding on to each other, forming a chain. At last Freeman reached them and was pulled on to the sand. The other twelve had drowned, eleven of them leaving widows on the shore.

The men of the *Merchant* were finally saved when the rocket-firing apparatus was taken on to the pier and a line thrown to the ship. The whole crew was then hauled to safety. Before Sunday evening three more ships had run on to Whitby sands. The crew of one simply climbed ashore as the dropping tide left them high and dry. The others were rescued by the old Whitby lifeboat, manned by volunteers from the town.

This is the background to Whitby, the inescapable presence of the sea. The best way to come to this town is not the easy landward way, but to walk along the cliffs on the footpath from Robin Hood's Bay, six or seven miles to the south. It is all stone country, the farms and their buildings in rusty, iron-rich sandstone, chiselled with the diagonal marks of Yorkshire masons. Choose a day on which the path is smothered in mist, the drifting blanket of a sea-roak that comes in off the North Sea on windless days. The cormorants hang their drying wings out below you. The small thorn trees are twisted inward, away from the gales, burnt off by the salt. You will hear the foghorn near the village of Hawsker for miles before you reach it, a slight snuffle and then four large blasts. It is known in Whitby, where it will wake you from any dream, day or night, as the 'Hawsker Bull'. Between its nasal blastings, in the pauses, all you hear is the muffling quiet of the fog, and the exaggerated thump and flush of the sea.

Then, without announcement, beyond a small farm and some old coastguard houses, coming up out of the fog like whale bones, you will reach the ruins of Whitby Abbey, the tall medieval masonry rubbed at by the sea, niched and worn into the small fretted terraces and rounded nesting holes of a sea-cliff, the stone returning to its natural state. The decay is not all natural. For years the abbey was used as a quarry for the town and, during the First World War, to great indignation, some German cruisers fired a couple of shells at the abbey, destroying its west front.

Over to the left is the grey stone of the Abbey House, built in the sixteenth century by the successors to the abbey, the Cholmleys, who bought the estate at the Dissolution of the Monasteries and fostered Whitby's growth thereafter. The sea is inescapable. There is no shelter from it. Facing you are the blanked-out windows of a giant banqueting hall, added in 1672 and ruined in 1775 by a gale that first nibbled at the eaves, taking a tile off here and there, and then, in the most majestic and contemptous of ways, lifted the entire roof clean off, sending its timbers cartwheeling over the abbey lands. The only glazed windows now face the other way, inland.

Here you are on the defining edge of Whitby. In front of you the land drops steeply away to the crevice of the harbour, rising again almost as sharply on the far side. In between, squeezed in like grit under a fingernail, is the town itself. Go down to the churchyard, where lines of tombstones, each with its own curly, slight baroque coping, are ranged like rows of theatre seats on the turf—the people of Whitby are looking west. Sit among them. The town lies below you and everything is clear. This view, one of the most famous of all town prospects in England, is the single thing which makes Whitby so wonderful a place. Nowhere else in the country can match it. This is a natural bird's eye view, a vision of a town whose structure is immediately apparent, its details effortlessly part of the whole, a natural three-dimensional map. All Whitby needs—at least this is the flattering illusion it gives you—is one sweeping glance.

At your feet, jumbled up together, are the roofs of the east side of the harbour, a zig-zagging multiplicity of different pitches at different heights, some along the steep slope, some at right angles to it, the whole a visual jostle, a geometrical playing with regular shapes, like an Escher drawing in the making. And here, immediately, Whitby sets itself apart from the country around it. Almost nowhere do you see the rusty sandstone of which the farms and villages are made. Whitby—the very material of the town—has come from the sea. The buildings below you are made of brick and roofed in pantiles. Both these materials arrived on ships—the first as ballast, the second as cargo—coming originally from Holland and then up the east coast from Hull. Pantiles, with their double-overlocking edges, each tile hooked into its neighbours, give every house a rippled line to its roof, and are far more resistant to the tearing and ripping of the wind than flat tiles. Only in the middle of the nineteenth century, with the arrival of the railway, did Welsh blue slate become part of Whitby, and even now there are many more problems with these slate roofs in the winter gales.

Beyond the roofs, which are like an angular sea in a cross-swell, is the harbour itself. At high tide the sea fills it, floating and straightening the fishing boats lying askew on the sand, to flood a basin in the shape of an hourglass. A bridge is laid across its narrow waist, and on either side the two halves of the port expand into the width of bosom and hip, the Lower Harbour nearer the sea, the Upper tailing away inland towards the valley of the River Esk. The larger trawlers are gathered at the Fish Quay on the far side of the Lower Harbour, landing white fish for the many restaurants in the town and for the curing factories up on the industrial estate. Behind them, in the entertainment palaces, the slot machines and coin-operated racing car fantasies jangle and burp their 'Nudge Nudge Nudge' and their electronic crashes out across the water. These places, vastly popular with the summer crowds, are rather less popular with the planning authorities, who restrict them to a short length of the Pier Road and refuse any further applications. One shouldn't be too sniffy. No one who has tried them can deny that the games are great fun, perhaps the best entertainment to be had in Whitby. Above that neon strip, beyond the gathered roofs of the west side, are the long terraces and

crescents of the nineteenth-century holiday town, the West Cliff Estate. This marvellous piece of visual planning does not pastiche the half-medieval jumble below it, as a modern developer would almost certainly be tempted to do, but strings clean, classical lines against the northern sky. It is the work of John Dobson, the Newcastle architect, and his patron, George Hudson, the Midland Railway magnate who bought the fields on the West Cliff in 1848, then built a new station, speculated on the seaside property, pumped in holiday-makers from the industrial towns of northern England and established the business on which Whitby relies for survival today. Up there, slightly deserted now, you will find the wide streets and small boarding houses, the flaky cornices and 'Vacancy' signs of a holiday atmosphere which would have been familiar to Mrs Gaskell, who stayed here in 1859. The only customers now, you might imagine, are pale poets in search of some reflective melancholy. But you should not be too sniffy about this either. Whitby gets about 1,000,000 visitors a year and over 110,000 of them stay the night.

It is high tide. The swing-bridge is manned and, at the far end of it, the operator in his small pavilion rings the hand bell before closing the gates at either end and starting up the silent electric machinery. The two halves of the bridge slide away, first the western and then the eastern, leaving a gaping space between them. As tall as a street, a merchant ship, its deck laden with Finnish chipboard or Norwegian timber, steers through the gap without any hesitation into the Upper Harbour, the small black pilot boat bobbing in its wake, and two or three nonchalant crewmen walking the deck. The ship slows beyond the closing bridge, where people are waiting, temporarily herded behind the gates on either side. It moves past the motor-cobles tied up at the New Quay, the wake jangling them one against the other, and then on, slowing, to Endeavour Quay in the Upper Harbour, where the pilot boat, with a small, final nudge, eases the stern into the wharf.

All this is town as theatre, a place to wait and watch. And if you add one element, the passage of time, you can make the history of Whitby happen before you.

Clear the scene. Remove all the buildings and return to the beginning. The grassy banks of the estuary drop to the waters of the Esk. It is a calm day and at the harbour mouth—no piers—men in little oared boats (that come to a point at each end) are stringing their nets across the mouth of the river. The nets float on the inflated balloons of animal bladders, and there, after a

The ruins of Whitby Abbey and the pair of St Hilda's Cottages, high on the East Cliff above the town.

The 199 steps, often repaired, connect the church and abbey with the streets of the lower East Side. Coffins and brides all travelled this way. The steep cobbled path on the far side of the steps is known as the Donkey Road; fast young men, it is said, used to drive their coaches up the incline as one means of wooing the Cholmley heiresses in the Abbey House above.

while, the fishermen haul them in, bladder by bladder, black bags against the white of the painted strakes, until the fat bodies of the salmon land on the salmon-boat floor. These people are Danes. It is the ninth century. They have destroyed the small ancient monastery on top of the East Cliff and their fishing village is just below the east end of the bridge, the part enclosed by Bridge Street and Church Street, abutting onto the harbour. They have almost certainly brought with them the design of the coble, which resembles fishing boats used in Scandinavia today. They have named the town Whitby—the white place—perhaps because of their painted houses. It sounds unlikely, but no one is sure.

That place by the bridge, the narrowest part of the harbour, where the eastern shore turns in, protected even from northerlies, is the natural place for a settlement. Late in the eleventh century, the abbey above is refounded by the Benedictines and slowly the enormous buildings grow high above the harbourside settlement. Whitby is no more than a fishing village of about a hundred houses and remains that size until the 1500s. There are also some houses on the far side of the bridge (first mentioned in 1351) but no great spread of buildings over the hillside. It would have been limited to the east end of Baxtergate ('gate' simply means street in Danish) and the modern quayside known as St Ann's Staith just north of it, then probably no more than a sandy place where boats could be pulled up. Gradually one or two extra houses, in a growth as slow as lichen, gather on Flowergate at the western end of the bridge and in one or two streets, such as Sandgate, and Grape Lane, at the eastern.

There are certainly some quays here by the fourteenth century, and when Leland visited Whitby in the 1530s the harbour mouth was protected by a rudimentary pier. But the ownership of the town by the abbey had limited its growth—or at least not encouraged it. The abbot had a market house down in Church Street where local taxes on market goods and fish were levied. But this is all on a small scale. The abbey's real interests were miles away in the middle of Yorkshire, where giant flocks roamed giant sheep-walks.

The acceleration begins with the demise of the abbey in 1539. The Cholmleys, enormously energetic people, take over, and under their influence Whitby starts to move. Quays are improved and enlarged. Landing facilities are provided at St Ann's Staith in 1559; a

Sir Nathaniel Cholmley's Tollbooth or Town Hall dominates the recently re-cobbled marketplace on the East Side. It was designed in 1788 by Jonathan Pickernell, the engineer responsible for the Whitby piers. This, until the nineteenth century, was the site for public punishment: whipping in front of the Tollbooth, and other humiliations in the stocks in the right-hand corner.

century later these are extended to form a quay over 150 feet long. The protection of the harbour with timber piers at its mouth is improved by 1545. The West Pier, intended partly to prevent the drift of sand across the harbour mouth, is given an outer bulwark of timber by Sir Hugh Cholmley in 1632. The medieval bridge has become dangerous by 1609 and again it is the Cholmleys who, in the 1630s, provide a new drawbridge, allowing good access to the Upper Harbour.

The town has begun to teem in front of you. The medieval lassitude has given way to the beginnings of modern enterprise. Alum, a valuable mineral once used in dyeing and tanning, is discovered at several places nearby—at Saltwick and Sandsend, as well as further away at Guisborough. It is mined and the raw material shipped to the textile districts. The coasting trade, above all in coals from Northumberland, is on the increase. Whitby's small role as a market for the agricultural produce of the valleys inland also grows and, in 1640, the Cholmleys move the market from its earlier site at the western end of the bridge (now Golden Lion Bank) to a new site on the east side between Church Street and Sandgate, the lower end given over to butchers' stalls and their slaughter-houses, with drains out into the harbour.

The increase in tempo brings more people into the town. The population of about 750 in the early 1500s doubles by 1610 and again by 1700. On the west side, Baxtergate and Flowergate now fill with houses on the familiar burgage plots—long thin strips of land with a house at the head of each of them making the street frontage, and a long yard or garden stretching behind. On the east side too, Church Street starts to fill up both north and south of the bridge in the same pattern. The Cholmleys give long leases on the plots to encourage development.

There is a tangible excitement in all this activity,

like bees making a hive. The pace quickens. The population is now doubling every fifty years or so—3,000 in 1700, 5,000 by 1750, 8,500 by 1780 and more than 10,400 by about 1810. A small valley called Bagdale runs out of the estuary on the west side and here, on the sunny south-facing slopes, large and beautiful brick houses are built in slightly haphazard terraces. Rather smaller but no less pretty houses are built for the slightly poorer types in Skinner Street and Cliff Street. These Georgian extensions to the town are not enough to accommodate the mass of people. For them there is something else: not the sunlit terrace but the sort of development which happened later in Alnwick and in many other small Victorian towns. Here in Whitby it occurred very early, during the second half of the eighteenth century, and it has left (at least in those parts which have not been demolished in the last few decades) the remains of a fascinating thing: the Georgian slum.

The poor could not afford to build new houses on the edge of town. Nevertheless, within the town itself there was land widely available—in the form of the back gardens of the burgage plots. It was on these areas, often steeply sloping as the gardens climbed the estuary banks, that the tenements of the poor were packed.

It is now that you must descend from your surveyor's seat in the churchyard. Before coming down the long, worn steps of the Church Stairs to the town below, you must see the church itself. It is a Norman building, dedicated to St Mary, and only the windows—like those of a large house, with clear square panes and Georgian glazing bars—can prepare you for what is inside. It is quite extraordinary. There is no church like it in England, but it is exactly right, a microcosm of what happened to Whitby itself. The medieval shell is treated with no antiquarian respect, and huge holes have been punched through masonry half a millennium older than the lighting windows themselves, which are the nearest the eighteenth century could come to plate glass. Inside, almost the entire space is filled with Whitby carpentry. In 1816, as some of the last of these wooden additions were being made to the church, there were 403 carpenters in the town, as well as 29 boat-builders, 17 block and mast-makers, 34 sawyers and 79 joiners. Expert carpentry and the ability to pack a great deal into a small space was Whitby's dominant skill. Here, in this tightly-fitted church interior, where every pew is boxed and baized, every space galleried, every corner trimmed and panelled, where the pulpit rises through three wooden storeys, you can see Whitby in the flood-tide of its existence—the medieval past obliterated, swamped by the vigour and volume of the sea-fed present.

If you walk along Church Street at the foot of the Church Stairs you will find the other side of the coin. Here (and the same is true too along Sandgate and on either side of Baxtergate on the far side of the harbour) Whitby is incredibly full. There is not a blade of grass to be seen. Behind every one of the houses on the main street—almost all of them built in the eighteenth or nineteenth century—you will find the living quarters of Whitby's poor. These are the yards or 'ghauts' (a word unique to Whitby and pronounced 'goats') where the gardens of the main houses were rapidly turned into tiny self-enclosed urban landscapes. The ghauts usually open out at their bottom end, facing on to the harbour, bringing some light and air into the tight little spaces, but the yards are utterly shut in. Stone staircases climb to galleries above or disappear up the hill, sometimes even through short tunnels, to further yardlets, where yet more buildings are stacked above them. Where down-pipes have broken, moss and ferns grow out of the brickwork. Makeshift repairs patch together the disintegrating fabric. Several of the tenements here have been smartened up and gentrified (and sold on, of course, as 'Georgian town houses'), but if anyone has forgotten why slum clearance seemed a good idea not so long ago, they should have a look at some of the less well-kept of Whitby's yards. They give the phrase 'urban fabric' a new meaning: here you are not coasting around on top of it; the sensation is more one of burrowing over the warp and under the weft, inside the very thickness of the cloth.

Whitby is still a poor place. Male unemployment rises to over thirty per cent each winter and the work on offer in the Job Centre on Brunswick Street is pitifully low paid. Nevertheless, nothing like the number of people live in the yards now as did before the Housing Acts which followed the First World War. At that time the concentration of people matched the density of the physical environment—and it is some measure of the improvement in living conditions here that although the population has scarcely grown in number, Whitby, including its modern housing estates, now covers something like ten times the area of the historic core of the town.

The people for whom these yards were first made had come in from the countryside for work, and the work focused on one place: the harbour. It was not a great fishing place—there were only nine fishermen here in 1816. It was for something more ambitious than that that they came: shipbuilding. The Lower Harbour nearer the sea was too exposed to wind and swell for any shipyards to be established there, but the Upper Harbour, beyond the drawbridge, was ringed with them. As one walked down the southern end of Church Street in the late eighteenth century, the way would be roofed with the bowsprits of ships that were in for repairs—like the arch of swords held up at a military wedding. The earliest yard, belonging to Jarvis Coates, was at the seaward end of the Baxtergate burgages, where the railway station was later built on infilled land. Coates's house still exists in Baxtergate next to the Post Office, swankily finished in dressed stone. Other small boatyards clustered along what is now the New Quay road and along the southern half of Church Street where it fronts the harbour, many of them building only the small cobles. (These are still made in two yards in Whitby, both a long way down the Esk, out of sight of the tourist crowds. The boat-builders still use no drawings, making everything by eye alone.) All the ancillary trades gathered too: timberyards, roperies, sail-lofts, sailcloth mills, iron foundries and the workshops of coopers and specialist blacksmiths were all here from at least 1730 onwards. Banks were founded, concentrated around Grape Lane. Watches, toys and jewellery could be bought in Whitby by 1800. Lawyers and physicians set up business in the town. The West Pier was repeatedly enlarged in an effort to stop sand drifting into the harbour mouth; the beach-like shores were converted into quays and a Fish Pier was built on the east side of the harbour. Sir Hugh Cholmley's bridge was rebuilt in 1766 and again in 1835. Sir Nathaniel Cholmley replaced the market hall with the present Tuscan temple in 1788.

At the heart of this boom were the ships. Indeed. Captain Cook, who had been a seaman and mate in colliers here, insisted on using Whitby ships on his voyages of discovery in the Pacific, and they became famous throughout the country. The *Endeavour* had been built by Thomas Fishburn in 1764, in the yard now covered by the railway station. She was a typical Whitby collier, stout rather than elegant, with a stubby look-to hull, bluff-bowed and incredibly strong. The colliers were roomy boats and had flat bottoms so that they could be beached and unloaded on the shore. They rolled horribly in a swell and their detractors said they were 'half clog, half coffin', but their great virtue was their toughness. One Whitby boat, returning from the whale fishery off Greenland in the early nineteenth century, with yards of her keel ripped out by the ice, was able to sail home with nothing but a sheet of canvas stretched around the hull until she arrived in the Upper Harbour. She settled on the mud, and at the next high tide the water rose as fast inside the hold as it did outside it. Most famous of all the survivors was the *Sea Adventure*, built in the Upper Harbour in 1724 and finally wrecked in a gale on the Lincolnshire coast eighty-six years later. She took it easily enough when the 'flood tide carried her into the midst of a field where she remained high and dry', her spars swinging among the bean-sprouts, her integrity unquestioned.

All the shipyards have gone now. The last, Turnbull's, lay far down in the depths of the harbour at the old Whitehall yard, where the *Discovery*, one of the ships on Cook's last voyage, had been built in 1774. Here, by the end of the nineteenth century, Turnbull's were building ships of well over 5,000 tons. They could only be floated out on the highest of spring tides and even then only without their engines installed. For decades the ship-builders had been asking the town council to replace the old swivel bridge (built across the harbour in 1835) because the gap it left when opened was not large enough to accommodate the width of ship now required. (This had been a problem ever since shipbuilding had begun here. The breadth in the beam of Captain Cook's *Endeavour*, for example, had been limited to 29 feet 3 inches, because the gap in what was then a drawbridge was only just over 30 feet.) The town did nothing about it. The number of ships that were produced here dropped from an average of twenty-eight a year in the early 1870s to eleven in the early 1890s and then to three a year by the turn of the century. Seven or eight hundred men were relying on the business. They had maintained the Whitby traditions of solid workmanship; re-fitters in Cardiff, for example, demanded extra money if it was a Whitby ship that was in for repair as the rivets were so extraordinarily well fixed. Despite the tradition and despite the town's reliance on shipbuilding, the council did nothing about the bridge. In 1902 Turnbull's closed their Whitby yard. The skilled men moved off to other places on the east coast. Only in 1908 was a new bridge installed, with the splendid opening-width of 75

The boarding houses of East Crescent on the West Cliff Estate, developed after 1848 when George Hudson, the Midland Railway King, began to transform the small port into a holiday town for the middle classes of the industrial north.

feet. This is the one that is there today. The council was too late and no important shipyard ever opened here again. Now, as a footnote to this story, the council is planning to transform the Whitehall yard (a beautifully melancholy place at the moment, with all the allure of industrial abandonment) into a Captain Cook theme park, complete with a full-size replica of the *Endeavour* floating in the dock.

Today, it has to be said, Whitby is a tourist town. Over three-quarters of the jobs are in the service industries and under four per cent in fishing. About twenty dockers and ten clerks work at Endeavour Quay. A few men build the motor cobles. Apart from that life revolves around cafés and trinkets, entertainment arcades and sticks of rock. It is impossible to move in the town during July and August. In the winter months it can be very empty. Whitby, unlike Hebden Bridge, for example, is not an immediately friendly place for an outsider to be. Too many visitors at one time, not enough work at another—this is a pattern which would degrade hospitality anywhere. Despite the armies of visitors, or in fact because of them, there is a self-protective indifference in the town, a rather charmless cutting-off which views Whitby people as human, the rest of us as ghosts with wallets. It is nothing new. In 1838, two years after the railway had arrived and while promoters were talking about the visitor-business as a replacement for shipbuilding (then in a temporary slump), a correspondent wrote to the local paper: 'Perhaps it is thought that a new house or two will attract settlers and that admiring visitors will come and teach us their fashionable foibles. Vain thought! and as undesirable as vain. Better endeavour to keep our bees in the hive than strive to entice butterflies into it. . . . No, Whitby is a town for business, not for pleasure.

A view of HEBDEN BRIDGE looking eastwar

HEBDEN BRIDGE
West Yorkshire

ross the Valley of the Hebden Water

EXPLANATION

A Nutclough Mill
B Hebden Works
C Eiffel Buildings
D Edward Street
E Birchcliffe Baptist Chapel
F 'Snob Row'
G Stoney Lane
H Stubbings School
I Zion Baptist Chapel
J White Lion Public House
K Bridge Mill
L Hebden Bridge Co-operative Hall
M Rochdale Canal

IT IS A SUNNY afternoon in the Calder Valley, the steep glacial cut that slices through the southern Pennines between the high and empty moors on either side. You lie back on the scratchy grass, your eyes on the horizon of the moor in front of you, and from far below, beyond the mossy stump of a disused chimney and the barrack of a five-storey cotton mill, you hear the thumping of the lorries on their way eastwards to the towns in Lancashire. This valley, with the narrow, twisted threads of road, canal and railway cabled along its floor like a nerve bundle, links the wide industrial districts that spread out in a complex and jungly ganglia of mill-towns to the east and west: Halifax, Bradford and Leeds in Yorkshire; Rochdale, Oldham and Manchester on the Lancashire side.

Here you are in the thick of the hills. It is a crux of valleys. Steep tributary streams, the Colden and Hebden Waters, drop quickly to the River Calder at the bottom. You know of their presence both from the map and from the contours around you, but their waters are hidden by the tall buildings, and their sound is obscured by the noise of traffic passing through.

It is steep country, in which nothing can slide comfortably from one state or place to the next; where suburbs are impossible because the suburban needs a site where seamless fluency is the norm, and it is definitely absent here. This is a place of sharp divisions and immediate change: where a chimney to carry away the noxious fumes from a dye-works stands erect and uncompromised in the middle of a wood high above the valley, while its underground flue climbs unseen from the blackened factory far below; where the double-decker terraces of houses built literally on top of one another (the gradient of the slope providing a ground-level front door for each of them) look out, in one direction, on the gritted roofscape of a nineteenth-century boomtown—Fustianopolis—and in the other at the moor and the sky; where there is nothing cosmetic. The feeling of raw practicality is scarcely softened by the little rows of pot-plants on the pavements outside the 'back-to-backs', built by the nineteenth-century mill-owners as industrial tenements without gardens.

There is a glamour of sorts in this, an unfuzzy straightness that appeals to a certain kind of modern nostalgia. Makers of advertisements for brown bread and banks—and of television series in which straight talking is the substance of life—choose HEBDEN BRIDGE as their location because it provides a visual metaphor for the integrity they want to convey. Look at the town and you think 'bluntness'. There is no southern backsliding here, no sneaking slickness, no idea, ironically enough, that 'marketing' is the thing.

This is, in large part, because Hebden Bridge has failed. Not long ago an old woman was killed by a lorry driving through the town; in her time she had been a weaver in one of the mills whose chimneys still stand like giant hitching posts above everything. That is, in a way, the recent story of Hebden Bridge: traffic has replaced the looms. The failure of the textile industries, undercut by foreign competition, has damaged all the mill-towns, not only those cramped like this one into the trench of a Pennine valley.
But while the bigger cities have gone on to do other things, Hebden Bridge has found little beyond the pinpricks of small enterprise to replace the cloth on which it once lived. Almost everyone who lives in the town now is either retired or commutes daily to the larger cities to the east. There is a special cheap fares policy on the railway to encourage them. In the late 1960s and early 1970s the economy of Hebden Bridge had sunk to its lowest point; many houses were empty and could be bought for £50 or less. It was this period that brought in the third element of Hebden Bridge's population. The new arrivals were quickly labelled hippies by the older people. They have now evolved into a self-contained artistic community, supporting a local theatre, running a wholefood co-operative, a bookshop with as good a poetry section as any in the country, and shops where oldish wooden proletarian furniture is stripped of its paint, waxed a kind of corpse yellow and sold as 'Pine'.

The town is a private place. The steep hills hedge it in, defining the narrow exits along the valley, or forcing the roads north to climb up out of it. If you come down the high road from Keighley or the steep lane from Heptonstall, it lies neatly smoking beneath you.
Hebden Bridge has always been a place apart. The turnpike road from Halifax had reached the town by 1771, the Rochdale Canal by 1798 and the Manchester and Leeds Railway by 1841. These were heavily used routes but most of the goods were not off-loaded here; they were carried *through*. Until about 1850 there was very little development of the floor of the valley. As early as 1792 one of the principal landowners had advertized land here in a Leeds newspaper as a suitable place to build a factory, but no one had taken him up. As long as sites were available in the easier

and more accessible flat land on either side of the Pennines, there was no need for an industrial town here. Its sudden boom in the second half of the nineteenth century, when over eighty factories could be found between the villages of Mytholm and Mytholmroyd on either side, was the result of land-shortage in the more suitable places outside the Calder Valley. Hebden Bridge was always on the edge of the industrial culture—one of the last to come, one of the first to go.

The late nineteenth-century town is surrounded by its predecessors. Up on the nose of high land to the west is the dark and beautiful village of Heptonstall. When settlements were first made here, the valley bottom was wooded, marshy and indefensible. Villages like this one were built on the high terraces overlooking the valley, where the inhabitants could control the approaches and where, despite the altitude (about nine hundred feet), they could still grow oats and wheat on the edges of the moorland. Just as Hebden Bridge has been left intact by the desertion of its industry during this century, Heptonstall remains—in its physical structures—an almost untouched example of the seventeenth- and eighteenth-century South Pennine village it once was. By 1600 the poverty of the farming here had turned most families towards part-time cloth-making. (Walk around the village now and you will hear Brahms coming out of one window and the soft clack of a word-processor keyboard from another. Sylvia Plath is buried in the churchyard.) In these streets of solid and blackened stone houses with many-mullioned windows, the dissenting, independent farmers-cum-weavers pursued their double life: a smallholding with a couple of cows and a patch of cereals; and a tiny, one-family cloth-making business. The poorer families would weave cloth for small-time master-clothiers, who provided the raw materials and took a cut when the piece was sold on. Throughout the village, men, women and children would be involved in the many processes of cloth-making. Some of these were arduous, all of them long: picking the raw wool clean, untangling the knotty mass with wooden 'cards' studded with iron pins, stroking and teasing it into long and fleecy slivers which were then spun into yarn by the women and children (one weaver needed six spinners or more to keep him supplied). The yarn would then be washed and dried, the warp greased and then fixed on the loom, the weft wound on to bobbins. Only then could the cloth be woven on the loom—the man's work. The cloth 'in the raw' would be soaked in stale urine, and then 'fulled' or hammered in a trough so that the fibres matted together and the cloth became weatherproof. It was then dried on tenterposts in the field, its loose fibres brushed up with teasels and the raised surface cropped with huge shears. The piece could then be taken to Halifax and sold as a finished kersey.

Despite the arduousness of the work, this is a picture of a domestic industry in which the man is his own man, not timed by a bell or factory hooter, able to walk in his garden or look to his cows, accountable for his own fate. He could pace his work so that in the first days of the week the loom went to the slow rhythm of 'Plenty of time, Plenty of time', quickening as the delivery day approached to 'A day t'lat, A day t'lat ' This independence of life became the great memory myth of these Pennine valleys in the nineteenth century. The textile factory had by this time arrived, with its discipline and time-keeping. The hand-loom weaver was either refused employment in the new mill because women or children could perform the job more cheaply, or he himself refused to become a factory hand and lose the honourable status of a self-motivated man.

By the middle of the century there were still two hundred thousand men in this situation in England—reduced to utter poverty, statusless outworkers for the industrial system in the valley below, which controlled the market and inexorably lowered prices.

Walk down the hill from Heptonstall on the old pack-horse track known as the Buttress into the centre of Hebden Bridge and you exchange one world for another: not the various and independent houses arranged haphazardly along the streets and lanes of a village, clustered organically around a churchyard, but instead, on a larger scale, the factory hugger-mugger with the housing, its many floors literally towering over the roofs of the dwellings next to it, its giant chimneys the flagstaffs of a new civilization. You have exchanged one kind of coherence for another. The first is organic, human and equable, coherent because its patterns emerge from the desires and aspirations of the people within it. The second is mechanical, rigid and imposed from above—by the mill-owners. This is the coherence of an institution, in which everything is arranged for one end: the efficiency of the mills. The houses are close to the mills not for sociability but to ensure good time-keeping by the workforce. Heptonstall is the

The Rochdale Canal is carried over the River Calder on the Black Pit Aqueduct, built in 1797 in the middle of Hebden Bridge. In the background, on either side of the water, are the town's two main schools: (left) *Central Street and* (right) *Riverside.*

flowering of independence; Hebden Bridge is a monument to obedience.

In the centre of the town is a small cluster of buildings left over from the pre-industrial age in which, through half-closed eyes, one can envisage the earlier scene: a picture of small-scale industry and farming. The first thing is the bridge itself, after which the original settlement was named. It was built in about 1510, to replace an earlier wooden bridge over the Hebden Water. The narrow, steeply pitched structure is made of millstone grit, the honey-coloured sandstone which has also been employed in the construction of the whole town. The bridge was a crucial link in the trans-Pennine pack-horse route from Halifax via Heptonstall to Burnley, the trade route for the early cloth industry in these hills. Just along Bridge Gate is Bridge Mill, dating mostly from the eighteenth century but built on the site of a much earlier corn mill. (It has been cleaned and dressed up recently as a conglomeration of boutiques and restaurants. For the older style, go round the back, on the river side, where the degraded mess is perhaps a truer reminder of how things were: the walls are broken down, and the alders hang over a millrace clogged with floating rubbish.) Beyond the mill is the White Lion, described to me by one of the town lads, who was not allowed in, as 'the boringest pub in the world for the youth of today'. He claimed that the landlord—actually a charming and witty man—had an 'Over-sixties policy'. It is in fact the nicest pub in the town. As you can still see if you go around the back of the main building, this pub was originally a farm and there is still a large barn on the other side of the street.

Lying in exactly the sort of arrangement you can still find in any more remote Pennine valley today, these few buildings represent the rural kernel, around which

the later town gathered. The first factories to be built in these little side-valleys off the Calder—during the first two decades of the nineteenth century—were driven by water wheels, which were set in the fast-running Pennine streams. Most of these have gone now, made redundant by the coming of steam engines, but a little way up the valley of the Hebden Water, tucked into a beauty spot called Hardcastle Crags, one of these early factories survives. Gibson Mill was built in about 1800. Water weeds cluster in the millpond and the trees stretch their arms out over the bed of the stream. What better model for industry than this—the renewable energy source, the refreshing surroundings, the integrity of work and place? But Gibson Mill is a liar. It absorbs the innocence of its surroundings. In 1833 the Factories Inquiry Commission interviewed the mill-owners throughout the Upper Calder Valley, including those at Gibson Mill. It was reported that the labourers at this cotton-spinning mill worked on weekdays from 6 a.m. until 7.30 p.m. (a 13½-hour day), with a 20-minute break for breakfast and 40 minutes for dinner, while on Saturdays the working day was a mere 9½ hours long. In times of drought, when the motive power from the stream was weaker, the working day was proportionately longer. There was no sick pay. There were two days paid holiday at Christmas and an unpaid holiday on Shrove Tuesday and at Whitsun. Most of the people who had to work these hours (a 72-hour week) were children. Of the 21 workers employed here, 11 were under 21, and 6 of them under 16.

This was far from untypical. Moreover, while these may have been the sort of hours children were forced to work in the earlier domestic weaving industry, the requirements of the new machinery, the heartlessness, regimentation and the violence to which they were subjected, all lowered the experience to another plane. The Halifax Worsted Spinners, an employers' organization, had passed a resolution in 1831 to the effect that 'Operatives aged between 7 and 14 are more capable of long continued labour than those aged 14 to 21.' Walker and Edmondson, worsted spinners in Mytholmroyd (just outside Hebden Bridge), employed 17 'operatives' who were between 6 and 8 years old, and 50 more who were under 10. These children were paid 3s. 8d. per hour. Boys over 17 expected higher wages but this meant that almost none of them was employed in the mills. These were the young men who were forced to return to the penury of hand-weaving in their cottages on the hillside. Many of the children who were employed were either the sons and daughters of these men or paupers from larger cities.

Children were not only cheap, they were also unable to resist the strappings they were given when they were late, or when they became drowsy at the end of the day. They were even more useful because they could be squeezed into places where a larger adult body would not fit. An overlooker in a worsted mill described in 1832 what happened to boys who laboured as human adjuncts to the workings of the machine: 'At the top of the spindle there is a fly goes across, and the child takes hold of the fly by the ball of his left hand, and he throws the left shoulder up and the right knee inward; he has the thread to get with the right hand, and he has to stoop his head down to see what he is doing; they throw the right knee inwards in that way, and all the children that I have seen, that I could judge that are

The Church of St James the Great in Mytholm, consecrated in 1833, on the western edge of Hebden Bridge, where the graveyard is full of the adolescent dead.

made cripples by the practice of piecening worsted, invariably bend in the right knee.'

The long hours and the cruelty were quite simply the products of the market. John Crossley, whose mill next to the canal in Hebden Bridge has only recently been demolished, told the investigators in 1833 that he was obliged to run his mill for more than twelve hours a day simply because his competitors were habitually running theirs for fourteen or fifteen hours.

The mill-owners' replies provide damning enough information about the situation. The reports made by those intent on reforming the factory system go further: the screams of children being strapped in the mills could be heard outside them, they reported. In Cragg Vale, a small and beautiful side-valley off the Calder, children were working sixteen hours a day and occasionally all night. The minister in the church there told one of the investigators in 1833 how he had recently buried an eleven-year-old boy, Sutcliffe Wilcock. The child had been found fast asleep as he stood, with his arms full of wool, having been working seventeen hours in the mill, and he had been beaten awake. The boy's father had carried him home but he was unable to eat his supper. He awoke at 4 a.m. the next morning, and asked his brothers if they could see the lights of the mill, as he was afraid of being late. Then he died. A week later the minister buried his nine-year-old brother, dead for the same reasons.

Go to the graveyard of St James the Great in Mytholm, on the western edge of Hebden Bridge, lying just above Colden Water where it drops to the River Calder. The church, consecrated in 1833, was once surrounded by mills but all of them are now demolished. Only a chimney or two remains. The churchyard, in the shadow of its large, dark church, is packed with blackened tombstones, set back to back in rows like the houses, with hardly a slit of air between them. One word occurs again and again on the stones, carved in small capitals: 'ALSO . . . ALSO . . . ALSO . . .', five or six times on each stone, each time recording the death of another child or teenager broken by the life to which they had been subjected. The stonemason resorts to little mottoes: 'Thy Will Be Done', 'God is Love', 'Life is Short'.

Ferocious criticisms of the factory system were published in the *Leeds Mercury*. The mill-owners challenged their critics, setting up placards along the valley which demanded evidence and witnesses. The reformers, led by Richard Oastler, responded with their own placards which they fixed to the buildings: 'You are more Tyrannical, more Hypocritical than the slave-drivers of the West Indies. . . . I shall prove to be *Tyranny* your boasted *Piety*. . . . Your system of "*Flogging*", of "*Fines*", of "*Innings up Time*" [the system by which production-time lost in the mills through mechanical breakdowns or lack of water had to be made up later by the operatives for no extra money, despite its being done in overtime], of "*Truck*" [paying not with money but second-rate goods], of "*cleaning machinery during mealtimes*", of "*Sunday workings*", of "*Low Wages*" . . . shall all undergo the Ordeal of "*Public Examination*" . . .'. 'Why,' the tirade ended, 'You stink over Blackstone Edge!' It was all too much for the masters. A great public meeting was held on 24th August 1833 in the White Horse, a pub in the middle of Hebden Bridge, now demolished. The place was packed, the people overspilling into the street, but none of the great men dared attend. They were vilified and exposed in their absence until, at the height of all the emotion, one of the local employers was found hiding in another room at the inn. He was forced through howls of contempt and anger to emerge and then to crawl back home through the crowds in the streets outside. The meeting closed at 10 p.m. and as Oastler himself rode back home he 'saw two mills blazing like fury in the valley. Their inmates, poor little sufferers, had to remain there until 11.30 o'clock, and the owner of one of them I found to be a noted sighing, praying, canting religionist . . .'.

There one finds the next crucial element in the town: the chapels. They are everywhere. God is as prevalent as work. When, for example, there was a musical procession through Hebden Bridge in the summer of 1883, the following bands lined up:

Hebden Bridge Brass Band
Independent Order of Rechabites (Temperance)
Old Temperance Society
Cross Lanes (Wesleyan Methodist)
Hope Chapel (Particular Baptist)
Nazebottom (Baptist)
Birchcliffe (Baptist)
Mytholmroyd (Primitive Methodist)
Mytholmroyd (Wesleyan)
Salem (Wesleyan)
Zion (Strict Baptist)
Heptonstall Slack (Baptist)
Cragg Vale (Wesleyan)

This, for a total population of about six thousand people. Some of it might be explained by sheer geography—it was convenient for the people in Cragg Vale or Heptonstall Slack, for example, not to have to come to the town to worship. But men, women and children all came easily enough from those hamlets every day of the week to work in Hebden Bridge itself. It may also be partly due to a natural tendency of nonconformism—a doctrine with a tradition dating back to the sixteenth century in this part of the world, where parishes were huge and ill-regulated—to disintegrate as soon as any sign of coherence appeared.

If you walk up the steep streets on the eastern side of Hebden Water—the area known as Birchcliffe—you will come upon one of Hebden Bridge's most expensive and glamorous monuments, a palatial if rather heavy building with pink granite columns and a giant two-storey auditorium with room for hundreds. It has now been cut up into little offices for community projects, but when it was opened in 1899 it was the new Baptist Birchcliffe Chapel.

Chapels were paid for largely by the mill-owners, the descendants of Oastler's 'noted sighing, praying, canting religionists . . .'. Even at that time, there was profound cynicism among the working people here about the true faith of their employers. Oastler met a group of mill-workers as they passed a Methodist chapel built by one of the Sutcliffes, for many decades the biggest men in the town. The men 'looked towards the chapel and wished it might sink into hell, and Mr Sutcliffe go with it. . . . I said it was too bad, as Mr Sutcliffe had built the chapel for their good. "Damn him," said another. "I know him, I have had a swatch of him, and a corner of that chapel is mine, and it all belongs to his workpeople." ' It was a common theory, and still is, that the chapels built by the mill-owners were paid for by the fines levied on the workforce for their unpunctuality or carelessness.

Some propagandists were quite explicit about the usefulness of the moral discipline of chapel for those wanting to run a factory. The lack of such discipline 'may be readily detected in any establishment by a practised eye, in the disorder of the general system, the irregularities of the individual machines, the waste of time and material. . . . It is therefore excessively the interest of every mill-owner *to organise his moral machinery on equally sound principles with his mechanical* for otherwise he will never command the steady hands, watchful eyes, and prompt cooperation, essential to excellence of product. . . .' Chapels and Sunday Schools—attended by boys up to fifteen and sixteen in Hebden Bridge until as least the Second World War—were the tools by which the workforce could be moulded.

Capitalist piety lasted well into this century. 'Of course the owners were the big bugs at Chapel,' an old lady in the town said to me, remembering her youth as a sewing-machinist in the 1920s in Hartley's Linen Works. 'They'd always be there in their Come-to-Jesus collars and their Go-to-Buggery ties. And some of the others, if they worked in that mill or machine shop, they'd nearly bow down in front of them. But I wasn't one of them.'

This is the authentic voice of Hebden Bridge. It is a weird paradox. This woman, like many others in the town, with an uncompromised sense of her own independence, and her knowledge that the power behind the chapels—particularly that of the Methodists—was in many ways hypocritical and repressive, was nevertheless a devout and active member of her own chapel congregation. In an extraordinary and scarcely understandable coming-together, the chapels could satisfy both parties: the mill-owners' need to control every part of their workforce's lives, from work itself, through education, housing, religion, morals and free time (largely arranged through the chapels); and the people's belief in their own independence, their non-conformity in *all* senses, going far beyond the purely religious. Come-to-Jesus and Go-to-Buggery walk hand in hand.

The boom came to Hebden Bridge in the very last moments of the nineteenth century. Only in 1893 was a replacement for the old pack-horse bridge over the Hebden Water built upstream. This opened up a whole new area of the town on the floor of the valley and new streets were named without any sense of irony: Bond Street, Regent Street and Sackville Street. Elsewhere you can find Eton, Oxford and Cambridge Streets, Balmoral, Osborne, Windsor and Queen's Terraces. This last, high above the town on Heptonstall Road, is perhaps one of the most remarkable constructions in the town. It is a double-decker terrace. The lower level is built, as usual, with its back wall dug into the hillside, so that the rooms at the back—before the invention of vertical damp-courses—were consistently mildewy, and were lit only by an internal window, borrowing light from the front rooms. These were always—and still are—the cheapest houses in a terrace. Bernard Ingham, later Margaret Thatcher's Press Secretary, grew up in one of them. On the upper storey, the builders erected two rows of houses back to back. One is accessible from the road, the other only from a balcony strung along the front. As a result, none of the houses, in this place of expansive views, has more than one wall in which there are any windows. Not one has any garden next to it, and none on the road side of the upper storey, which faces north, ever felt the sun.

Down the many staircases and cobbled paths that net the hilllsides here—the snickets or guinnels as they are called—the workforce walked every morning to the mills and machine shops of the boomtown. Hebden Bridge's great product was *fustian* (in its various forms), a cloth with a linen warp and cotton weft, that is best known today in the form of corduroy, but which in its heyday stretched to 'Corduroys, Moleskins, Drills, Cantoons, Twills, Gambroons, Diagonals, Bedfords and Whipcords'. In these materials the British working-man was clothed along with many millions across the empire. Hebden Bridge became Fustianopolis, producing everything here from the yarn to the finished ready-made trousers, jackets, overalls, boiler suits, even riding breeches. The works at Nutclough Mill, a worker's co-operative established in 1870 and run by the Hebden Bridge Fustian Manufacturing Society, were the biggest. In 1900 there was an annual turnover of £50,000; 350 men and women worked here, all with shares in the enterprise.

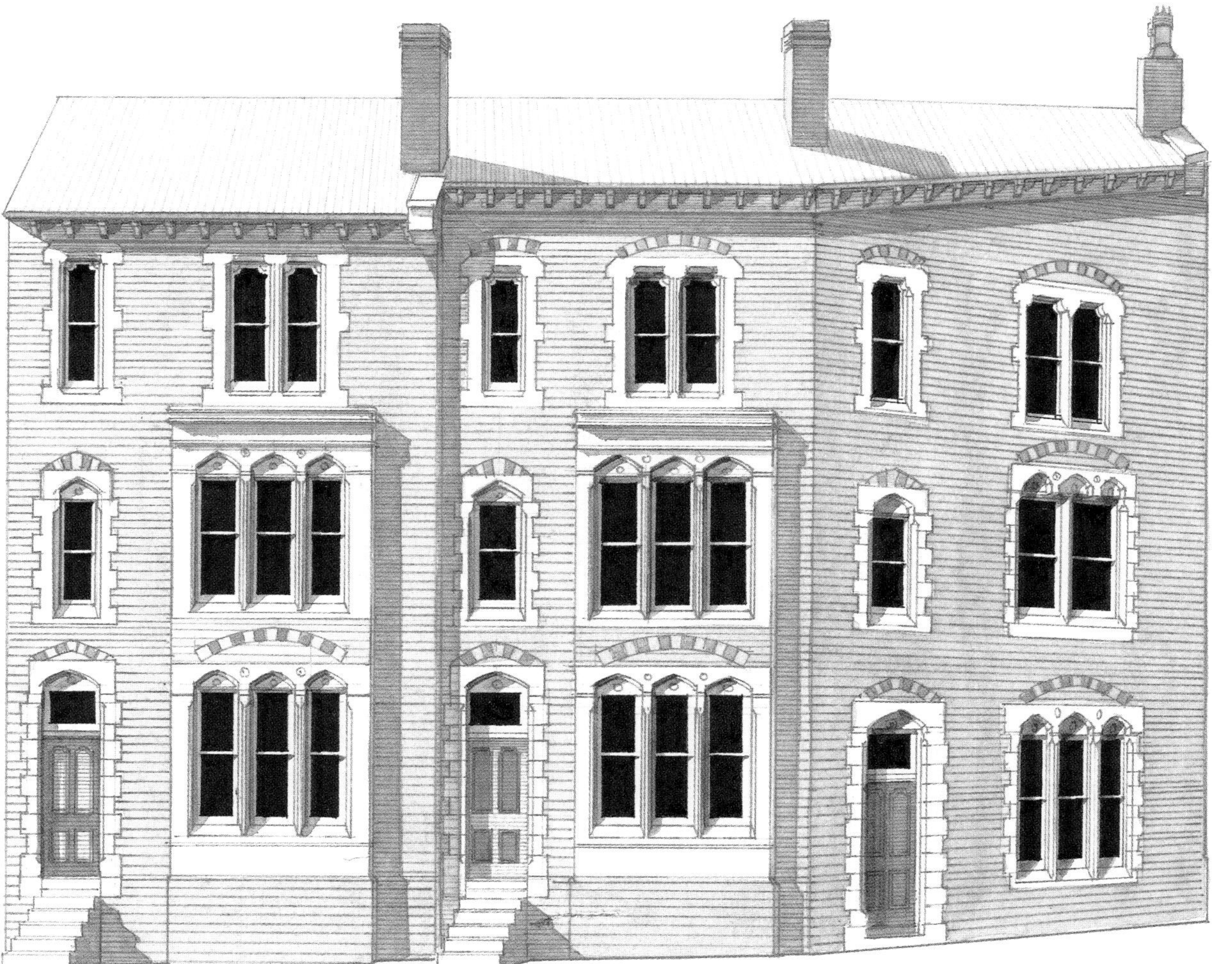

The relatively elaborate façade of Barker's Terrace just off Market Street at the foot of Hangingroyd Road reflects the middle-class status of this part of town at the end of the nineteenth century. It has since gone downhill.

Talk to anyone here who is over sixty years old and they will people the streets for you. Take the scene at 7.30 a.m., some time after the First World War, for example. The town is suddenly crammed with people, walking, cycling, coming off the buses, most of them iron-shod in clogs, crowding the pavements so that you could not walk against the stream, pouring into the factory mouths, and then—at 8 o'clock—suddenly nothing, the streets empty. There are only one or two people around the shops in Market Street (the smarter end) and Crown Street, where the great Co-op Hall is to be found, and where the air of the Victorian lady shopkeeper, the buttoned bust, the cameo at the throat, is still to be felt today. The machinery is now working in the mills, the constant undernoise of the town—a percussive edge to it from the looms, a deeper underbass from the engines which drive them. And there is not only noise. You could stand in a house across New Road from Crossley's down by the canal and feel yourself shuddered by the works around you. Nevertheless it is the noise inside the mills that they all remember: it was *so* loud. A painter and decorator told me that if he was working in a weaving shed during the day, the noise would not leave his head when he came home at night, and he would be kept awake for hours by the sound of the looms. The weavers themselves got

The dense industrial landscape along the quays of the Rochdale Canal. The last commercial barge to make the full journey from one side of the Pennines to the other did so in 1939. This short section was re-opened for pleasure boats in 1984.

used to it, although many of them went deaf. All of them can now lip-read because that was the only way of communicating above the rattle, after an initial 'Yoo-Hoo, right loud, like that'. I have seen old weavers on either side of the street talk silently to each other, exaggerating their lip movements, as the traffic passed between them.

When business was good, each of the weavers—and they were mostly women—would have four looms to run. The women to whom I have talked certainly claimed that they were far better at the job than the men: the women kept the looms running, while the men clumsied around, the wife often prompting her husband next to her, or standing in for him when he went off to the loos to have a smoke. In some mills, the men's urinals were deliberately built without a roof so that the overlooker could see the smoke rising from them, and so that the men would not stop there talking if it was raining. It was the men who worked at the heavy jobs, above all in the dye tanks which stood beside the Hebden and Colden Waters, colouring those Pennine streams bright blue when the 'Bluette' overalls were being dyed, or brown when it was corduroys.

The young women staffed the machine shops too, where the finished garments were sewn together. It is a measure of the poverty of the time and the occupation that payment was measured not in pounds or shillings but in pennies and fractions of them: 7d. for a boiler suit, a whole 10d. for a pair of 'black moles' (miners' trousers made of moleskin fustian so thick that the needles smoked as the women struggled with a flap-front, two side-pockets and flies in the intractable material). Worst of all were the schoolboys' corduroy shorts (lined), known among the girls as 'little shits' because you were only paid 2⅝d. a pair.

There was another element to life in the machine shops at which perhaps one should not be too surprised. It was simply another part of the culture of obedience. It was perfectly well known that after the girls had finished work at the end of the day the boss would keep one of them back for 'a bit of business in the office'. Exposure to 'jiggery-pokery' with the sewing shop-owner was almost a condition of employment for the young women and many bastards were fathered on them, often enough by a man who played his faithful part in chapel on Sundays. Such a pregnancy often forced the girl into an early marriage with a man of her own class, and then on into the likelihood of more children.

In the 1920s and 1930s, the social divides in this town were as great as ever. At the lower end of Birchcliffe Road, there is a climbing terrace of continuous villas known as Snob Row. Mr Tucker, the painter and decorator, was not allowed to enter the front door of one of these houses—or even the tradesman's entrance at the back—in case he sullied the interior. If he was to decorate a bedroom on the first floor, he had to reach it and leave it by a ladder propped against the window.

The food for the working people was often terrible—dock-leaf pie, half a sheep's head which would make broth enough for two days—the housing bad, the education narrow and often only half-time. The other side of life in Hebden Bridge, however, the spirit of independence, must not be forgotten. Even if the bitten down ethic of 'Nowt said needs no mending' governed many families' lives, there were others who lived a wilder existence. The pubs opened at 6 a.m. and men would go on all-day blinders there—'on the rant' as it was called—only to be dragged out of the police cells in Hope Street the next morning to go to work. Boys played endless and rather innocent tricks, putting slates on top of smoking chimneys and dog mess on door handles, shining up the winter roads to make them slippery before the policemen came round on his beat—all games remembered with unadulterated delight sixty or seventy years later. The excitement of such naughtinesses was outdone only by the Monkey Run on Sunday nights after chapel. Along the dark road between the railway station and Mytholmroyd, the boys and girls would walk up and down, at first in their separate sexes and then mingling, and then breaking up again in pairs, down by the gasworks, where it was quite dark and where F & H Sutcliffe's, makers of pre-fabricated sheds, provided scores of secret places.

And what of the future? The District Council has grand schemes for the regeneration of the whole of the Calder Valley, plans founded mostly on tourism. House prices in Hebden Bridge are presently rising faster than anywhere else in the area, fuelled by the employees of the Halifax Building Society, for whom a new headquarters has recently been built down the road at Sowerby Bridge. Old buildings are refurbished and the soot scrubbed off them. Plans exist for walkways; undertakers and garages are encouraged to move their businesses out of sight. No one here hankers after the sort of life recreated by the television-makers. There are other things to be got on with.

Some of the Birds Hill cottages in LETCHWORTH design

LETCHWORTH
Hertfordshire

Parker & Unwin for Garden City Tenants Ltd in 1906

YOU HAVE to practise a sort of archaeology in LETCHWORTH today. Almost everything it set out to achieve in 1903 as the first Garden City has now faded from the surface. It could be almost anywhere in the developed world, the comfortable middle ground where hamburger stores have 'Smile Zones' and a Business Park is well under way. It has, in a strange reversal, become part of exactly the process it was meant to arrest—the spreading uniformity of the megalopolis, the 'functionless congestion and formless sprawl', which the founders of the Garden City movement considered a threat to southern England even in the early years of the century. Here you can find the first cul-de-sac in the world, the first roundabout, the first setting of a housing estate around a 'green', and the relics of the first Ideal Home Exhibition (or its forerunner). Sometimes Letchworth seems to have been buried under its own progeny.

So you must allow your historical imagination to work here on that most difficult of areas, the quite recent past. Then, in the light of what existed at the time—the inhuman slums, the vacuous suburbs, the derelict countryside—the ideal of an entirely new town with its own industry, its own farms, its own way of living and—all importantly—its own possession of the land on which it is built, becomes an extraordinary and courageous experiment. There was no need here to bend the ideals to whatever had come before. A rather dull stretch of Hertfordshire farmland thirty-odd miles north of London, and comprising nearly four thousand acres, could be treated as an open prairie, a wax tablet on which the shining optimism of the Letchworth pioneers could be cleanly impressed.

But nothing ages faster than declared newness and Letchworth now hovers, rather uncertainly, on the boundary between the second-hand and the respectably old, hesitating somehow between the antique and the simply out-of-date. But that wonderful idealism of the first decade—beginning with the founding of Letchworth and lasting until the outbreak of the First World War—is what any visitor here must rediscover. It is, in fact, only just hidden. You need a hoover not a trenching tool to find it, just a blowing off of the dust. Come here on a spring morning, with the white paint on the pebbledash shiny and the red tiles warm and the bloom out on the thousands of flowering trees planted by the pioneers on their Arbor Days (an idea frankly stolen from the Beautiful Oldham Society), and I would defy anyone not to think Letchworth at least extraordinary.

It began with a book. *To-morrow: A Peaceful Path to Real Reform* was published in 1898. Its author was Ebenezer Howard, a stenographer and inventor of typewriter mechanisms, who at one time had farmed in the United States. While he was there he had seen the development of Riverside, Illinois, now a suburb of Chicago. A new town had been built here in the 1860s which consciously included in its plan large slices of countryside.

Howard's scheme in *To-morrow*, however, is far more than the purely aesthetic one of setting greenery among the houses. His intentions were larger and more embracing than that. He aimed, in short, to bring about a social revolution, not by Utopian dreaming but by a practical, empirically-based working-out of the mechanisms required for the Good Life. Howard was no philosopher and in many ways *To-morrow* reads like an inventor's book. It was not the first in the field. Ever since the beginning of industrialization attempts had been made and schemes suggested to alleviate the conditions imposed by industry on its workforce. J.S. Buckingham's *Victoria* and Benjamin Ward Richardson's *Hygeia* had both, earlier in the century, suggested the creation of new towns on the same sort of philanthropic principles which motivated Howard. Robert Owen at New Lanark, Sir Titus Salt at Saltaire, Sir William Lever at Port Sunlight and George Cadbury at Bournville, all of them immensely rich industrialists, had already created model industrial villages outside large cities to the great benefit not only of their employees but of their businesses too. None of these schemes was on a very large scale and all of them depended on the continuing philanthropy of the industrialist concerned. (The whole of Port Sunlight, for example, continued to belong to Lever Bros; George Cadbury described the setting up of Bournville as 'my hobby'.)

In many ways Howard shared the ideals of this tradition. *To-morrow* describes how each garden city—it was to be a national movement—was to have a population of about 32,000 people. In an estate of 6,000 acres, 5,000 would be devoted to agriculture and only 1,000 to the city itself. Within the city, a hospital, library, theatre, concert hall, museum and gallery, all set in a central park, would give way to a crystal palace—we would call it a shopping centre—and then to wide and spacious housing estates, to schools with playgrounds and generous boulevards and avenues. Beyond the houses would be the factories and warehouses, next to the encircling railway which defined the boundary of the city. In the agricultural belt outside it, which would thrive on the large new market brought to its doorstep and with crops liberally manured with sewage piped out from the town, the farmers would find allotments and smallholdings, convalescent homes and asylums for the blind and deaf all scattered among the fields. The Garden City was to arrange a new marriage between town and country in which the beauty of nature could be allied to social opportunity, and high industrial wages with low rural, or near-rural, rents; in which pure air and water would accompany good drainage, no smoke, no slums and all the attractions of urban amusements.

It is the most humane of visions but how dreamy it all sounds! *The Times* called it 'an ingenious and rather entertaining attempt', and added: 'The only difficulty is to create such a City, but that is a small matter to Utopians.' The *Fabian News* was worse: 'His plans would have been in time if they had been submitted to the Romans when they conquered Britain.' As it was, boringly, 'We have got to make the best of our existing cities, and proposals for building new ones are about as useful as would-be arrangements for protection against visits from Mr Wells's Martians.'

What this sort of complacent contempt ignored was Howard's own recognition of one crucial element: his Utopia would make money. The laying-out and development of a town on land which is bought at agricultural values will always yield more than what is spent on it. There will be an automatic rise in the value of the estate as soon as people start to come and work in the new city. Almost no investment could be safer than one which plans to transform a rural into an urban property.

But this was not speculation for its own sake. An all-important aspect of Howard's scheme emphasized that the freehold of the estate was not to be sold but to be kept in the hands of a Board of Trustees, who would administer it for the eventual benefit of the Garden Citizens themselves. Plainly, any initial loans and mortgages would have to be paid off, but after that and after essential services were paid for and capital expenditure made, any surplus from the ground rents would be returned to the benefit of the community. The people who had created the added value would be the ones to get the benefit of that increase. (Although the arrangements are not quite as Howard saw them, Letchworth continues to fulfil this obligation to itself. In the year ending March 1987, a total of £795,000 was paid out by Letchworth Garden City Corporation to a string of community projects.)

This was the blueprint. Despite the establishment poopooing it, the idea of a Garden City moved extraordinarily quickly towards its realization. A Garden City Association was formed. Conferences were held in Bournville and Port Sunlight. A Garden City Pioneer Company was set up to look for a suitable estate. The whole country was searched—in secrecy to avoid driving the price up—and 6,000 acres at somewhere called Chartley in Staffordshire was almost settled on. Would Chartley, if it had been chosen, be any different from Letchworth as it is today? Would all the garden city lives have simply happened there instead? How odd, the transplantability of this idea, of these streets and the lives lived in them!

At the last minute the pioneer company was told of the Letchworth estate. It was far nearer London than Chartley, it was on the Cambridge-King's Cross railway, and it had a good water supply and good drainage. Throughout the summer of 1903 negotiations were held, sometimes openly in the name of the company, sometimes in the name of a proxy to prevent a particular farmer raising his price on the grounds that his portion was essential to the scheme. In the end 3,818 acres were purchased—very much less than Howard originally envisaged—in 15 separate lots, at an average cost of £40 15s. per acre.

It was a time of great excitement and trepidation for the promoters of the scheme. For techical reasons a formal trust could not be set up and instead a prospectus for shares in a limited company called First Garden City was issued. It not only spoke of 'a sound investment at a cumulative rate of five per cent per annum' (such a dividend was not actually paid until 1923 and the arrears on it not paid off until 1946) but, in an attempt to meet its investors on their own ground, it also described how, 'In the face of physical degeneration, the existence of which in our great towns is incontrovertible, imperialism abroad and progress at home seem alike an empty mockery. Sound physical condition is surely the foundation of all human development.' The Garden City alone, it claimed, was the solution to the problem of: 'How to maintain and increase industrial efficiency without impairing the national physique.' Nevertheless, the market responded poorly and the directors of the company were forced to produce £40,000 themselves and borrow a further £83,934 via mortgages on the freeholds of the estate. It was not the most promising of starts.

On a day of pouring rain in October a lunch was held in a marquee pitched on the corner of Letchworth Lane and the Baldock Road. As the contents of the clouds fell heavily on the canvas, Earl Grey spoke of the old world where 'streets upon streets of sunless slums [had] little provision for recreation beyond that which is supplied by low music halls and still lower public houses'. In all the writing and speaking that accompanied the birth of Letchworth one phrase consistently recurs, spoken with a relishing, shuddering delight in the knowledge of a dead demon well-buried. Whether it is houses, furniture, clothes, food, domestic habits, social systems, attitudes to women, animals or foreigners, everything that could possibly be bad about them seems to be summed up in the one phrase: '*nineteenth-century*'. Letchworth would be different. Here, in the glorious dawn of the twentieth century, 'the rents of a population of 30,000 souls will not go to enrich any individual landowner, but will be spent in such a way as will tend to refine the lives, ennoble the characters and exalt the minds of all who reside on the estate.' It is the classic Letchworth marriage of self-interest and community spirit,

The Spirella factory on Bridge Road by C.H. Hignett, 1912–22—a place full of Letchworth paradoxes—Arts and Crafts pavilions tacked on to concrete and a workforce of 2,000 modern girls making something they would never wear— ladies' corsets.

breeding self-help on the communal scale, the achievement of community through the release of individualism, in a town small enough for its citizens to identify themselves with it and yet large enough—they hoped—to make that sense of community worth having. This subtle and narrow line—between the claims of the individual and of the town of which he was to be a part—governed the thinking, planning and building of Letchworth's creators.

After lunch the thousand shareholders and their friends tramped through the rain to see what it was they were now embarked on. They found a few rather broken farms, a patchy network of unmade roads connecting the hamlets of Letchworth, Norton, Radwell and Willian, a small dribble of a stream running through the middle of the estate, a railway that bisected it east to west and a great deal of mud. It was not this that was promising. Moreover the severe under-capitalization of the company made it daunting to say the least. It was—and this can hardly be overstated—the burning vision of what they were doing that in some ways glossed over the mundaneness of the enterprise, and in others actually lifted it on to a plane which they at least felt to be heroic. Ebenezer Howard, soon to be known as Ebenezer the Garden City Geyser, had set a quotation from Blake's *Jerusalem* at the beginning of his book. Within a year or two of Letchworth's foundation, one of its inhabitants could write the following about the housing estates, boulevards and sewage works that were in the process of construction:

> I see a City being wrought
> Upon the rock of Living Thought.
> Upon her rising walls I look
> And every stone is like a book
> Of my milk-white pages, fair
> Imprinted, with a loving care,
> While on each lovely page is set
> Words of wisdom lovelier yet.

Letchworth? You have to believe it. Norton Way South and Ridge Road, Leys Avenue and Sollershott West—these were the lineaments of the New Jerusalem.

The early years were wonderful. The pioneers' accounts resound with the sheer verve of liberation, foreshadowing those of people sixty years later who were to abandon the rigidities of their parents' lives. For this first decade of Letchworth's history, the town pursues a double track: on the one hand, committed libertarians live out all the desires of individual freedom that had been nurtured through the nineteenth century; and alongside them, less flamboyantly but perhaps even more idealistically, the architects, planners and surveyors whom Howard had gathered to convert his proposal into a real place—whilst being acutely conscious of the financial limits within which they had to work, and of the need to create a proper financial base for the town—place the main emphasis not on the fulfilment of the individual but rather on the achievement of a physical and social environment which would *ennoble* (another repeated Letchworth word) the lives of those who came to live there. These two groups—the self-fulfillers and the social engineers—in some ways fused but in others conflicted. Here was the dramatization of the paradox inherent in the very concept that a community could flourish by releasing the individuality of its members. That conflict—or at least that central division in the Letchworth idea—is still clear on the ground today.

The wilder elements soon attracted the attention of the press. F.W. Rogers, an official of First Garden City Limited, was showing some press men around the fledgling town in 1907 and talking about the social and economic advantages of Letchworth over any other, less rationally organized city. ' "Cut that stuff out, Rogers, and show us some of your freaks," said the *Daily Mail* man. I protested that the days of freakism were over, that maidens no longer walked about hatless, stockingless, shoeless, and that men now wore garments other than smocks.

'Just then there sailed into view . . . a tall, angular man robed in a flaming yellow djibba, with green lining, sans stockings and hat, but plus sandals.

'The eyes of the *Daily Mail* man bulged like hat pegs.' Rogers went on. 'Standing up in the motor and stretching out both hands to the object, he screamed, "My God! there's one!" You can imagine what type of report Letchworth got from the stunt press.' A year of two earlier, one of Rogers's colleagues had been attempting to show 'the stolid board of a large building society the first row of shops in Station Rd, with a view to a mortgage advance, when a half-nude procession of locals proceeded along in blissful ignorance that their presence caused the advance to be turned down.'

Blissful ignorance is the right phrase. They were having the time of their lives—dew baths on Norton Common ('Dabbling in the dew/Makes the milkmaids fair . . .'), sixty societies when the town still only had one thousand inhabitants (a total of three domestic servants among them), vegetarian banquets, Theosophist seminars, Independent Labour Party read-ins, and a 'Liberal Catholic' church—that most Letchworth of institutions—which, its manifesto blithely declared, 'combines the ancient form of sacramental worship with the utmost liberality of thought. It leaves its members free in matters of belief,' There was 'Skittles', the de-tox pub, or 'The Liberty Hall of the Letchworth Worker', where Cydrax was the best thing on offer, and where the publican Bill Furmston, when asked why he had been a vegetarian from birth, replied: 'Because I was a Buddhist in a previous incarnation.' Peppermint and marsh pennywort grew on Norton Common, bee orchids, agrimony and centaury around the site of the new Spirella corset factory, where the workforce of two thousand girls were, it was said, 'easy game'. In the winter the mud was atrocious; indeed, a builder's horse sank up to its belly in it and had be be levered out with planks.

For one or two timid creatures the new life was too much. One cockney mother decanted her entire East End family on the new Great Northern Railway Station and promptly—according to the rather smug testimony of a convinced pioneer—'went off the deep end. She took the next train back to London.' The parents of Hitchin children prevented them from going up to Letchworth because of all the goings-on there.

'Coming from a city of crowds and noise,' a less than enthusiastic latecomer recorded, 'Letchworth seemed so dead. I didn't take kindly to the aloofness of those early inhabitants. "Simple Lifers" we used to call them, walking about in sandals and short knickers.'

The Simple Lifers themselves couldn't have cared less. If they had had their way Letchworth might have been called Alseopolis, from the Greek for Garden City. There was, it has to be admitted, an element of self-satisfaction about them. 'If it is possible to summarize the character of our early citizens in two words,' one of them wrote later, '"mental alertness" would best express it. . . .' Pantomimes and the profoundly serious approach to Laughing At Oneself are somehow inseparable from this sort of world. Here, for example, is part of the *Song of the Spirit of Place*, from one of these innumerable productions:

> Or again at lunch, as you sit and munch
> your savoury cabbage fritter,
> Your tummy may turn and begin to yearn
> for a chop and a pint of bitter.
> Then you somehow feel that a high ideal
> is a thing much overrated,
> And you hint to your wife that the Simple Life
> is a wee bit complicated—
> Ah, then is the hour when you need my power
> to brace and fortify you.

The public apologists for the Garden City consistently and repeatedly denied that Letchworth was an asylum for cranks, but there is no doubt that an extraordinary, eccentric, egomaniac, idealist, pacifist, vegetarian, esperantist, naturist, spiritual and amorous collection of people did flourish here for a while, people who took one strand of the Garden City idea—the most romantic—and made it the core of their lives. The focus of this aspect of Letchworth was the most extraordinary building ever erected in Hertfordshire, a sort of Theosophist Monastery-cum-Swimming Bath Complex called the Cloisters. This building—discreetly described in the Official Guide as the 'Open-air School'—cost £25,000 at a time when a perfectly habitable cottage could be built for £150 and a mansion for £800. Its patron was a Miss A.J. Lawrence whose idea it was to have a meditative college whose classrooms were 'constantly exposed to the atmosphere. . . . Books and other necessaries, when not in use, can be placed in watertight cupboards.' Young people *of both sexes*—this phrase always included—slept in hammocks in a first-floor arcade open to the air.

Nowhere in Letchworth inspired quite the degree of hyperbole aroused by The Cloisters. Georgia Pearce, a visiting American journalist, thought 'The Cloisters bids fair to be a landmark, a milestone, on the Open Road to the Universe.' Alfred Dawson, Editor of the *Christian Commonwealth*, recommended his readers to visit Letchworth, to 'dispense with superfluous clothes, reject with scornful glee everything starchy, and enjoy unfettered intercourse with people who are asking questions of the universe. . . .

'You come into contact there with people who are making such amazing experiments,' he went on. 'Here

is a man who has made himself almost black by working in the fields in the scantiest of garb. This sturdy giant has been fasting for more than a dozen days, nothing but water having passed his lips for a fortnight. Yonder tall Californian lives on nothing but fruit; he has brought with him a crate of oranges and eats a dozen at a time.'

They are all but ghosts now. The Cloisters, with the ugliest brick box addition of a dinner-dance room tacked on at the back, is now owned by the Freemasons. What remains from Letchworth's glory days is the other side of the enterprise: the creation of a physical structure, the 'town architecture' as they called it at the time. Throughout the winter of 1903–4 Raymond Unwin and his partner Barry Parker, the two architects who more than anyone else were responsible for the creation of physical Letchworth, worked on the drawing up of a town plan. The abstract Utopian geometries which had appeared in the diagrams of *To-morrow* were never intended to be anything more than that. It was always understood here—not the case in many earlier schemes—that the plan of the Garden City needed above all to be responsive to the landscape on which it was to be planted.

The Cloisters by W.H. Cowlishaw, 1906–7, originally an adult school for Theosophical Meditation, where the most liberated of Letchworth's pioneers set out on their well-ventilated road to the Universe. The central tower contained an organ and open-air classrooms. The sun-heated swimming pool was on the far side.

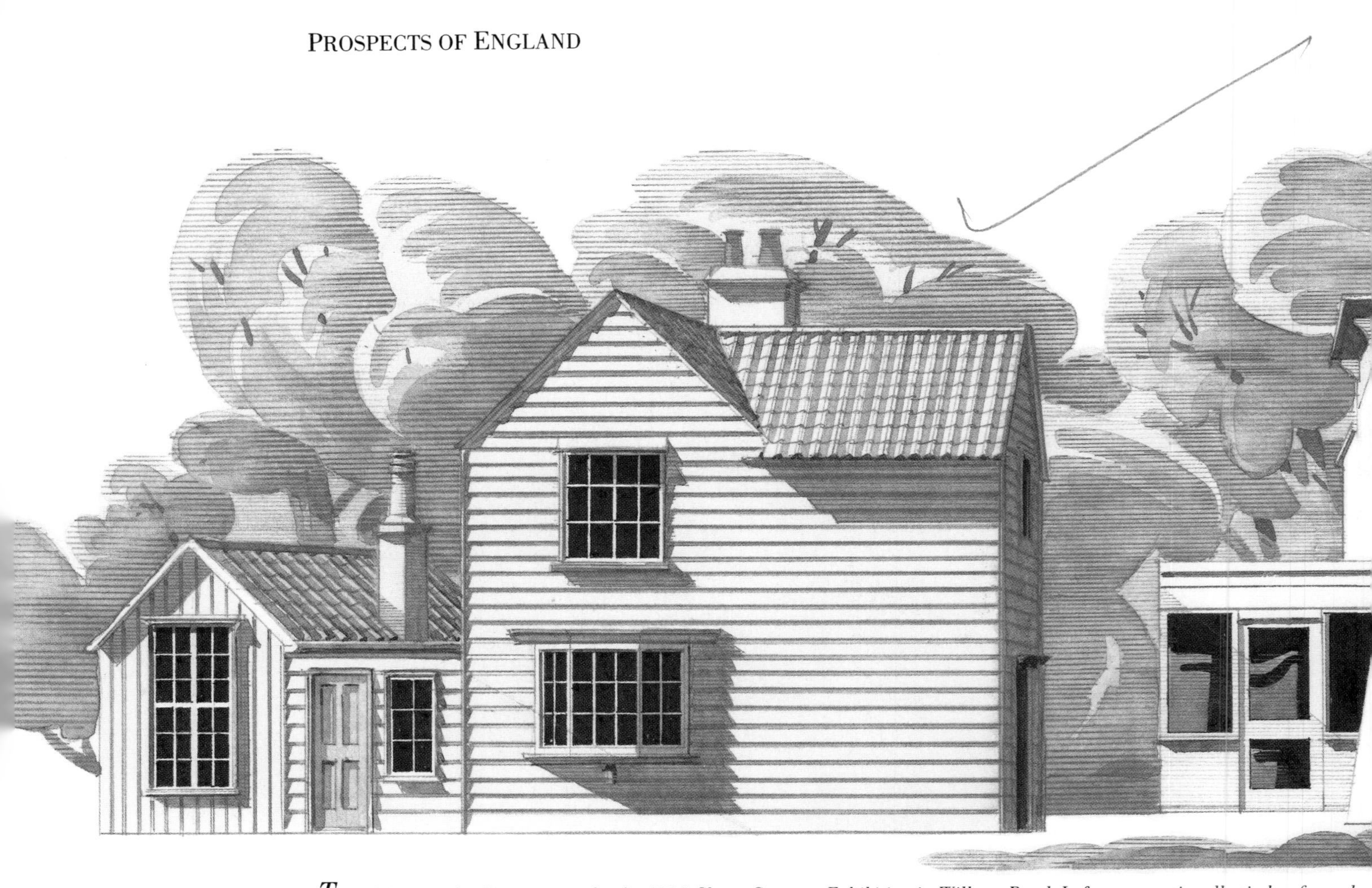

Two of the 121 dwellings put up for the 1905 Cheap Cottages Exhibition in Wilbury Road. Left *a conventionally timber-framed and clapboarded house,* Right *a more experimental design in pre-cast concrete slabs. The floor and ceiling of each room is made of one piece. The horrible sun-room on the left is a modern addition.*

You can still visit the place where these men worked. Their office—described as 'the holy of holies' by one of the pioneers—is now the First Garden City Museum, just off Norton Way South in a little copse by the Pix Brook. It is a thatched building, dramatically distanced from any recognized urban tradition, and designed as a conscious pastiche of a late medieval East Anglian hall house, the solar being reserved for the two partners, while the hall itself was given over to their assistants. More than anywhere else which is easily accessible, you can get some feel here for the aesthetic and moral milieu within which early Letchworth was made. Massive whitewashed timbers, left partly in the rough, support the high and open roof. The floors are open boards, the furniture all solidly and largely made, with scrolled ironwork fittings. There are some charming little stained-glass cameos in the windows and a copper hood over the fire. The air of the whole establishment is one of well-made near-austerity, a part-puritan medievalism which is rich not gaudy; it is *echt*, suspicious both of unnecessary ornament and the sterility of machine production.

This office was not built until 1907, but it sets Letchworth in the right light. The architecture shouts its morality at you, while the hierarchy of hall and solar (with a window in the solar from which Parker could oversee his subordinates below) reflects an important aspect of the Garden City scheme. Parker and Unwin's plan for the town was—perfectly realistically—drenched in the idea of social stratification; community maybe but no hint of communism here. Their plan is rigorously zoned: lower, lower-middle, and upper-middle classes are all allocated their separate areas, and each is placed in a suitable relationship to the station, the industrial sections and the town centre.

The plan was complete by early 1904 and building soon began. Almost immediately, however, progress towards the New Jerusalem was disrupted by the editors of the *Country Gentleman and Land and Water* and the *Spectator*. Together these two promoted the first Cheap Cottages Exhibition, which was held the following year. With the approval of First Garden City Limited, 121 dwellings were erected on both sides of Norton Common. The idea was to show how a healthy

and pretty cottage could be built for £150. Eighty thousand people visited the show to see the toy-town buildings sprouting in the land of the nut-eaters and banana-munchers. The more serious minded of Letchworth's promoters regretted the exhibition had ever come here (as they did again, to a slightly lesser extent, with its successor two years later, the Urban Cottages Exhibition.) Nevertheless, the cottages that remain, most of them now worth £80,000 or more, are one of the delights of Letchworth, lined up along Wilbury Road, and between Nevells Road and the Icknield Way. Here they stand, a souvenir from the age of experiment.

Most of the cottages were taken by 'people of small means, clerks, etc', as the report on the show described them. The housing for industrial workers, erected by new charities (like the Howard Cottage Society) which could borrow Government money at favourable rates for this purpose, lay on the eastern side of the town centre. It was separated from the shops of Leys Avenue by a park and from the main industrial estate itself by a belt of trees. It is here more than anywhere else that the Letchworth idea comes to fruition. In the streets designed by Parker & Unwin, and by their assistants and associates—Bird's Hill, Ridge Road, Rushby Mead and Hillshott—Howard must have felt entirely vindicated. They are beautiful. Everywhere you look the same elements reappear but always in a slightly different combination. Here is a constant and novel playing with the forms of an English rural tradition which was part of their vision: the gable above all, the continual peaking of the Letchworth skyline, a constantly surprised and optimistic 'Oh really?!' to the look of the streets; the clay tiles too, which the planners insisted should cover every roof in Letchworth—Welsh blue slates were banned because William Morris disapproved of them; the long catslides, bringing the roofs down almost to the ground, pegging the house into its place, as though Letchworth really were no more than camping; the pebbledash walls painted creamy white; the leaded casement windows, conversationally placed in the façades, squeezed in next to the porch, or tight up under a gutter like a swallow's nest; the down-pipes and gutters, terminating originally, and in some places still, in water butts; the flowering trees; the privet hedges.

More than these details, however, one can see here, where it is used for the first time, how excellent an idea is the cul-de-sac. Its success depends a great deal on the scale. Parker & Unwin's roads down the centre of a cul-de-sac—I am thinking of one in Rushby Mead—are both tiny and sunk beneath the level of the houses and their gardens. The privet hedges tower over them as though it were somewhere in Cornwall. It is a tight, controlled, intimate space, with its own drama, rather than the flattened out bit of utilitarianism it was so quickly to become.

Inside, too, the architects took immense care in designing the houses. They did not repeat the arrangement of rooms from one to another, but changed them so that the sitting room was always sunny, the larder always on the shaded side. Paths were made to thread between the houses and their gardens, so that one can still burrow around inside these tiny landscapes as though they were secret. Almost all of this area is still owned by The Howard Cottage Society. Many tenants apply to buy their houses but they are always turned down. There is a waiting list of four years and a thousand people—all of whom have *bona fide* Letchworth connections—for a tenancy here. It is not surprising; this is a sort of urban paradise.

The Parker & Unwin office on Norton Way South. In the right-hand block, built in 1907, the assistants worked in the main hall while the two architects supervised them from the solar at the far end. Barry Parker added the two-storey block in 1937.

Almost the only original complaint was from those new arrivals who had brought their Victorian furniture with them: it was impossible to get it either up the cottagey stairs or in through the cottagey windows. Nevertheless this was widely interpreted among the Letchworth intellectuals as a metaphor for the real newness of the world they were inventing.

Away from the industrial estates, on the southern side of the town, between The Cloisters, the golf course at Old Letchworth Hall and Sollershott Circle, the famous first roundabout (little more, in fact, than a *rond-point* from the seventeenth-century French gardening tradition) are the large properties on which the rich built their pretty and innovative houses. Here, if you could get into them, you would find the first open-plan layouts in England, the remains—now unused—of the highly *echt* private drainage system by which the waste pipes from 'Glaed Hame' (only in Letchworth!) were directed straight out on to the vegetable patch, and all the familiar enthusiasm for Fresh Air. Parker and Unwin's own shared house at 'Arunside' on Muddy Lane—now part of a vegetarian school—has a 'sleeping tower' attached, in which Parker and his family would sleep with all the breezes of Hertfordshire blowing about their nostrils.

This southern section is the smartest but also the most disappointing part of Letchworth. It is little more in the end than another turn-of-the-century suburb—Surrey with a fringe on top, Bel-Air gone damp. Each property affects to ignore the existence of its neighbour and its neighbour its neighbour's neighbour, and the totally arbitrary way in which Queen Anne Revival follows Black Forest Chalet or Deep Suffolk Backwoods destroys any idea of a town.

There is one building down here, however, which has something of the true Letchworth spirit about it. Just off Sollershott Circle is a large, brick, gabled building now surrounded by much later additions and slightly ridiculously called Sollershott Hall. This is the remains of one of Ebenezer Howard's own schemes 'to overcome', in the words of C.B. Purdom (one of the most active of the Garden City's promoters), 'the difficulty of the domestic servant.' Thirty-two houses were planned to surround a quadrangle, all served by a common hot-water system and all linked by telephone to a central block of a dining room, smoking room, reading room and kitchen. The idea was partly feminist—or at least proto-feminist—in wanting to

release the housewife from the repeated drudgery of cooking, while partly being an attempt to preserve the luxuries of a cook and maid at not too great a cost, by sharing them between houses. At a time when the rent for a working-class house was anything between 4s. 6d. and 8s. a week, a three-bedroom house in Homesgarth—as this cooperative venture was called—cost about 24s. 6d. a week, all services included.

It was an idealist scheme (there was another like it for 'business women' in Meadow Way), tempered to the requirements of class and seclusion, but from the beginning there were problems. 'The tenants,' Purdom warned, 'need to possess and cultivate a friendly spirit, and the common rooms should be a centre of common life and pleasant social intercourse. But it is essentially a group of separate homes, and the preservation of the privacy of each of those homes is the very first need. To secure this combination of absolute privacy and of the benefits of co-operation and communal action in certain things is the chief object of the management.' Outside moments of peculiar inspiration, it is perhaps impossible to ride both these horses at once. Homesgarth failed. The practical efficiency of modern cooking gadgets turned out to be far more convenient and preferable to the enforced clubbability of a shared dining room. The communal sections were closed first and were later turned into a club for the town, but the residents complained about the noise, and the types who frequented it. Now even that has been split up into flats; the triumph of privacy.

This rich residential district lies south of the area designed by Parker and Unwin to be the monumental centre of the town. The road network is there as they intended, a star-burst of avenues focused on the Town Square. On the map it looks fairly convincing, the bringing to fruition of Howard's civic dream, the embodiment of the communal idea. In reality it is a disaster: a mess of empty lots, ugly trees, intrusive car parks, differing architectural styles and scales, gimmicky baubles recently added to a confusion of ugliness that was already worse—ironically enough—than almost anything put up before 'town-planning' was 'invented' here at Letchworth. First Garden City Limited was desperately short of capital from the beginning. The suspicion of the financiers and the urgent need to install all the essential services in a completely agricultural district meant that there was nothing left over for the central grandeur they needed. They delayed and delayed, pushing in the Town Hall here, a post office there, until eventually the idea of what Letchworth town centre might once have looked like disappeared from view. Most of the pioneers had moved off to try out their schemes in Welwyn.

But I think there is more to the failure in the centre of Letchworth than a lack of cash at the right time. The whole ethos of the town, or at least the drift which the Garden City idea took here, works against the notion of a city centre. Here ideally was a rural, individualistic community, self-expressive not sober-suited, dispersive not self-concentrating, expressed by a move away to individuality in the expensive houses in the southern section and a declared liking for the eccentricities of the Exhibition Cottages. This ideal, to my mind, reaches a form of balanced perfection in the Birds Hill and Rushby Meads estates, where its sense of mild, unenforced urbanity is perfectly married to its idea of the rural; where the democratic instinct—to make industrial housing habitable and enjoyable—is allied to an originality and inventiveness in design; where that sense of what is morally right sits exactly with what is aesthetically and socially right; where it is a pleasure to be; where there is no guff. Anything more than that, any banging of the municipal drum, could never be quite right here. The grand would always degenerate into the grandiose. Letchworth never got a town centre because, in the end, it did not want one.

In some ways, and quite ironically, this marks the end of the town. The ideal admired by the Garden Cityists was the one proposing precisely the sort of small town which has been the subject of this book, which was contrasted with the anonymity and inhumanity of the large industrial city. But the idea that these towns represented some kind of spontaneous 'organic' expression of healthy sociability was a profound if understandable misapprehension. The towns they admired were held together not by a desire to be happy but by economic need on the one hand and by the rigid impositions of an urban oligarchy on the other. In the prosperity and comparative liberalism of twentieth-century England, both the need and the control diminished. You could now afford to be on your own and were also allowed to be. Even the tenants in the Homesgarth Cooperative communicated with the communal kitchen by telephone. The shape of things now is not the beautiful continuity of Chipping Campden High Street, but the separate houses lining Letchworth Broadway, each one slightly different in its pastiche of some inherited style or other.

Bibliography

General

Martin Carver, *Underneath English Towns*, 1987
Peter Clark (ed.), *The Transformation of English Provincial Towns 1600–1800*, 1984
W.L. Creese, *The Search for Environment*, 1966
Ralph Hyde, *Gilded Scenes and Shining Prospects: panoramic views of British towns, 1575–1900*, 1985
John Patten, *English Towns 1500–1700*, 1978
Graham Parry, *Hollar's England*, 1980
Nikolaus Pevsner and others, *The Buildings of England*, 1951–74
Colin Platt, *The English Medieval Town*, 1976
Susan Reynolds, *An Introduction to the history of English medieval towns*, 1977
P.F. Smith, *The Syntax of Cities*, 1977

Chichester

David J. Butler, *The Town Plans of Chichester 1595–1898*, 1972
Barry Cunliffe, *Fishbourne: A Roman Palace and its Garden*, 1971
Barry Cunliffe, *The Regni*, 1971
Alec Down (ed.), *Chichester Excavations*, five volumes, 1971–81
Alec Down (ed.), *The Archaeology of Chichester*, annual reports
S.S. Frere, *Britannia*, 1967
Eric Gill, *Autobiography*, 1940
Joan Liversidge, *Britain in the Roman Empire*, 1968
L.S. Mazzolani, *The Idea of the City in Roman Thought*, 1967
Pallant House, Guide, n.d.
J. Rykwert, *The Idea of a Town*, 1976
J.S. Wacher, *The Towns of Roman Britain*, 1975

Glastonbury

[SANHS: Proceedings of the Somersetshire Archaeological and Natural History Society]

L. Alcock, *Arthur's Britain*, 1971
Geoffrey Ashe, *Avalonian Quest*, 1982
M. Aston and R. Leech, *Historic Towns in Somerset*, 1977
Neill Bonham, *Glastonbury Town Trail*, n.d.
James P. Carley (ed.), *The Chronicle of Glastonbury Abbey*, 1985
R.W. Dunning, 'Revival at Glastonbury, 1530–9', *Studies in Church History*, 1977
P. Ellis, *Excavations at Silver Street, Glastonbury*, 1978
F.A. Gasquet, *The Last Abbot of Glastonbury*, 1895
I.J.E. Keil, *The Estates of Glastonbury in the Later Middle Ages*, Bristol PhD, 1964
I.J.E. Keil, 'The Garden at Glastonbury, 1333–4', *SANHS* 1960
David Knowles, *The Monastic Orders in England*, 1963
Michael Mathias, *Glastonbury*, 1979
Adrian Moon, *The First Ground of God*, 1978
Stephen C. Morland, 'The Glastonbury Manors and their Saxon Charters', *SANHS* 1986
Stephen C. Morland, 'Hidation on the Glastonbury Estates: a study in tax evasion', *SANHS* 1970
Stephen C. Morland, 'Glastonbury Twelve Hides', *SANHS* 1983/4
C.A. Ralegh Radford, *Glastonbury Tribunal*, 1984
H.F. Scott-Stokes, *Abbot Bere's Terrier and Perambulation*, 1909
William Stukeley, *Itinerarium Curiosum*, 2nd edition, 1776
Victoria County History, *Somerset*, 1911
Rev. Richard Warner, *An History of the Abbey and Town of Glastonbury*, 1826
Dom. A. Watkin, *The Great Chartulary of Glastonbury*, three volumes, 1944–50
M. Williams, *The Draining of the Somerset Levels*, 1970

Alnwick

Alnwick Castle Guidebook, 1985
M.R.G. Conzen, *Alnwick, Northumberland. A Study in town-plan analysis*, 1960
William Davison, *Descriptive and Historical View of Alnwick*, 1822
Frank Graham, *Alnwick*, 1973
R. Rawlinson, *Report to the General Board of Health on . . . Alnwick*, 1850
P.B. Sansum (planning officer), *Alnwick Town Centre, Written Statement*, 1980
George Tate, *The History of the Borough, Castle, and Barony of Alnwick*, two volumes, 1866

Chipping Campden

C.R. Ashbee, *The Last Records of a Cotswold Community*, 1904
T.L. Elsley, *Chipping Campden, Today and Yesterday*, 1931
Charles and Alice Mary Hadfield, *The Cotswolds: a New Study*, 1967
Fiona MacCarthy, *The Simple Life: C.R. Ashbee in the Cotswolds*, 1981
Geoffrey Powell, *The Books of Campden*, 1982
D.H. Pennington, 'Chipping Campden', *History Today*, January 1952
Eileen Power, *The Wool Trade in English Medieval History*, 1942
Percy Rushen, *The History and Antiquities of Chipping Campden in the County of Gloucestershire*, 2nd edition, 1911
Claire Sandry, *Town Trail*, n.d.
Robert Welch, *Design in a Cotswold Workshop*, 1973
Christopher Whitfield, *A History of Chipping Campden*, 1958

Woodbridge

P. Carthew, *Short History of Woodbridge*, 1950
Mark Mitchels, *Woodbridge Tide Mill*, 1983
V.B. Redstone, *Bygone Woodbridge*, 1893
V.B. Redstone, 'Woodbridge, its history and antiquity', *Proceedings of Suffolk Institute of Archaeology* 9 (1895/7)
Robert Simper, *The Suffolk Sandlings*, 1986
D. Symon, *Woodbridge in Suffolk: a Tribute*, 1934
Suffolk County Council, *Conservation in Woodbridge*, 1978
Carol and Michael Weaver, *Woodbridge, a Short History and Guide*, 4th edition, 1985
Carol and Michael Weaver, *The Seckford Foundation*, 1987

Blandford Forum

John Adams, 'The Bastards of Blandford', *Architectural Review*, June 1968

John Bastard, *Fire Survey*, notebook in Dorset County Record Office, MS PE/HON:IN, 1
Malachi Blake, *A Brief Account of the Dreadful Fire at Blandford Forum in the County of Dorset*, 1731
Benjamin G. Cox, *The Book of Blandford Forum: the story of the town's past*, 1983
Benjamin G. Cox, *The Ancient Borough of Blandford Forum, Dorset*, 1988
Benjamin G. Cox, *The Great Fire of Blandford Forum, 1731*, 1987
H.G. Harrison, *Blandford Forum*, 1931
J. Hutchins, *The History and Antiquities of the County of Dorset*, 1774
Donald W. Insall & Associates, *Blandford Forum, Conserve and Enhance*, 1970
William Jeans, letter in Dorset County Record Office MS D396/L23
John Piper, 'Blandford Forum', *Architectural Review*, July 1944
Royal Commission on Historical Monuments, *Dorset*, Vol. III, 1970
Christopher Taylor, *Dorset*, 1970

Monmouth
Sir Cyril Fox and Lord Raglan, *Monmouthshire Houses*, 1951–4
G. Griffith and T.G. Davies, *Monmouth Town Centre Plan Review*, 1981
Charles Heath, *Historical and Descriptive Account of the Ancient and Present State of the Town of Monmouth*, 1804
James Kegie, *Monmouth Town Centre Draft Plan*, 1965
Keith Kissack, *Monmouth, The Making of a County Town*, 1975
Keith Kissack, *Medieval Monmouth*, 1974
A.J. Taylor, *Monmouth Castle and Great Castle House*, 1951
Yvon Waters, *Customs and Folklore of the Lower Wye*, 1969

Weymouth
Anon., *Royal tour to Weymouth and places adjacent in the year 1789*, 1789
Maureen Boddy and Jack West, *Weymouth: an illustrated history*, 1983
P. Delamotte (ed.), *The Weymouth Guide*, 1792
The Gentleman's Magazine, 1789 and 1798
J. Hemlow (ed.), *The Journals and Letters of Fanny Burney*, 1972
M.R. House, *The Structure of Weymouth Architecture*, 1961
J. Hutchins, *The History and Antiquities of the County of Dorset*, 1774
Eric Ricketts, *The Buildings of Old Weymouth*, 1975
Royal Commission on Historical Monuments, *Dorset*, Vol. II, 1970

Buxton
W. Bray, *Sketch of a tour into Derbyshire and Yorkshire*, 2nd edition, 1789
W. Bott, *A Description of Buxton and the Adjacent Country*, 1792
Vera Brittain, *Testament of Youth: an autobiographical study of the years 1900–25*, 1933
J. Byng, *The Torrington Diaries*, C. Bruyn (ed.), 1936
J. Denman, *Observations on the Effects of Buxton Water*, 1793
Sir J. Floyer and E. Baynard, *The History of Cold Bathing*, 5th edition, 1722
A.B. Granville, *The spas of England, and principal sea-bathing places*, two volumes, 1841
Ivan Hall, *Georgian Buxton*, 1984
A. Jewitt, *The History of Buxton, and visitor's guide to the curiosities of the Peak*, 1811
J. Jones, *The benefit of the auncient bathes of Buckstones*, 1572
M. Langham and C. Wells, *Buxton Waters, A History of Buxton the Spa*, 1986
John Leach, *The Book of Buxton*, 1987
W.H. Robertson, *A handbook to the peak of Derbyshire, and to the use of the Buxton mineral waters*, 1854

Whitby
Rev. J.C. Atkinson, *Memorials of Old Whitby, or Historical Gleanings from Ancient Whitby Records*, 1894
Rev. G. Austen, *The Story of Whitby's Old Parish Church*, 1950
J.R. Bagshawe, *The Wooden Ships of Whitby*, 1932
H.B. Browne, *Chapters of Whitby History 1823–1946*, 1946
G.H.J. Daysh (ed.), *A Survey of Whitby*, 1958
R.T. Gaskin, *The Old Seaport of Whitby*, 1909
Hugh P. Kendall, *The Streets of Whitby and their associations*, 1976
National Maritime Museum, *The English Coble*, 1958
Bernard McCall, *Whitby Modern Seaport*, 1988
Edward Perry, *Whitby Inns and Yards*, 1988
C. Preston, *Captain James Cook and Whitby*, 2nd edition, 1970
Robb Robinson, *A History of the Yorkshire Coast Fishing Industry 1780–1914*, 1987
Bill Eglon Shaw, *Frank Meadow Sutcliffe*, 1974
Dora Walker, *Whitby Shipping*, 1971
Dora Walker, *Whitby Fishing*, 1973
Colin Waters, *Bygone Whitby. The Haven under the Hill*, 1988
Rev. G. Young, *A History of Whitby*, two volumes, 1817
Rev. G. Young, *A Picture of Whitby and its Environs*, 2nd edition, 1840

Hebden Bridge
Chris Aspin, *The Cotton Industry*, 1981
Chris Aspin, *The Woollen Industry*, 1981
Tony Dyson and others, *Hebden Bridge Trail*, 1979
Leslie M. Goldthorp, 'The Fustian Weavers' Strike at Hebden Bridge 1906–1908', *Hebden Bridge Local History Booklets*, n.d.
Leslie M. Goldthorp, 'Child Labour in the Local Textile Mills', *Hebden Bridge Local History Booklets*, n.d.
John Hargreaves, *Factory Kings and Slaves*, n.d.
H.W. Harwood, *As Things Were. A Social Study of the Upper Calder Valley*, 1968
Jennifer Holt, *Cloth for All*, n.d.
Frank Horsfall and Terry Wyke, *Looking Back at Hebden Bridge*, 1986
Bernard Jennings, *Pennine Independency*, n.d.
Maria Murtagh, *New Ways, New Cloths*, 1982
Maria Murtagh, *Handlooms and Cloth Halls*, 1982
E.P. Thompson, *The Making of the English Working Class*, 3rd edition, 1980

Letchworth
Thomas Adams, *Guide to the Garden City*, 1906 and 1986 (facsimile edition)
Ebenezer Howard, *To-morrow: A Peaceful Path to Real Reform*, 1898
Brian G. Hull, *Letchworth Conservation Area*, 1977
Kenneth Johnson, *The Book of Letchworth*, 1976
John Moss-Eccardt, *Ebenezer Howard*, 1973
F.J. Osborn, 'Sir Ebenezer Howard—The Evolution of his Ideas', *The Town Planning Review*, October 1950
F.J. Osborn and A. Whittick, *New Towns*, 3rd edition, 1977
C.B. Purdom, *The Garden City*, 1913
C.B. Purdom, *The Building of Satellite Towns*, 1925
C.B. Purdom, *The Letchworth Achievement*, 1963
Sir Freshwater Spray, *How Sir Gadabout Came To The Garden City*, 1922

Index

Page numbers in **bold** refer to illustrations or their captions